T0121933

From Mindfulness to
Heartfulness

*A Journey of Transformation through
the Science of Embodiment*

Dr. Alane Daugherty

BALBOA.
PRESS

A DIVISION OF HAY HOUSE

Copyright © 2014 Dr. Alane Daugherty.

All rights reserved. No part of this book may be used or reproduced by any means, graphic, electronic, or mechanical, including photocopying, recording, taping or by any information storage retrieval system without the written permission of the publisher except in the case of brief quotations embodied in critical articles and reviews.

Balboa Press books may be ordered through booksellers or by contacting:

Balboa Press
A Division of Hay House
1663 Liberty Drive
Bloomington, IN 47403
www.balboapress.com
1 (877) 407-4847

Because of the dynamic nature of the Internet, any web addresses or links contained in this book may have changed since publication and may no longer be valid. The views expressed in this work are solely those of the author and do not necessarily reflect the views of the publisher, and the publisher hereby disclaims any responsibility for them.

The author of this book does not dispense medical advice or prescribe the use of any technique as a form of treatment for physical, emotional, or medical problems without the advice of a physician, either directly or indirectly. The intent of the author is only to offer information of a general nature to help you in your quest for emotional and spiritual well-being. In the event you use any of the information in this book for yourself, which is your constitutional right, the author and the publisher assume no responsibility for your actions.

Any people depicted in stock imagery provided by Thinkstock are models, and such images are being used for illustrative purposes only.
Certain stock imagery © Thinkstock.

Printed in the United States of America.

ISBN: 978-1-4525-2183-1 (sc)
ISBN: 978-1-4525-2185-5 (hc)
ISBN: 978-1-4525-2184-8 (e)

Library of Congress Control Number: 2014916172

Balboa Press rev. date: 09/19/2014

To Frank

Contents

Exercises and Reflections

Practices

1

The Promise of Heartfulness

Introduction – The invitation

Journal entry – March 1997

I have this vague gnawing in my gut. Intuitively I know that the gnawing must be the key to reclaiming my life, but I have a part of me that is terribly frightened to listen to it, or even acknowledge its presence. Maybe it is afraid of the unknown, comfortable in every day existence, or wondering why my life, as it is, is not enough. Or perhaps it is just too paralyzed to entertain a different way of being.

I have this other part that is so entrenched in its reactive ways of being and seeing the world, it is doing everything it can to make me believe its version of reality, and act accordingly. It is got me convinced that all my skewed perceptions are true, and the best I can do is just react to the outside world and all it throws at me. And it seems to be throwing a lot.

Maybe the gnawing is yearning. I know there is something more, and I long for it to be reflected in my outside world. I long for heartful connection to others, and for engagement with life itself; and I long for the feeling of expansiveness and flourishing that go along with it. I long to live in a larger way, where there is energy flow from my vital Inner Being to my external existence, and I want to engage with life in a different way. I want to engage with life to its fullest potential.

Mostly, deep down, there is a profound stirring in my heart waiting to be released, and waiting for a guide to help me do so.

We may have an occasional glimpse of it. We may know there is a deeper way to be connected to life, and we recognize it when we feel it. We know

1

those times when the life force within us is thriving; we feel it in our internal world and we live it in our external existence. We feel it in our hearts, our souls, our brains and, indeed, every cell in our body. Our body reflects it back and it becomes the reality we live. It is truly an embodied phenomenon. It is filled with passion and purpose, calmness and clarity; being grounded in this life force is what gives us the experience of being fully alive. As we fully embody this life force within us, our external world adapts accordingly and there seems to be a flow of harmony from the life at our core to the life we live. We feel connected and engaged with both our Inner Being and our outer world.

And yet.

And yet most of us only get an occasional whisper of this existence. If we do at all. This divine flow from our inner heart to our outer world seems absent from our daily lives, or just experienced happenstance. We know there is another way to be, but we just cannot quite grasp it.

Many of us live our lives consumed with stress, chaos and anxiety, blame, shame and judgment. We live in constant reaction to the circumstances our external life provides, as if we have no choice in the matter. We may be our own worst enemy. Our perceptions and reactivities color the lens of our existence, and we behave and further react accordingly. We seem to be victims of our own reactions and emotional programming, and in a large sense we are. We might even try to force our outer life into attunement, when our inner life is still in chaos, and wonder why we are not happy. We long for the understanding and guidance to intentionally cultivate the life force deep within us, so it can flourish to its fullest potential.

This book offers a path to do just that.

It offers the promise of heartfulness.

In it, you will see that heartful awareness and engagement offers us a profoundly different way of being in the world. It offers us the opportunity to engage with life in a way that automatically reduces the stress and emotional chaos that so often consumes us, and allows a sense of expansiveness in connection with life itself to flourish. It offers the opportunity to truly embody a different way of being. When we look at human experience through the science of embodiment, we can see that the cultivation of heartfulness foundationally changes who we are, and who we are becoming.

We can see what blocks us from experiencing the life force deep within us, and how to calm, clear and heal those blocks. We can see that the intentional cultivation of, and true embodiment of heartful ways of being can potentially affect every cell in our body, and short-term changes become long-term operating patterns. This way of functioning in the world makes us more capable of connection to our own life force or Inner Being, as well as to others and our outside world. The way we see and behave in the world begins to transform in direct correlation to our own inner transformation, and we see tangible and specific ways to cultivate it in our everyday existence. In short, we can see, and intentionally embody, all that heartfulness has to offer.

The cultivation of heartfulness completely transforms our inner and outer lives to states of calm, clarity, connection, expansiveness, full inner potential, and a larger way of living. Heartfulness, embodied, profoundly changes who we are and how we function in the world. It gives us greater access to our Inner Being, or whatever life force lies deep within you, and greater, and more meaningful connections to others, and our outside world. It allows us a more expansive, larger way of being in the world. It changes the experience of being alive.

Using the science of our humanness, as reflected in the adaptive processes of our human body, we see that it is inner experience that profoundly determines who we are becoming at any given point in time. We see that life is indeed an embodied phenomenon, and, in fact, at this very moment we are the sum total of all of our life experience. We see how our past programming and perceptions were developed, and how and why we see the world in the way that we do. We see how we can begin to 're-program' ways of being that are no longer serving us, and how easy and 'doable' it all is.

This science shows us that deep in our psyche there are embedded two very strong drives, or systems. One is a fear response drive that is hyper-reactive to any perception of threat, and is responsible for feelings of emotional chaos, stress and anxiety. The second is a calmer, much more

3

stable drive; its desire is to bond and connect. Heartfulness stems from, and further cultivates this second drive.

These two drives are responsible for how we see the world at any given moment in time. Both were necessary for our species to survive, however physiologically it is impossible to be rooted in both drives at once. Both are continually being developed and perpetuated by our inner experience, and the one that we pay attention to is the one that dominates, and more strongly develops. At any given point in time we perceive our existence through the lens of the dominant drive. Through the 'spiral of becoming' this perception becomes our inner experience, and our inner experience becomes who we are.

Although our fear response system is most often dominant, and is responsible for our all consuming stress, anxiety and emotional chaos, it is really our calm and connection system that allows our deepest sense of life to flourish. When we are rooted in our calm and connection system we are not only drawn into attachment and communion with others, and our outer world, we are also more capable of being in communion with our own Inner Being. However, since our fear response drive, physiologically, is hyper-reactive and will override and hijack us when it gets a chance, it takes overt intentionality to nurture, sustain, and fully develop our calm and connection system. It takes active and heartful engagement. Heartful awareness is our path to do this. Living a life of heartful awareness matters immensely, and profoundly changes us.

The transformative powers of heartful awareness are evidenced, through the 'science of embodiment', throughout this book. Through it we can see how we have become 'who' we are, and how heartful awareness helps us to re-align ourselves to a life of thriving. We can see the importance of the nature of engagement we bring to every moment, and we can see how it helps us heal. We can see tangible and specific ways to incorporate it into our every day lives, and the transformations that occur when we do so. We can also see that when we define heartful awareness through the science of embodiment it requires truth and authenticity. Deep down our bodies and psyche's know. This requirement of truth necessitates greater depth in understanding and embracing our heartful experience.

When we look at heartful awareness through the lens of our human existence, that it is truly an embodied way of being, we can clearly see how it transforms us. All at once this 'science of embodiment' shows us how our human bodies are not only evidence of, but are vehicles for, transformation. We can plainly see that being heartfully engaged with our world creates very specific and measurable changes in how we receive and perceive our existence. It affects the choices we make, the behaviors we exhibit, and the lens through which we see our world. As long as we are humanly alive, our bodies are the instruments through which we experience life; and they are constantly adapting to every moment of every day. These adaptations are taking place whether we know it or not, and whether we like it or not.

Looking at heartful awareness through the science of embodiment shows evidence of the transformative powers of our day-to-day choices. It shows the profound power of intentional heartful engagement, and the power of that engagement in every moment. It demonstrates the efficacy of specific and prescribed ways of being, practices, and choices we can cultivate in our day-to-day life, and a blueprint for overall change. The science of embodiment validates tangible and specific steps we can take, and the tone of intentionality we can bring to all of the moments of our lives. It not only shows us the 'why', it shows us the 'how'. The 'why' and the 'how' are conveyed throughout the journey of this book.

The embodiment of heartful engagement also offers us an alternative way to heal. When we heartfully engage our world, we are not only engaging others, we are engaging ourselves as well. Our bodies, including our brains, psyches, and spirit, are beautifully designed systems of adaptation. Our human systems, or bodies, are constantly adapting to any experience that we give them. Unfortunately, however, throughout our lives many of us have had traumatic or challenging life experiences that have had an impact on our ability to be grounded in our calm and connection system.

When we look at this dynamic from an embodied perspective, we can see how, even through trauma, our body's adaptive processes have always been there to protect us. As a response to trauma or other life challenges we may have adopted perceptions, behaviors, or choices, that were originally protective in some way. Quite often these adaptations have far outlived their purpose and we begin to blame, shame, or judge ourselves for feeling or behaving as we do. This blame, shame, or judgment only further cements our fear response system, and leads us further from the physiological state of healing.

Embracing this process from a posture of heartful awareness and engagement for our selves, and our adaptive processes, is the first step in being able to heal and reprogram a different experience. In other words, we can hold ourselves in a place of self-understanding, or self-compassion for our perceptions and behaviors without letting them consume us or perpetuate our inner experience. Once we can gain a little distance from the reactivity, we can hold our self in a state of heartful engagement, and offer an alternative, healing inner experience. Heartful engagement, directed internally, heals us at our core.

The way we engage every moment permeates our life. Because we are constantly adapting to every moment of every day, the words we speak, the stories we tell, about ourselves and others, the scripts we write and the willingness we bring to every moment profoundly determines who we are, and who we are becoming. When we look at these dynamics through the lens of heartful awareness, for our selves and others, we see how immensely they matter. Because every inner or outer feeling, thought, word and choice leads to more of the same, we can see the transformative powers of intentionally and heartfully engaging our selves, and these practices. The way we engage in, and the things we expose ourselves to on a daily basis powerfully impact who we are becoming at any moment in time.

Lastly, the science of embodiment is honest. Our bodies know and will reflect the truth even if we are not consciously aware of it, and somehow this truth will find its way into our existence. Heartful awareness and engagement must be authentic or it is not heartful engagement at all. Looking at the requirement of truth in heartful engagement invites us to a new level of depth in the heartful experience. The requirement of truth leaves no room for self-blame, shame, judgment or 'shoulds' if we are feeling less than heartful. It merely offers the invitation, in the moments we can, to deeply engage in what that moment has to offer. And if we cannot, heartful awareness directed back at our self offers the opportunity to heal or clear what may be blocking us.

What does it really mean to be heartfully present with our self, others, and our Inner Being in this very moment?

Through this book I invite you on an embodied journey. I invite you on a journey to the truth and the transformative power of heartful awareness and engagement. We will look at what it means, and what blocks us from it. We will examine how to intentionally cultivate it, how to heal through it, and how to embody it in our day-to-day life. We will look at how it profoundly changes us, from the inside, out.

Our heartful path

The promise of heartfulness through the science of embodiment assures us that through its practice we can cultivate a more expansive, larger way to live in the world. We all at once have greater access to the inexhaustible source of wisdom, radiance and power at our core, and are more capable of having that power manifest in our external reality. Heartfulness is experienced as a deep FELT SENSE of engagement with that of which we are heartfully aware; it may be in communion with our own Inner Being, others, or our outside world. In a large sense it is ineffable, or beyond all words.

At its most profound sense it is experienced as a whole body knowing, a coherent integration of bodily systems where there is a felt sense of surety. This is, in fact, what is going on. When we heartfully engage in its profoundest sense, our bodily systems form a coherence where, working as an integrated whole, our mind, body and spirit become one and it feels like we become one with the universe. We may know and understand things we may not even be able to formulate words for.

Maybe you've experienced this phenomenon, in big or small ways. Maybe this is a typical way of being for you and you want to cultivate more. Maybe you've experienced it intermittently, you know it exists, but have no idea how to intentionally cultivate, or even begin to give it voice and let it guide you.

Maybe you have a faint inkling that it might exist, but it certainly has never been your way of being in the world.

We all have the capacity to reap the foundational and transformative powers of heartfulness, and indeed, it is where our true power lies. Heartfulness offers us a path to live the lives we were meant to live.

So what is stopping us? If there is this perfect and ineffable heartful core built into every one of us, and intentionally cultivating it can profoundly change our lives, why are not we consistently living from this state? Why are heartful awareness, and its substantial benefits, not the operating forces in our lives?

Stress, anxiety and emotional chaos often so consume our existence that we are not capable of feeling or perceiving anything else. Our perceptions of stress and chaos in our every day reality color the lens of our existence, and we see our whole world through those states. We cannot seem to find solid ground from which to change. The effects of anxiety, worry, fear and other ungrounded emotions are in direct biochemical opposition to positive loving emotions and a sense of inner calm; it is physiologically impossible to feel both states at once. Too, these states of threat, anxiety and reactivity perpetuate themselves as we consistently and routinely expose ourselves to them. Our bodies and brains adapt and continue to worsen the cycle. We literally become more biologically capable of experiencing more stress, more anxiety, and more emotional chaos. This 'feedback loop" of emotional states fosters more emotional chaos, and heartfulness seems an impossible ideal. Simply put, stress, anxiety, and emotional chaos counteract heartfulness, all its foundational benefits, and any ability for us to connect to others, our outer world, or the deepest parts of ourselves. Authenticity in heartful engagement, a prerequisite for its foundational benefits, seems completely elusive.

We know there is another way and we yearn to be different. Even though we know heartfulness is the answer to curing our stress and anxiety and allowing us to live the lives we were meant to live, our stress, anxiety and emotional chaos seems to be exactly what is blocking our ability to be heartful. To worsen the cycle, we may be blaming, shaming or judging ourselves for not being able to authentically feel anything remotely heartful. Our threat, or fear response system is in overdrive, and our calm and connection system seems nonexistent. We long for an answer.

The miracle of being human, and existing in our human bodies, may all at once be the answer to what blocks us, and the solution for clearing those blocks. It certainly provides for us a frame of understanding of how stress, anxiety, and emotional chaos become programmed ways of being for us, and how those states prevent us from realizing and living from this powerful source at our core. It also provides us with a blueprint for how to intentionally cultivate more life generating, and heartful ways of being in the world, which allow us to flourish to our fullest inner potential.

So what does the science of embodiment tell us about the typical ways we respond to life, and what is possible through heartfulness? An embodied look at life shows us how our inner experience is paramount in the transformative process and creates who we are becoming at any given point in time. It shows us why stress, anxiety and emotional chaos cut us off from states of heartful awareness, and how to clear those blocks. It shows us the life transforming power of heartful awareness and a path to manifest heartfulness as our lived experience.

The science of embodiment

"Listen to your heart." " What does your gut say?" " I'll need to sit on it." "I am happy living in my own skin." "The eyes are the windows to the soul." The mind, body and spirit cannot be separated. And we know it because we feel it.

Our bodies may be the greatest spiritual, and transformative tool we have. As long as we are humanly alive, it is our all-inclusive bodies that define human existence. Our bodies, including our brain and body proper, are what receive for us, perceive, interpret, and tell us stories about our reality. They tell us how to think, feel, respond and behave, and then further facilitate our capabilities to do all of those things. They allow us to feel, and experience love, compassion and other deep states of heartfulness; even advanced states of consciousness, mystical experience and peak moments are facilitated through the workings of our body and brain.

In short, without our bodies, our human existence ceases.

This is not meant to be a philosophical or theological discussion about what happens to our soul after our body dies. The impermanence of the body does not mean the impermanence of the soul, and the body is not the soul itself. However, as long as we are humanly alive, it is the body that is the receptor and facilitator for experiencing the soul. As long as we are alive in our human bodies it is through our bodily processes that we interpret, and engage in all of human life. Our bodies are truly the incarnation, or human receptor, of all that is seen and unseen.

While many traditions view transcendence from the body as their goal, an embodied approach to heartfulness offers us another path. It offers the idea that the duality of "I am not my body", is, in fact, myth. It offers the possibility that the 'spirit incarnate' may be exactly what the gift of humanness is about, and we can, in fact, use the 'science of embodiment' as a path to engage life in a whole different way. It allows us to see that there "is no body separate from process, or process separate from body[1]" and encourages us to look at the body as an experiential space in which heartfulness is allowed to flourish, grow, and transform our inner lives, outer lives, and world.

It is the best 'field of transformation' for the 'seeds of consciousness' to grow, and heartfulness, embodied, profoundly changes us. Joseph Campbell said: "We are not really seeking the meaning of life, as much as the feeling of being fully alive. We are seeking the experience of aliveness on this physical plane, in deep resonance with our innermost being.[2]" It is our bodies that facilitate this feeling of aliveness and the experiential state that Joseph Campbell was talking about. And it can be intentionally cultivated. An embodied approach to heartfulness provides for us both evidence of, and vehicles for this transformative path.

Living embodied

As long as we are alive in our human bodies, everything we think, do, say, experience, and feel can somehow be measured in our body and brain. All of our life experience, and everything about the universe around us, is filtered through these human systems that we live in, and is reflected back through some physiological process. As such, we can learn from these physiological dynamics to understand the transformative process, and further facilitate growth and healing. We can see how it all works together, and we can manipulate it to flourish. We can understand it is programming, heal what may be harming us, and create optimal conditions for growth. Our bodies are designed to take care of us, and facilitate all the wonder that the human experience can offer us. Life is truly an embodied phenomenon.

Our bodies are also beautifully designed systems of adaptation. Part of what it means to be human is that we filter all of our experience through our bodies, and they adapt to what we give them. The beauty of the human body is that it is constantly growing, changing and transforming through new experience. Our bodies are constantly adapting to life's experience, as we know it, and making us more capable of living the texture of that experience. They are great caretakers of our existence, but can only prepare us for what they know.

They can only respond to, and grow from what they are exposed to. Transformation is completely dependent upon experience. It is happening every moment of every day, whether we know it or not, and whether we like it or not. Every thought we think, every word we say, every emotion we feel, every moment of our existence is reflected, and then encoded in our bodies and used as operating patterns for future experience. Routine experience profoundly matters, and if we want a more heartful existence we need to allow for regular heartful experience.

Our bodies are the instruments through which we experience life, and the instruments through which transformations are constantly taking place. Most of us go through life completely unaware of this phenomenon and, as such, fail to see one of the greatest tools of enlightenment at our disposal. Every moment we are training our human systems through personal experience, and most of the time we do not even realize it. Worse, we may be training ourselves to experience more of our habitual ways of reacting.

The science of embodiment shows us that whatever inner states we authentically, and most often experience, become the operating forces in our life. When we truly 'embody' a specific way of being, through our adaptive human processes, it becomes our primary way of being in the world. The process of transformation is a constant 'spiral of becoming.' This spiral is a constant circular process from our perception in any given moment in time, to the meaning we attach to that perception, to the neuro-physiological responses (brain and body) that meaning generates, back to further influencing our perception.

This process is going on every moment of every day, whether we know it, or not, and whether we like it or not. Our human capabilities for experiencing life, through the adaptive processes of our body, are molding themselves from all the momentary experiences of our life. Moment to moment internal experience becomes our reality. There is no room for blame, shame or judgment of our self in this dynamic, as those just further exacerbate the cycle of self-harm. What this cycle does offer us are endless moments where heartful engagement, with our self, or others, has the potential to truly transform our existence.

There are three important pieces to understanding how this forms, and reforms our human existence. Once we understand this process, we can see how merely reacting to the outside world only perpetuates our 'status quo' way of being, and we can see specific and tangible ways to cultivate it for our thriving.

The first piece invites us to look at how our perceptions, or 'programming' were initially developed, for it is not reality that drives us so much as our perception of reality. Our perceptions are the lens through which we see, react, behave, and further cultivate our existence. The second piece invites us to look at how our internal reality creates foundational adaptations in our whole human system that further perpetuates that way of being. In other words, how experience, from an embodied perspective, just molds more of the same experience. The third, and most important piece invites us to build from the first two, calm a system consumed with stress and emotional chaos, and intentionally cultivate a different, more life generative way of being. In essence, we look at how we were programmed initially, look at how that programming just perpetuates itself if we remain in the status quo, and then offer life changing, alternative programming. This is our path to heartfulness.

Life as usual

Why do we see the world the way we do? What causes us to have such strong reactions to life's circumstances? Why are we so often consumed with stress, anxiety, or emotional chaos?

As a species we are programmed for survival, and sometimes that programming gets way out of balance.

When we live life in 'status quo' most of us have no idea how much a product of our own programming we are, and how much our day-to-day life just perpetuates that programming. We also do not realize how much states of heartful awareness can re-program us. As was stated earlier, deep in our human make-up are built two very strong drives. One is a drive designed to be hyper-responsive to threat, and one is a drive to create community, bond and connect. We had to have both drives built into our humanness, for without either we would not have survived as a species. And, again, physiologically it is impossible to be rooted in both drives at once. This is both the problem that blocks us from, and the answer to, creating a life of flourishing.

What this means is when we are consumed with stress, anxiety or reactivity it is physically and psychologically impossible to be in any grounded and loving state. It is impossible to be calm, see clearly, or form deep connections with others, or our own Inner Being. This is by design. The neural connections of our fear response drive are stronger, quicker and more numerous than those of our calm and connection drive. In other words, they react, and react quickly. For our species to survive, our threat response drive had to be overpowering, all consuming, and capable of overwriting any other state of being. Imminent dangers, like the threat of a tiger, had to immediately and completely overpower any state of calm. This is the way we are wired.

Also, it had to be 'programmable' to those threats that were likely to be manifest in our environment. In other words, if a tiger ate my friend the week before, and I saw a large cat, it would be advantageous for my brain to instantaneously react: "Big cat, react!" without much further thought. It had to be programmable to those threats we were likely to encounter, and react instantaneously and overpoweringly to keep us safe. We had to have an overwhelming and all-consuming inner experience of threat built into our physiology.

Furthermore, the science of embodiment tells us that the more we experience any 'inner state of being' the more we adapt to that state being as our routine programming. We are wired to program to any past threat so we can react appropriately in the future. But what our threat response system deems as appropriate is quite often skewed from the emotionalism of our past experience.

What does this mean? As we shall see in the next few chapters, our human bodies are designed to keep us safe and thriving. Our 'threat response system' has been programmed since birth to deeply encode all of our past experiences, especially those that have been threatening in any way, and use those as the 'database' deep in our brain to make meaning of all future circumstances. They are like the fire alarm system in our brain to alert us anytime anything looks remotely like that which has hurt us in the past. The greater the original threat was, the more deeply they are encoded. But it is only a warning system. And most of the time we react as if our current skewed perception is the only true reality.

Our skewed perceptions, then, create an all over system rush of threat biochemicals, chaotic heart wave patterns that permeate our body and brain, and further cement 'threat wiring' in our brain. Basically our body and brain respond to the illusion of threat, even when there may not be one, and further our threat capabilities. Our system further adapts, and reactivity, skewed perceptions and emotional chaos become the operating patterns of our life. It is a function of neural and biochemical coding and recoding, and even though the process itself is protective in nature, it now may be the exact thing that is causing us distress.

For example, in chapter 2 we will learn the story of Joey. Because of the past abuse Joey experienced from his mother, his emotional programming led him to see any woman, by nature of her gender, as a serious threat. The more he perceived and reacted negatively to any woman, the more this became ingrained as his primary operating pattern. This developed threat response to women in general far outlived the threat of his mother, and became a life-debilitating pattern for him.

When we look at these dynamics from an embodied perspective we can clearly see how this programming process is a protective mechanism designed to keep us safe, but parts of its programming may have far outlived their usefulness. We will see how the coding takes place, how the process itself is a beautifully protective response, and how to reprogram it when it is out of balance. We will see how heartfully aware ways of being help ground and reprogram our over-reactive threat response drive, and nurture the development of our drive to be calm and connect. We will see how heartful awareness and engagement profoundly changes how we function in the world. And we will see that it takes overt intentionality to develop the calm and connection drive, as it has fewer neural pathways, and is slower, and less reactive than our fear response drive.

Intentional heartful awareness foundationally changes us from the level of our cells all the way to our perception of expansiveness, and to a larger way of living in the world. And we can see, then, that through heartful ways of being our calm and connection system is allowed to flourish and be the dominating force of our life.

What is Heartfulness Awareness?

Living a life steeped in heartful awareness has the capacity to reduce the stress, anxiety and emotional chaos in our lives, and completely transform us from the inside out. We know it when we feel it. But what is it? What is its relationship to, and how is it different from mindful awareness? What are its requirements, and how are we changed because of it?

Heartful awareness is a sense of grounded and connected presence we bring to every moment. It is paying attention to the present moment experience with non-reactive acceptance as in mindfulness, and then intentionally connecting with whatever life-generating emotion deep within us that moment may offer. It is a non-reactive, non-judgmental present moment awareness that is acutely attuned to each momentary opportunity to foster a sense of deep love, compassion, understanding, connection, joy, gratitude or whatever life-generating emotion may be available to us. It is an active and intentional engagement of deep and heartful states that are nurturing and life-sustaining. It is dependent upon, and yet distinctly different from mindful awareness. As such, our journey of transformation through heartful awareness invites us to acknowledge the inextricable relationship of mindfulness and heartfulness, as well as make some distinctions between the two.

The concepts of mindfulness and heartfulness are like two halves of a transformative and healing whole. The life-generating powers of mindfulness are incomplete without heartfulness, and heartfulness is dependent upon mindfulness to be practiced in its truest sense. The science of embodiment shows us how this is true.

Mindfulness, or mindful awareness, is a concept and practice gaining widespread popularity. It has been shown to have numerous health, mental and emotional benefits. Mindful awareness is most often described as a very specific type of presence we bring to each moment. It is a full presence of mind, from a non-reactive, non-judgmental, fully accepting posture. In its purest sense it is void of the emotional reactivity that so often consumes our moments. Sometimes it is described as 'cultivating the witness,' or 'becoming the observer' of our own impulses, the impulses of others, and our outside environment – maybe, even, with a little curiosity. It is a nonreactive, nonjudgmental, wholly accepting, full presence we bring to each moment. Although when we are in a mindful, nonreactive and accepting posture, deep spaces of love or compassion may open up, that is not necessarily the overt intention.

The dynamics of mindful awareness will be covered much more in depth in Chapter 4, and there we shall see how the cultivation of mindful awareness calms our fear response drive, and re-wires our ingrained reactive patterns. We shall see that continually practicing this type of awareness causes foundational changes in our chaotic emotional response systems, and reduces their hold on our perceptions, behaviors, and ability to be grounded in the present moment. The practice of mindfulness reduces our automatic threat response, which further fosters nonreactive and accepting ways of being in the world. It allows us the gift of full presence.

But it is only one half of the story.

Heartful awareness is about active engagement with life-generating emotional states. And when we look at what defines 'life-generating' through the science of embodiment, we can clearly see that there are specific states of being that lead to a dominant calm and connection system and nurture life, and there are those that do not. Authentic and deep love, compassion, gratitude, and joy are but a few that lead to life generation. Pretense, self-blame, shame, or judgment, or those that are grasping or whimsical, are not life generating states. Our bodies know, and our bodies will reflect the truth. Too, to authentically engage in life generating emotional states, we first need to be grounded in non-reactivity. In other words, mindfulness is the first step to heartfulness, but heartfulness has the overt intention of active and full engagement.

Heartful awareness, then, is that place of nonreactive awareness where our heartfulness is allowed to emerge, and connect to our own internal processes, the people around us, or our external circumstance. While mindful awareness is a non-judgmental acceptance and awareness we bring to each moment, heartful awareness goes one step further. It is grounded in non-reactivity and acceptance, but then actively and intentionally seeks, and engages in whatever life generating opportunity that moment has to offer. It is grounded in intentional love, connection, compassion, and other heartful states of being. It holds truth and it embraces acceptance, and it also holds intentionality, engagement and possibility. By definition, and when examined through the science of embodiment, it also requires authenticity and stability.

Heartful awareness is a specific type of presence. It is an intentional engagement and heartfelt communion with our self, others, and our surroundings. It is grounded in the intentionality of engaging in life generating emotional states. When we look at heartful awareness from an embodied perspective we can see that some emotional states can be stabilizing, and life generating, and others destabilizing, and life depleting. The question is not so much whether emotion itself is good or bad, as much as which emotions lead to life, and which do not. Life generating emotional states, such as deep love, compassion, for our self, and others, joy and gratitude lead to a dominant calm and connection system, a more expansive view of life, and a larger way of living.

The science of embodiment is inherently truthful. Although some emotional states, on the surface, may masquerade as heartful awareness, our bodies know the truth. Those that are grasping, whimsical, come from our shallow heart, or mask our attempts to fill a hole in our own being are, in truth, not heartful at all. In other words, I may intensely think I love something, but my body, in its physiological response may tell me otherwise.

Too, because the science of embodiment reflects the truth, there is no room for blame, shame, or judgment if we are feeling less than heartful. Heartful awareness merely offers us the opportunity of engagement in each moment, with no blame or coercion if that moment does not present itself. In other words, a pre-requisite of heartful awareness is that it be grounded in life-generating emotional states. Physiologically, self-blame, shame or judgment is not a life-generating state. Beating ourselves up for not loving, is not loving to ourselves – therefore not heartful awareness. Self-understanding, or self-compassion for what might be blocking our capabilities in that moment may be the most heartful action we can take.

Furthermore, the science of embodiment shows us that it cannot be done out of duty, or pretense. Because, again, heartful awareness is grounded in the truth of experience, authenticity is also a prerequisite. Coercion or pretense is not authentic. As we shall see further in this text, the science of embodiment shows us that states of self-judgment or coercion are not heartful at all. It also offers us a whole new opportunity for self-compassion, and heartful awareness for our self, and our own programming when we experience those states. If we pretend to feel something we do not, or hate ourselves for not living up to some impossible ideal, we are not experiencing authentic heartful awareness. And our bodies will know.

Heartful awareness is comprised of those states where we most fully, and authentically, experience, and are guided by love, compassion, a sense of purpose, and a larger way of living. We may experience it in regard to others, to ourselves, or our world. If it is not true, it is not heartful awareness.

Heartful awareness is most deeply grounded in the momentary choice to engage in life-generating states of being. As such, it invites us into a whole different way of responding to life's reactivities. When we look at our own personal programming and reactivities through the science of embodiment, and a heartful lens, we see that our programming was originally developed to protect and serve us in some way. While it may be out of balance and causing us chaos now, 'holding' even our chaotic programming in a non-reactive, intentionally loving, or compassionate state leads us to the physiological state of healing. It is not about blaming, shaming, judging, denying, or even 'being with' our reactivities as much as directing heartful awareness back at our self, and our own internal processes. It is from there that true healing can take place. Even when our programming may be out of balance, heartful awareness offers an opportunity to engage in life in a whole different way.

When we look at the possibilities of heartful awareness, and its embodiment, through the activity of our fear response drive as opposed to our calm and connection drive, we can see the profound impact the sense of presence we bring to every moment can truly have. If each moment spent in one or the other drive contributes to which drive becomes the dominating force in our life, we can see the power, responsibility and opportunity each moment holds. 'Holding' our self, and all the moments of our life in reactive judgment, either for our self, or others, only perpetuates a threat and fear based life. Heartful awareness, on the other hand, offers moment after moment of opportunity to cultivate a life-generating sense of presence. All of our moments are full of opportunity and responsibility.

Heartful awareness also requires honesty. The science of embodiment shows us that for heartful awareness to have a profound impact on our calm and connection system it needs to tip the scales of time when we are residing in it. In other words, if we can bring a heartful presence to more moments of our life than not, we begin to see profound changes. Sometimes the most heartful response may be that it is OK to feel less than heartful, momentarily. Heartful awareness directed internally is the pre-requisite for external heartful awareness.

The heartful experience

We know heartful awareness when we feel it.

It is an integrated sense of harmony with our body, psyche, spirit and outer world. It is the 'felt sense' and inner experience of connection to deep and profound spaces, and is reflected in the awareness we bring to our outside world. We feel it in all aspects of our being including the emotional, spiritual, and physiological aspects of ourselves. It is an embodied phenomenon of 'holding' that which is in our awareness in states of deep love, understanding, and compassion. The object of our 'holding' can be our self, others, or our external world. And it can be nurtured and allowed to grow.

It is not removed nor is it shallow. Neither is it chaotic, ungrounded, grasping or whimsical. It is not distant, or cold or only observed. It is a truthful and full presence of mind, body and spirit. It is the awareness and experience of deep love, compassion, and other heartfelt emotions, for our selves, others, and outside world. And it needs to be in truth.

When we are heartfully engaged we are changed people. It can literally unite our brain, our heart, and all the cells in our body. It feels harmonious and expansive – like we are all at once in touch with the depths of our being, and connected to a much larger way of living. Our biochemicals are bathing the cells of our body in the hormones of connection, love and compassion, our brain is being activated to greater states of calm, clarity and reduced stress, and our hearts are responding with a corresponding, coherent wavelength. And, physiologically speaking, because what we continually experience, especially states that are deeply felt, become the way we function in the world we begin to live this existence.

The embodiment of heartful awareness calms our limbic, or emotional system and creates body and brain integration that leads to a higher sense of wellbeing. Our nervous system changes regulatory mechanisms, and we begin to look at the whole of life through life generating, rather than life depleting emotional states. We can better distinguish between chaotic emotional appraisal and the truth of any moment. Heartful awareness allows us to reclaim emotion in its most generative sense. While a chaotic and reactive emotional system can be our greatest foe, life-generating emotion may be our greatest asset.

Our fear response system, and the perceptions that stem from it, are no longer the driving force in our life. Anxiety, stress and emotional chaos diminish with a calm fear response system, and life becomes a choice instead of a reaction. Living a life of heartful awareness has the capacity to impact every cell in our body. And, because as long as we are humanly alive, our bodies are the instruments through which we receive, perceive and interpret life, life itself changes.

Heartful awareness profoundly changes us in all areas of our lives. Its cultivation is appropriate for deep thriving in the most intimate of relationships. When we are grounded in our calm and connection system we are grounded in the deepest sense of who we are. Bringing this loving, radiant self into our deepest relationships allows the relationship itself to flourish. As heartful awareness changes us at the deepest sense of who we are, the self we bring to our workplace and vocational life also flourishes. We are all at once grounded in clarity and purpose, and better equipped to connect with those around us. Heartful awareness gives us the opportunity of every moment. As such, that opportunity extends itself to all we do, and all we see. It provides for us a different lens from which to see the world; from those we see often, all the way to the stranger on the street.

Heartful awareness creates the capability to rest in the ineffable. As our calm and connection system better allows us to connect to others, and the outside world, it also allows us to connect to the inexhaustible source of radiance, wisdom and power at our core that Lama Surya Das professes we all have deep within us[3]. Whether for you it is experienced as a spiritual presence, your deepest sense of Self, or some form of your own Inner Being, we all have some core radiance that is our source of internal luminosity, and it is ineffable, or beyond words. Heartful awareness better connects us to this source and increases its presence in our life.

Heartful awareness is a momentary choice, moment after moment, to let our truest essence emerge into our lived reality, and have it intersect with our outside world.

Our journey as a labyrinth

Our journey through the hope and promise of heartful awareness will be much like a labyrinth. A labyrinth is an ancient symbol built on the image of a spiral as a meandering, but purposeful walking path. It can be thought of as a symbolic pilgrimage, a metaphor for the journey to the heart of our deepest self, and then out again into the world with a broadened understanding of who we are, and what we can bring to the world. A labyrinth is not a maze. A maze has twists, turns, blind alleys and dead ends; the labyrinth is a circular path that has one through route and is not designed to be difficult to navigate. The requirement of the labyrinth is that one has a willing and receptive mindset to keep following the path to the center and deeply engage in the invitation of the experience as it unfolds.

The labyrinth is designed to teach us about ourselves through our journey inward. As in a labyrinth, our journey to heartfully engaged awareness will follow a purposeful and specific path.

With a labyrinth the outer paths set the foundation for the inward journey, and so it will be with ours. On the outskirts, in chapter 2, we will look at what it looks like – from an embodied perspective - when we operate from 'status quo' or merely reacting to what the outside world offers us. We will look at how our perceptions are developed, how they are stored as our internal programming, and how they perpetuate our reality unless we offer them a different experience. We will see how they most often block us from our ability to be heartfully aware.

As we travel further into our labyrinth, in chapter 3, we will explore the workings of our two dominant systems or drives, and discover that it is physiologically impossible to have both drives dominant at once. We will see that it takes intention to cultivate our calm and connection system and subdue our fear response system, and heartful awareness does both. We will see that it is our calm and connection system that facilitates our connections to others, as well as our own Inner Being, and we will see that this is the place of reduced stress and anxiety, healing, and inner potential. We will look at tools and practices to calm the threat response, such as Mindful Awareness, Present Moment Awareness, the Power of Pause, and the importance of fostering non-reactivity.

As we near the center we will look at the power of intentional and heartful ways with which to engage the world. In chapter 4 we will shift from mindfulness to heartfulness and we will see that the degree to which we are able to heartfully engage, may directly determine the degree to which we experience transformation in our lives. We will see that it is intentional heartful experience that is the key to change. We will see the profound opportunity every moment offers. We will learn easy and 'doable' heartful shifts that tip the scales of our inner life to generating states instead of depleting states, and we will see how heartfulness changes us from the inside out. The crucial importance of the degree of heartfulness we bring to our moments and days will become evident.

In chapter 5 we will see that length in, and depths of experience are what change us most, and learn specific techniques and contemplative practices to promote that depth and length. These techniques and practices were developed from all the scientific concepts presented in this book, and with our western culture in mind, to be most effective. They are designed to be done in and transform our moments of reactivity, they are designed to be done as sustained practice, and they are designed to help us heal. They are the Heartfully Engaged Awareness Reprogramming Tools (HEART) and they are like pushing the 'reprogram' button to rest in, and further develop our calm and connection system. HEART are a set of practices that intentionally cultivate heartful awareness often enough and deep enough that they become our 'new programming' from which to engage the world.

Deeper in our labyrinth, and also in chapter 5, we will be invited to take a healing and self-compassionate look at our own personal programming. We will see that this programming was initially developed to keep us safe and thriving. When it is reactive or out of balance it is most often an indication that something in our implicit memory is asking for our loving and healing attention. Understanding the process of our personal programming, and the fact that the process itself is good and meant to keep us safe, helps us hold ourselves in a loving and compassionate state even within the difficulty. Directing heartful engagement back to our selves, even within our reactivity, is the first step to healing and rebalancing our systems. We can then re-program a new way of being. HEART for Healing specifically leads us through this process.

When one walks a labyrinth, it is customary to pause in the middle and reflect on the journey. As the path in quite often reflects the journey to our own center, the path out can reveal specific and tangible steps we might take to outwardly manifest the lessons learned. Such will be our process. The rest of our journey, throughout chapters 6 and 7, we will consider specific and tangible ways we might cultivate heartful awareness in the moments of our every day life.

First, we will examine the question of authentic willingness. Many of us profess to want change, but at a fundamental level we are not really ready, or willing to accept that change. We will look at ways to discern this question and move forward if it is appropriate to do so. We will also consider the power, opportunity and presence we bring to every moment, and the incredible impact of our inner chatter, outer words, stories we tell, scripts we write, and interpretations we make.

We will look at the ever-pervasive challenge of action, and the fact that until action happens everything remains the same.

Simple daily changes, and attention to our every day involvements create new neural networks and establish new habits of being 'us'. How do we, more often than not, and not just in the midst of practice, live from that state in our everyday lives? Sometimes, it is the simple things we do that best ground us in our calm and connection system and make the most powerful difference. Small changes add up, and we can intentionally create the conditions, or the fertile soil, for our 'seeds of consciousness' to grow in life generating ways. We can create the circumstances to better allow our heartful awareness to blossom, for our self and others.

As such, we will look at our 'energy diet', or the things that we expose ourselves to on a daily basis that either detract from, or add to our overall ability to ground ourselves in our calm and connection system. We will entertain the idea that our overall level of 'wellness' profoundly affects our ability to engage in heartful awareness, for both ourselves, and others, and examine what comprises true 'wellness.' Finally, we will focus on gaining some clarity on how we might move forward to create heartfully engaged awareness as a foundational part of our existence.

Personalizing the journey

Finally, the process of this book is designed to guide you on your own transformative journey to heartful awareness. All at once it invites you to learn about the scientific process of what heartfulness has to offer, as well as engage in the miracle of how it may play out in your own life. Mostly, it encourages you to create your own heartful journey.

It is my desire to tell you what it means, why it is worth doing and lead you through a process of concrete development through heartful experience.

I encourage you to fully engage in the journey by doing all the activities and reflective writing exercises included in each chapter. The reflective exercises challenge you to take the journey from cognitive knowledge to lived experience, and the miracle of heartful awareness through action. The reflection exercises are designed to have you take the abstract concepts being presented and reflect, personalize, and process at a much deeper level than you would by merely reading the material alone. They are designed to be done in a 'stream of consciousness' style of writing in which the writing process leads you. These exercises facilitate the experiential nature of fully embracing heartful awareness.

Reflective writing all at once quiets our inner chatter, reduces the stress, chaos, and anxiety in our lives, and brings our deeper feelings to conscious awareness. By bringing this type of awareness to our emotional lives we promote brain integration and a more balanced way of experiencing reality. Heartful awareness is more accessible; we are better able to connect to what we intuitively know to be true, and with our Inner Being. Too, reflective writing gives us insight and guidance for further heartful awareness, and the powerful life transformations that come from it. You might find it helpful to keep a personal journal dedicated to the process offered here, and include in it thoughts or insights along your path. The heartful transformation offered here is completely dependent on your level of engagement with it. Do what feels comfortable for you.

Heartful Practices for life

Throughout this book there are also various centering practices, heartful awareness tools and re-programming techniques. These are designed for practical use and deep application of heartful awareness, and may be the most transformative material on our journey. Because it is experience that changes us, and deep and sustained experience most of all, routine and consistent use of these practices has the potential to truly transform us, have us most often rooted in our calm and connection system, and experience the world accordingly.

But like the rest of the information in this book, they need to be experienced. Routine and consistent practice is what produces foundational change, and the benefits of routine and consistency cannot be overstated. These practices are designed to be done in the moment of reactivity, and also done as sustained practice. A large part of the appendix is dedicated to diving deeper into the practices. In it is a diagram to help you visualize how the practices are interconnected, a review of each of the specific practices, and a record log to chronicle your experience with them. Each of the practices are also available in audio format, and in the appendix is a reference on how to obtain them.

Finding heartful opportunity

Heartful awareness invites us one step beyond being mindfully aware. It is the other half of a whole way of being. Beyond fostering a non-reactive and accepting presence, it invites us to see every moment as an opportunity for active, and intentional heartful engagement. In heartful awareness every moment offers an opportunity to actively and heartfully engage with life.

The embodiment of heartful awareness requires authenticity. It is not about pretending to feel something we do not, positive thinking when we really do not believe it, or forcing or judging the moments when it is not available. There is no room for blame, shame or judgment, as these states are in direct opposition to what heartfulness has to offer. Your body knows the truth and will adjust accordingly.

It is about finding the opportunity – in more moments than not – to intentionally and genuinely notice and engage in a deep and heartfelt way with what that moment has to offer. It may be heartful engagement with yourself, your Inner Being, others, or the outside world. Too, when we remember that every moment of every day we are molding, or transforming to our inner experience, and cultivating the capabilities for more of the same, we can also see the responsibility that every moment carries.

The moments add up.

And every moment is an opportunity.

Heartful awareness is found in momentary opportunities for full presence and loving engagement, and each moment we are able to heartfully engage is a moment of heartful transformation. The opportunity for heartful awareness presents itself moment after moment, and day after day. And the moments and days add up.

But we need to be aware.

Presented throughout this book are specific and tangible ways to cultivate heartful awareness. The opportunities are as numerous as the moments in the day, and the type of presence we bring to every moment is paramount. But it takes overt attention and awareness to truly be fully present in the moments of our lives. How do we remind ourselves? How do we truly recognize the opportunity when it presents itself?

There is a concept called in-attentional blindness, which basically tells us that we are blind to the things that we do not pay attention to. It also tells us that the things that we do pay attention to show up for us full force. The concept of in-attentional blindness is closely related to a practice I call Present Moment Awareness. Present Moment Awareness invites us into a way of being fully present and aware in each moment, but then also invites us to recognize the opportunity for heartful engagement it may provide. In-attentional blindness and Present Moment Awareness will be presented more in-depth shortly, but first, a story of a time the practice of Present Moment Awareness gave me one of the most meaningful moments of my life.

It was a challenging morning getting the kids off to school and I was pressed to make it to work on time. Everything that could go wrong seemed to be going that way. It was raining and I just had enough time to make it to my class if there were no travel hitches. The stress was building, and I could feel its impact. Immediately I was delayed by construction on the road leaving my town. When I got to the university there was another construction zone, and I was beginning to feel the stress of time furthering the frustration of the morning. Although at the University where I teach parking can be a major challenge and quite often requires several extra minutes built in to commute time, that was never an issue for me. There was a faculty parking lot right next to the building I taught in. I could ALWAYS find a parking spot there.

That is, until that morning. I was beyond shocked and dumbfounded when there were no spaces and I had to drive all the way around to another lot where I would have to cross several muddy grass athletic fields in the rain. Too, when I go to work I typically have numerous bags to carry. I teach both movement classes and lecture classes, which require separate changes of clothes. That fact, coupled with the books, etc. I need for classes, makes it look like I am packing for the weekend every time I go to work. As I began to make my way, with all my bags, through the mud and the rain some voice deep within me said: "Bring yourself heartfully present, Alane, look for the opportunity".

Something incredible happens when you can bring yourself truly present. For me the shift was palpable, and, given the emotional state I was starting from, what happened in the next several minutes was nothing short of amazing. My 'brain chatter' and the over-exaggerated appraisal and emotional significance I was bringing to one day of being a few minutes late began to quiet. Immediately I began to feel the soft rain on my face and appreciate its texture. For the first time I saw the loveliness of the morning. The fields were actually beautiful, and behind them I could see the snow topped mountains. I felt a measurable shift in both my physical and emotional state of being, and, for the first time since I woke, my laser focus of stress dimmed and I began to let in the expansive beauty of life. I was able to distance myself from, and even find great amusement in all the mishaps of the morning. My emotional shift made me much more available to the opportunity of the moment, and that moment offered something surprising.

I ran into my dad. We both taught for the same department at the University, but because I always came in from the other side I almost never saw him. I had no idea he had a class in that space, or at that time. He was teaching a golf class, on the grass fields, in the rain. I cannot explain exactly what happened at that instant, all I can say is that sometimes life intervenes and makes magic. I wish I had the words to describe the heartfelt connection that took place. There are those moments in life where we have heart to heart connections with another that are impossible to put into words. This was one of them.

Although I was peripherally aware that there were over 50 people still waiting for me to begin my class, being fully present in this moment with my father seemed more important. I dropped all my bags and playfully held the umbrella for him as if he was a king and the most important person in the world. I will never forget that moment of genuine eye contact, full presence, and heart-to-heart engagement. He laughed. I laughed. His class laughed. The rain became downpour and he excused his golfers for drier conditions.

I entered the building, and while I was walking down the hallway to meet my class I reflected on what a transformational moment that had been. Even though I was wet and muddy, and a few more minutes later to my class than I would have been otherwise, what I was bringing to my class in the way of my emotional presence was night and day. Instead of coming in to my class frazzled, harried, stressed out and emotionally unavailable, I came in fully present, full of love, and ready to connect with my students.

If the story had ended there it would have been enough.

It didn't.

After my dad canceled his class he started not feeling well. He decided to leave work for the day and go home to rest. While at home he had a massive heart attack and passed away. That was the last time I saw or spoke with him.

I have thought of that story many times since, and the absolute grace I was given to hear that deep voice within reminding me to be present in the moment and look for the opportunity. I can only imagine how different the story would be if my last words to him had been: "Dad, I cannot talk right now. It is been a horrible morning, and I am late for class. I am sorry, I just do not have the time."

The moments of our lives are rich with heartful opportunity, but we need to be present with what they have to offer. When we are, those moments transform us. Cultivating the transformational powers of heartful awareness profoundly changes who we are, and who we are becoming. That is the journey of this book.

Exercise and Reflection # 1 - In-attentional blindness, or "What are your gorillas?"

Imagine this. You are watching a group of people, some with white shirts and some with black shirts. They are all weaving in and out of each other in a group and throwing basketballs. You have been instructed to count the number of bounce passes from someone wearing a white shirt to another person wearing a white shirt. Since there are several balls, and several types of passes being thrown within and between the groups, you are so focused on the counting you completely miss a gorilla walking through the middle of the group, pounding on his chest and continuing on! This phenomenon is true for at least 75% of the people participating in this scenario.

This phenomenon is called 'inattentional blindness,' or 'selective attention.' This concept tells us that when we are hyper-focused on one thing, we literally may miss what is right in front of our faces. Research has shown over and over again that we perceive only those objects that receive our focused attention. I have shown this video on many occasions. Participants are always shocked when, on the third or fourth time through the video, I point out the gorilla pounding on it is chest standing in the middle of the basketball players.

Selective attention plays itself out over and over again in our daily lives. Your brain can only pay attention to so much at once, so if you are giving all the things in your life that are challenging more emotional attention than they deserve, you may completely miss the good things that are right in front of your face. Literally. When we are so focused on what we think is wrong, may go wrong, could, should or would go wrong - **whether those thoughts are rooted in reality or not** - we can literally miss the wonderful things that comprise our lives. And neuroscience tells us that what we pay attention to wires us to see more of the same. We not only miss seeing the wonderful things right in front of our face, quite often we miss the opportunity to cultivate more of their presence. Paying attention to the gorillas in our midst – the daily graces we tend to overlook, or not see at all, can profoundly change the way we see the world.

What graces in your life are you overlooking? What are your gorillas?

Write and brainstorm about the wonderful things in your life you may be overlooking because your awareness is directed at your many life's challenges. Write 'stream of consciousness' style, and let the writing lead you. What are you overlooking? What might be different if you gave it more of your heartful attention? How can you stop and remind yourself to see your blessings as well?

Practice: Present Moment Awareness

When we bring our awareness to the present moment, or are very mindful of the present moment like an observer or a witness, we begin to break the typical stimulus / response patterns that usually carry us away into a state of reactivity. Too, our awareness begins to integrate and balance our brain activity to states of calm and non-reactivity. It allows us to calm our hyper-arousal and see opportunity where we had only perceived threat. Present moment awareness, or mindfulness in the moment, usually involves bringing awareness to our senses of sight, smell, touch and sound in a way of hyper experiencing them without really being engaged in thought about them. Again, we are acting almost like an observer of our self, and what it feels like to be fully present, mind, body and soul, in any given moment.

Present moment awareness, also means that we are not hijacked by our thoughts, emotions, or implicit memory patterns. We may notice the reactivity without getting caught up in it, possibly, even, with a little curiosity. We become more aware of heartful opportunities as they present themselves.

1. Disengage from the reactivity and breathe
2. Bring your awareness to the experience of your senses without really engaging in thought about them.
3. Pause and feel what it feels like to be fully present in this absolute now moment.
4. Notice if the moment presents for you a heartful opportunity you might have not been aware of in your reactive state.

Practice present moment awareness 3-4 times a day for the next week. Record your experiences in the record log in the appendix.

Conclusion – Embracing the journey

This book is about the transformational powers of heartful awareness. It is about transforming and healing the stress, chaos and anxiety in our lives through heartful awareness for our self, others, and our world. It is about healing and reprogramming reactive, destructive and threat based emotional patterns that are no longer serving us, and replacing those patterns with ones that encourage us to thrive and connect with the world around us. It is about intentionally cultivating a way of heartfulness that changes us from the inside out.

It includes what I have learned academically, personally and relationally from working with the thousands of people I have been blessed to share this information with. What I have come to know through this journey is that you have it within you. Inside you is a life of heartfulness waiting, and yearning to be born. You have within you the ability, knowledge, passion and emotional know how; you have within you the possibility of a heartful transformation, whatever form it takes and however it is calling to you.

Ultimately, it is experience that transforms. This book leads you on a transformational journey to heartfulness, and it is designed to be an experiential process. This journey, if you authentically and heartfully engage, will all at once better connect you to your Inner Being as well as with others and the outside world. By consistently experiencing moments of authentic heartful awareness we create measurable changes in our bodies, brains, spirits and psyche that profoundly affect our life and the lives of those around us. Beyond knowledge, this process requires action.

If nothing changes, nothing changes.

We all have it within us, but it takes an about-face, a change of heart, and a choice of love. It takes calming the chaos of our lives enough to hear our heartful voice, and it takes enough self-trust, self-love and self-compassion to acknowledge its presence and heal what may be blocking it. It takes reprogramming some of our emotional patterning that is no longer serving us, and it takes attention, intention and action, to heartfully engage with what each moment is offering us. It takes willingness, and choice, and intentional engagement of the heartfulness within, and all around us. And it often takes a guide or facilitator and a blueprint for change. This book offers you that.

Journal entry - March 1997-2

I had this dream last night that I came upon a big, beautiful carved wooden door. I knew intuitively that what lied inside was a symbol for my internal life. I paused knowing that opening the door was an irreversible step. I knew that whatever I discovered would be knowledge gained forever, that I could not unlearn whatever I might discover. Maybe I should just walk away and go back to status quo. And yet I needed to know. I needed to know if there were answers for me in there. I needed to know if what lied inside was the key for moving forward, for direct answers to the key of life, my life, and how I might engage it.

When I opened the door I found a room of such potential beauty, yet it was incredibly dusty from years of neglect. A couple of realizations hit me hard. One was that I now knew that this room existed. I could not just walk away and go back to my external life as if I had never made this discovery. Going back to my external life, as if all answers were to be found there, was no longer an option. I knew that the key to recovering my life was somehow associated with this room. I intuitively knew that my external life would begin to flow the way that it was supposed to, almost in direct correlation to the degree to which I could engage with what this space had to offer me.

It was also evident that to really tap into the life waiting for me there, I needed to pay attention to what might be blocking me from truly experiencing it in all its glory. I could not be truly immersed in its beauty until I figured out how not to be immersed in the dust. I needed to be able to turn off, reroute or heal the external noise and distractions so I could truly trust and rest in this space and soak up whatever wisdom it held for me.

Lastly, there was this feeling of profound peace. Accompanying this profound peace was a slight sense of anxiety and fear of the unknown, but these were peripheral pieces. Acknowledging the fear, and still having the courage to step into the room, trusting that the room would provide the answers was my only choice. And even though it felt uncomfortable, and a little scary, I knew this was a step I needed to take. It felt like surrender. It felt like surrendering the idea that I could somehow force my life into attunement, and what I really needed was an awareness and engagement with life, and this room, in a whole different manner. This way of engaging life was where the answers were, and I needed to be present with all that it had to offer.

This was the room of heartfulness.

And it offered me everything.

2

Who We Are and What is Possible

Introduction – A blueprint for change

This book is based on the concept that the intentional development of heartful awareness foundationally changes who we are, and who we are becoming. It shows us that heartful engagement helps calm our fear response system, and allows our calm and connection system to flourish. With the reactivities of our fear response system quieted, and our calm and connection system dominant, we are better able to connect with our outside world, others around us, and our own Inner Being. For deep within each and every one of us is an Inner Being; a reliable source of inner wisdom, radiance and truth, and being able to tap into and live from this state creates transformational changes in our lives. The ability to cultivate heartful awareness profoundly connects us to life itself, and matters immensely.

However, the reality is that most of us live our lives in constant reaction to the external world with all its challenges, pitfalls, and troubles, feeling ungrounded and believing we have no other choice. Our fear response system dominates, and stress, anxiety and internal 'unsettledness' are ever present. What is more, when we are in this state of constant reactivity, merely bouncing around in response to all the external world gives us, we cannot even remotely grasp, or tap into this grounded way of being. We seem to be faced with two ways of being; we know one is 'The Way', but we are consumed with the other. So what happens?

As hard as it may be to accept, our lives at this very moment are the sum total of our life experience, a complete record of our personal past. Because part of being human means we are systems of adaptation, every moment of every day we are transforming, or adapting, to life experience, whether we know it or not, and whether we like it or not. As we shall see throughout this chapter, inner experience forms us, and life becomes any repeated internal state. Of course you probably know that the major experiences of your life have had an impact on who you are; the much more subtle influences have also. As we shall see, every internal experience, process of an event, every thought, behavior, word, choice and action creates more of the same and has brought you to this very moment. Our bodies, brains, psyches, and spirits, indeed the totality of our beings, are constantly adapting to every moment of every day and delivering back a model of its experience.

Quite often the first impulse people have when faced with this reality is to blame, shame or judge themselves if they are not in a comfortable life space. Or blame life circumstance, understandably so, for external events that have been traumatic, and wounded them in some way. This part of our journey together is intended to share with you how this process takes place, to form a genuine understanding and deep appreciation for how we have become who we are, and to inspire you to take action in areas you would like to transform. You will see that your original 'programming' – as limiting, chaotic or destructive, as it may seem now – was originally developed to serve you, or keep you safe in some way. You will see that this very moment, welcomed with self-love and compassion, is the first step to transformation and healing.

Embracing this process from a state of heartful awareness, acceptance and gratitude gives us the necessary tools for change and healing. Looking through a lens of self-love, we can all at once appreciate how past reactions, patterns and behaviors have helped protect us in the past, and 'update' the parts that are no longer serving us. We can see how these reactions, patterns, and ways of being can truly be transformed, and we have a blueprint for change. This transformational process will give you greater access to your Innermost Being, and your Innermost Being will begin to guide you through greater transformation. Your life experience will change, and so will you.

The focus of these next two chapters is to learn how our bodies, brains, psyches and spirits work together in an integrated sense. Essentially what it means to be living in our human bodies and experiencing life the way we do. Once we have this foundation of understanding we can see why, when our systems are in chaos and out of balance, it is impossible to live from heartfully aware or grounded states. Too, we can see scientific evidence of transformation and healing when we cultivate those states, and we can see specific steps of how to do that.

In this chapter we will look at perception, or how and why we see life, and all it comprises, the way we do. Also included is how unique or individual our perceptions are to us, and our past experience. In other words, two people can have a profoundly different perception, or inner response to the same experience, which then can deeply affect the way they are in the world. We will look at how and why this happens, the important significance of it all, and how to begin to transform, or heal what it is in you that may be nudging for attention.

The truth is that it is not reality that drives us as much as it is our perception and interpretation of reality. In other words, we see our world through any past experience programmed in our psyches, and any emotional state that we are currently experiencing. Understanding how perception is formed and guided originally is paramount to healing the perceptions and reactions that keep us out of balance, in chaos, or out of connection with Anything Larger.

Too, understanding, embracing, and even appreciating how this process has formed us – even as out of balance as it may seem now – is an all-important step along our path. In essence, we will learn to give ourselves, and our 'programming', the same degree of love, compassion and heartful awareness as we would our best friend. When we can look at this process void of any self-blame, shame, or judgment, in fact, through the lens of self-love and acceptance, we can clearly see the road to transformation and healing.

Chapters 2 and 3 work together to tell a comprehensive story about how we have come to this very moment in a neuro-physiological sense, and how this sheds light on the path for change.

In chapter 3 we will look at how our life experiences perpetuate themselves. Our perceptions guide our everyday reality, which, in turn, molds who we are becoming - which then circles around and guides our further perceptions! We will see how our day-to-day existence is guided by the version of reality this process wants us to believe.

Through what I call the cycle of adaptation, or 'spiral of becoming' we will look at the primary physiological systems that play a major role in who we are at any given point in time and how they change and adapt to ongoing life experience. By looking at the neuroscience, biochemistry, and electrical aspects of transformation, we can clearly see that human life is an embodied phenomenon, and adapts as such. Embracing it in this way, we can heal and cultivate intentional experience so those systems create true and foundational transformation. This all leads to a better connection with our Inner Being, and the ability to cultivate a larger way to live.

We will look at how our programmed reactivities have molded who we are, and we will look at ways to bring a non-reactive awareness to them – the first step in re-encoding them. In short, in the next two chapters we will look at how it all works, what happens when it goes wrong, and how to begin to cultivate it so that we can thrive. This material sets the foundation for our journey from mindfulness to heartfulness.

This is the most scientific and difficult material in the book. I urge you to take some time to digest the material and stick with it. I will do my best to make it understandable, and help you see how the neuroscience behind the 'spiral of becoming' plays out in your everyday life in very deep and meaningful ways. The foundation built in this chapter, and the next, will serve as the basis for our transformative process. From there you will be able to clearly see how heartful awareness, and engagement, leads to healing and thriving, and how living a life grounded in your deepest potential or Inner Being is possible.

There may be a point in these two chapters where all of this information may seem dismal, and the 'spiral' beyond hope of any healing or higher functioning. When we were at this point in a course I teach at the university I once had a student raise her hand in the middle of class and say "Dr. Daugherty you are just pissing me off! Every time I get in a fight with my boyfriend all I can think about is how my amygdala is firing, his amygdala is firing and we are both being totally hijacked by our own perceptions and interpretations of what is going on. From the material, now I understand we are both completely off-balance and seeing the chaos from our own reactive and emotional lenses, but there is nothing I can do about it!" Thankfully she stuck with it long enough to learn, and embody, another way.

The information in these two chapters is designed to give you a good understanding of what really is going on in the chaos of our lives, and give you a vision and hope of what to do about it - a blueprint for heartfully engaging, and tapping into a life force we know is possible.

We know there is another way, so what is blocking us?

Before we look at this process in its life giving, or life-generating form, however, it is helpful to look at our patterns at status quo - the way we routinely act and react to every moment of every day. As we shall see, fear response states, and states of calm and connection, are two profoundly opposing and different biological realities. Living immersed in stress, reactivity and emotional chaos profoundly impedes our connection to Anything Larger. Much of the time we live life at status quo; on automatic pilot, merely reacting to the external world as if we have no choice. It seems our chaotic emotional systems are in control and want us to see and believe only disorder.

In a large sense they do.

Or at least in part.

Stress, anxiety, reactivity, and emotional unease pervade our day-to-day life. They affect our perceptions of happiness, our ability to operate from a grounded state, our physical health, the health of our heart and our immune system, and create an often-skewed perception of reality. The physiologically detrimental effects of anxiety, worry, fear, and other ungrounded emotions are in direct biochemical and neural opposition to positive loving emotions and a sense of inner calm - and it is physiologically impossible to feel both states at once.

The static of stress, anxiety, emotional unease, and reactivity block the path to our own internal wisdom, calm, and ability to function from grounded, centered and heartfully engaged states. How can you tune into your heart, or deep inner wisdom if the static of your life is screaming so loud that you cannot even hear it? Any repeated internal state becomes who we are and how we function in the world, and staying immersed in states of reactivity, stress, or anxiety, only further the distance between heartful awareness for ourselves, others, or our Inner Being.

So what is this sense of emotional unease that seems to dominate and dictate our lives? How do we not be victims to it? How do we intentionally create a different way of being, thrive and live the life we were intended?

First, I use the term 'stress' as an all-encompassing state of emotional un-easiness, including all the ungrounded emotional states that cut us off from the deepest parts of ourselves. I use it as an umbrella term including feelings of anxiety, to describe times when we are consumed with emotional reactivity or triggers; basically as an over-arching term to describe all the states that throw us off balance. Whereas the opposite, a sense of thriving, may include a sense of 'oneness', groundedness, feelings of clarity, coherence, passion or purpose, the state of stress is decidedly absent of these. What I am describing as stress is any state of being that is in direct opposition to that felt sense of thriving.

When I pose the question 'what is stress?' to my university students, I get a variety of answers including bills, relationships, work, money, time, health; the list goes on and on. But then we get deeper into it I will get more answers like overwhelm, anxiety, worry, fear, self-hatred, anger, feelings of inadequacy, feeling like there is something more, and that list goes on. Once we can pull apart the difference between the things that stress us out, our reactions, and that 'felt sense' we carry in response, we come to the understanding that stress is an overall feeling of emotional unease. We cannot really find the words to accurately describe the debilitating effects, but we know it because we FEEL it.

And it feels horrible.

Stress is the combination of a perception of threat, and then the all-consuming physical and emotional reactions to that threat. The bigger the perceived threat, the more overpowering is the emotional and physical response. And overpowering is an appropriate word because it literally does overpower any system in our being trying to find balance or coherence. In other words, the more threatening the perception, the more chaotic the response, and the less likely we are to find any solid emotional ground. Furthermore, our perception of threat is formed by anything that has been threatening to us in the past, and may have little to do with current circumstance.

Reactivity, and the stress and anxiety responses in our beings are very real, scientifically measurable, physiological responses to perceived danger. In other words, anytime we perceive anything to be a threat, be it internal or external, our bodies react in physically and psychologically predictable and measurable ways. Physical, emotional, and, ultimately, behavioral responses to threat and anxiety are intimately related. The more intense the emotional response, the stronger the physical response, and it is always the perception of the danger's severity that determines the emotional response.

In other words, anytime we sense something that causes us to feel vulnerable, or in danger in any way, and it could be very simple, very subtle, or severe reactions to conscious or subconscious past experience, our bodies get absolutely hijacked with the fear response. The problem is, how our brains and bodies perceive or determine what a threat is comes from a very primitive part of our brain that only wants to keep us safe – and will use any means it can to get our attention. This includes flooding our body with hyper-alert reactions of fear, anxiety and apprehension.

41

What is more, threat, anxiety and reactivity perpetuate themselves. As we consistently and routinely expose ourselves to the physiology, biochemistry, and energetics of these states, significant physical adaptations occur in our bodies and brains that continue to worsen the whole cycle. We literally become more biologically capable of experiencing more of the same, and begin to suffer increasingly negative effects. We begin to see the world through the lens of reactivity and these negative effects can have significant implications for our physical health, our mental health, our relationships, and our lives.

Living from a heartful and grounded state of inner power is virtually impossible from these reactive states. We feel out of control. We feel like we are not living up to our potential. We feel a yearning for a different way of being, and we know there must be something more. We know there is another way and that somehow the path to it lies in our own being, but our inner 'operating systems' seem to be programmed for something different. If most of our days are consumed with stress, reactivity, and emotional chaos, yet we know there is another, larger way to live, how do we begin to cultivate it? How do we be intentional about it, so we can all at once, remove the blocks to better heartfully engage with our world, and Inner Being, and further guide our transformation?

The great difference in these two ways of being lies in our internal programming, our on-going day-to-day perceptions and reactions, and the psychological, physiological and spiritual adaptations that occur from these states. After a basic understanding of brain dynamics, three fundamental questions will be addressed 1) How are our original programming and perceptions developed? 2) How do the continual adaptations in our beings take place? And 3) How can we be intentional about creating a different paradigm? The answers to these questions are paramount in creating foundational change. If I could give one thing to everybody in the world, it would be the answer to these three questions.

The contribution of our brain

The tip of the ice-berg

We can learn a lot from the brain. Brain activity tells us a lot about what is going on with our inner experience. However, I belong to the "camp" that believes in a reflective view of science rather than a reductionist view of science. That is, the brain is reflective of experience not the experience itself. In other words, we may have a thought, or experience that can be reflected and measured in our brain, but it is not the thought or experience itself. Sometimes you hear this referred to as the difference between the mind and the brain. The mind thinks, the brain reflects that thought. The brain may reflect the soul, but it is not the soul itself.

There are some scientists that will have you believe if you have an experience of God, and it is reflected in your brain, it is really only a malfunction of your brain. Therefore they 'reduce' the experience to the workings of the brain itself. However, a good counter-example is the experience of sex. If I have a sex spot in my brain that is activated during sexual activity, it does not mean I am not having a sexual event. It merely means it is reflecting a sexual thought or experience I may be engaged in at the moment.

There are limits to what we know, and what we can articulate about brain science. Brain science is constantly shedding new light on old concepts. However, it is important to remain in awe and wonder for what we do not know. The felt experience of heartful awareness, and the transformations that occur from its practice, are nothing short of miraculous. The ability of brain science to be able to document some of those transformations, and give us a blueprint to create more, is nothing short of amazing. But I believe it is only the tip of the iceberg. The transformative potential of heartful awareness, at this point, is immeasurable and ineffable.

What I believe to be true about the nature of science is that it is like an iceberg. When you see an iceberg, what you actually see above the level of the water is only a small portion of it. It is believed that more than 70%

of the iceberg may be submerged; we do not see it, yet we know it is there. Embedded in my view of science, then, is the notion that we can use what is being discovered by science as a great enlightener, validator, motivator, and guidepost for further exploration, yet still remain in reverence and awe for the mystery of healing, spirituality and the sacred.

That being said, the brain is an entirely awesome and fascinating organ that allows us to register all of our lives' experiences. It works in conjunction with the body proper to facilitate what it means to be fully alive in our human bodies and live our human existence. The brain and the body work together in an awesome and staggering system that facilitates and defines human life. The body proper is far more integral to the system the most of us realize, and will be addressed shortly, but for now let us focus on the brain.

Brain dynamics

Your brain is made of neurons, which are nerve cells responsible for transferring information and encoding experience. Information is carried by electrical charge down the length of a neuron and transferred to other neurons by a synaptic connection helped by a neurotransmitter. A synaptic connection is similar to a lightning bolt between the neurons, and a neurotransmitter is a type of biochemical that helps the synapse fire and transfer information. Your brain has approximately 10 billion neurons with 10,000 to 100,000 synaptic connections for each neuron. Neurons are responsible for encoding and transferring all of the information in our brain including past experience, how we evaluate and give meaning to circumstance, and advisable ways to react.

Every thought, feeling, word, behavior, and interpretation of life events is made possible by the activity of our neurons.

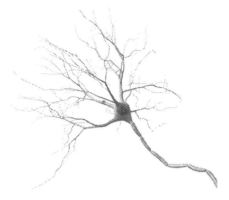

Fig. 2.1 Neuron

In addition to neurons you also have cells called glia. Glia have been estimated to match neurons in number anywhere from 1:1 to 10:1, and are believed to be responsible for holding the neurons together, helping transfer information, and pruning ones no longer in use. Neurons, with the help of the glia, form connections with other neurons, grow, and change throughout our life depending on experience. Together with Glial cells, neurons literally encode the 'operating system' in our brain and tell us how to function, perceive, react and make meaning of our lives. They also allow us to change. It is all done through the connection and function of the synapses, assisted by the 'glue' of the glia, and these information transfer processes shape the reality we live.

Neural networks are interconnected neurons that together perform a function. There maybe 10,000 neurons firing together in one neural network that is responsible for transferring a thought, feeling, response pattern, or behavior. External experiences, internal experiences, and experiences of our past are all reflected in our neural networks. Once these neural networks reflect an experience, they then encode it for future reference. They then begin to form connections with other neural networks called associative memory, and this tells us how to make meaning of new experience. These neural nets look like intricate spider webs firing and transferring information and experience. They tell us how to make meaning of our world, and the more they fire in specific patterns, the more those patterns become a long-term way of being for us.

Let us say I have a typical reaction pattern that I let consume me most every day. It may be feelings of anger, jealousy, abandonment, insecurity, feeling not good enough, etc. Instead of listening to the nudging for healing or transformation that it may be calling for, I routinely let the pattern consume me. My neural nets would be consistently firing in patterns reflecting these feelings, and anything done routinely would become a typical operating pattern for me.

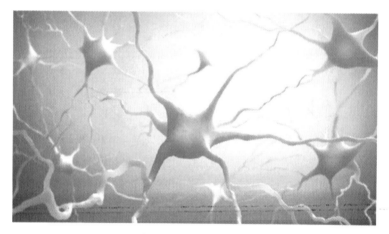

Fig. 2.2 Neural Nets

Being your own electrician

Scientists often say "nerve cells that fire together, wire together". What this means is that anytime we have a repeated thought, experience, or interpretation of events, the repeated firing of the neurons, in concert with the glial cells, starts to form long-term connections and create our individual life operating patterns. Joseph LeDoux, who has done a substantial amount of work in this area simply puts it "you are your synapses"[1]. But the good news is, your synapses can change. Nerve cells that cease firing together cease wiring together.

Providing new, or healing experience fundamentally changes the way our brain operates.

One of the greatest discoveries regarding the brain is the concept of neuroplasticity. Simply put, neuroplasticity means that our brains are malleable, or have the capability to change with new experience. Neuroscience used to tell us that the brain was a physiologically static organ, meaning once connections were made they never changed. Now we know that is not true. Also, we not only see changes in the brain's function, or physiology, meaning how it works momentarily, we also see changes in the brain's anatomy. What this means is that you actually are changing the structure of your brain, and all its intricate workings, with new experience.

With new experience we create new neural connections, new neural nets and associative memory, and break old patterns and connections because they are no longer firing together. Now we can see true potential for transformation and healing, as evidenced through neuroplasticity and the working of our brains, and it is staggering.

Shortly we will look at how all this plays out with emotional memory and look deeper into how our individual perception is developed and stored, but first let us recap in an easy and understandable way the workings of our brain.

All the experiences of our lives are reflected, and then encoded, in the neurons and the neural networks of our brain. Every thought, experience, behavior, interpretation, and choice are coded, and then used as operating patterns for future circumstance. Our individual perception of reality stems from what is coded in our neurons. And, as we shall see shortly, a large part of this process is subconscious. This is our 'programming' and it is how we make sense of our world. The events and experiences of our lives are no longer tangible, but the encoding in our neural networks is, and it is responsible for the version of reality we perceive.

For example, if I were severely bitten by a dog when I was a child, all my future perceptions of dogs would somehow be colored by that experience. I might not even be aware of the tinted view. I just see dogs as dangerous. Compare this with someone who raised puppies as a child, and has only had very fond and nurturing experiences with dogs. Their responses and perceptions associated with dogs would be quite different. Immediately upon seeing a dog they would most likely have a rush of fond and nurturing feelings that may or may not be even be consciously associated with the circumstance.

This is just a simple example, and this process is going on every moment of every day in very big, and small ways. It is how we make sense of our universe. All of our past experience wires us to make meaning of future circumstance. All past experience becomes the 'operating system' through which we filter our world. However, we shall soon see that because of the concept of neuroplasticity our brains are malleable. We shall see that new experience creates new connections, and when the old connections no longer fire they actually break off and die. With new experience our brains, and then our lives, begin to change. And a good deal of this transformation takes place at the level of the subconscious.

Embracing the subconscious

There is a man near a light-post searching and searching for the keys he has lost. He's frantically looking around and feeling frustrated because he cannot find them when a woman comes walking along. She asks him what is wrong, and he says, "I lost my keys!" Because he looks so desperate she begins to help him and together they look and look, but to no avail. Exasperated because she cannot seem to help him she tries to reason with him. She asks him, "okay, where was the last place you saw them?" He stops and points, "over there, by the rose bush" he responds, pointing to a spot several yards away. Exasperated that she been wasting her time helping him look in the wrong space she asks, "Then why are we looking here?" He responds, "Because its dark over there!"

The key to perception

Before we get to how our individual perceptions are developed, it is important for us to address the general idea of the subconscious. There is a non-conscious part of our brain, meaning beyond conscious awareness, which serves as sort of an 'automatic pilot' and is largely responsible for the way we perceive and behave in our world. It is responsible for storing and synthesizing large amounts of information. It is estimated that the subconscious mind processes 20 million environmental stimuli per second as opposed to a mere 40 total by the conscious mind[5]. What this means is that our subconscious mind is constantly assessing our entire environment and telling us what to think, and how to feel and behave in response to what it picks up, and we may not even be consciously aware that this is happening. It is hyper-vigilant, and, as we shall soon see, the way it evaluates our environment is completely due to our individual programming. In other words, it sees all and reacts according to its past experience. The subconscious is the key to perception.

When presented with the idea of the subconscious, many people feel defeated and disillusioned. It seems to carry this inherent idea that because it is the system that is in control, and subconscious in nature, no-matter how hard we try there is nothing we can do about it. It is almost like we have this big bad monster somewhere in the dark of our psyche, and the best we can do is suppress it or ignore it because there is nothing we can do about it anyway. There are several very important reasons that this is absolutely false, and they give us great hope for healing and reprogramming how our subconscious sees and reacts in the world.

First, subconscious programming or subconscious knowledge is not *unconscious*. It is most often referred to as implicit memory or implicit programming, meaning that at some level it is felt, and that is where the key lies. The subconscious is intimately connected to the rest of our body through biochemical, electrical and neural reactions, which are responsible for that 'felt sense' that we experience when we feel threat, or fear, or conversely security, trust, or bonding. The body is the gauge of the subconscious. At some level, our body is always aware of what our subconscious is feeling, and is, in a large sense, more honest than our conscious mind.

Second, as we shall soon see, the subconscious is simply like a database of programs or response patterns stored in the neural networks of our brain. These response patterns are stored from experience, and the more deeply felt, or repeated the experience the stronger the storage will be. The subconscious is like a vast 'hard drive' that has been programmed with all the experiences of our life.

Third, and most importantly, the hard drive of our subconscious can be re-programmed. All the programming in our subconscious brain is done by way of information contained in the neural networks, or wiring system of our brain, and our neural networks can be re-wired with new experience. But it is not the conscious mind that does the rewiring, it is deeply felt *experience*, internal or external and *experience is an embodied phenomenon*. We need to find the key at its source.

As we shall see in the next chapter the body both encodes subconscious information, and registers subconscious activity through strong biochemical reactions, and a strong 'felt sense' in response. This may be exactly how the subconscious brain becomes conscious – and re-programmable. The biochemistry of deeply felt experience is responsible for the encoding and re-encoding of our subconscious brain. When an experience is deeply felt, it is deeply stored. Once it is deeply stored, it is released as a subsequent deeply felt response to a similar circumstance. The interconnectedness of our bodies and brains is all at once the instrument that detects subconscious reactions, and the tool to create subconscious healing. When we create a deeply felt alternative experience through heartful awareness we begin to re-code our subconscious.

Our unique interpretations of the world

At this point it would be helpful to look a little deeper at how our individual perceptions are created, and the ways that we begin to use them to attach meaning to our day-to-day circumstance. Our individual perceptions are completely unique to us, and they tell us how to see, react, and behave every moment of every day. We all filter our world, our every day circumstances, reactions, and interactions, by what has been programmed in the 'meaning making' center of our brain. There is an enormous amount of information there, and a complex filtering system, but understanding the process of how it is created, stored and activated gives us important information about how and why we see the world the way we do, and a foundation to understand how change and healing occur.

A simple explanation of brain dynamics will help illustrate how the perception systems in our brains are developed.

LIMBIC SYSTEM STRUCTURES

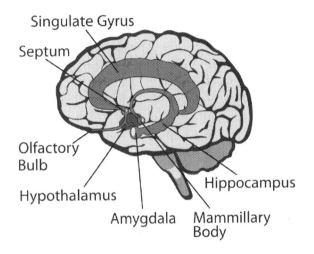

Fig. 2.3 A split view of the inside of the brain

From the diagram of the brain notice the outside layer. This is the neocortex, and is quite often referred to as the thinking part of the brain. It is responsible for most executive functions like logical thinking and planning ahead, and the storage of information we would typically classify as 'knowledge'. The neocortex was the latest part of the brain to evolve.

The limbic brain is between the brainstem and cortex. It is the inner structure right below the neocortex, and includes everything inside it, except for the brain stem (the portion of the brain protruding down from the limbic system). It is associated with learning, motivation, memory and emotion. It is the intersection of our external and internal world. The limbic brain holds our emotional drive, and is the system that provides feeling and meaning to our day-to-day experience. It also houses our subconscious. It, by its close association with our biochemical system, is associated with any 'felt sense' we experience throughout our day.

When we feel joy, passion, purpose or groundedness, that is the limbic system in its calm state. Conversely, when activated in a fear response, it is responsible for flooding our body with a cascade of physiological reactions that seem to literally hijack our body and brain. While a well-grounded limbic system can be our greatest ally, an out of control limbic system can be our biggest challenge.

The brain developed from the inside out, so the inside parts of the brain are more primitive, but are also the most captivating in terms of powerful emotional drives. This is manifest both from a standpoint of a fear/protective system, as well as a system that invites us into caring for one another, bonding, socialization and community. For our species to survive we had to have these two opposing drives, or emotional systems; a system designed to react quickly when threatened or faced with fear – either in retreat, attack, or halt - and a system designed to draw us into attachment and communion with others – both in pair bonding, and social groupings.

When we are grounded in the system that draws us into attachment and communion with others, we are also more capable of being in communion with our deepest potential or Inner Being. That is when we experience the 'felt sense' of unconditional love, compassion, agape, or are resting in that ineffable state that is beyond words. I love the word ineffable. Ineffable basically means that something is felt so deeply, or is so enormous in meaning, that words fall short in being able to accurately describe it. However, for our species to survive the fear response system had to be much quicker and much more reactive.

Why is this so? Lets imagine a tiger were threatening my village. I would need to have an immediate, overpowering and all-consuming innate impulse to react, and react quickly for my village's safety. It would have to be so hyper-responsive it would mobilize me before a fully developed thought process kicked in. Compare this with the drive to love and create community. Although this second drive is incredibly strong, and most people cannot emotionally survive with out it, it did not have to be wired for immediacy and all-consuming mobilization the way our fear response drive did.

How we perceive, make meaning, and filter our world is largely done through the workings of the subconscious, limbic system and these two drives. The limbic brain, from the time we were born, and many believe during the latter parts of gestation, begins to store experiences as implicit memory patterns that are then used as 'blueprints' to interpret and make meaning of future circumstances. What this means is that our subconscious and limbic brains are like very archaic computers. The computers are blank until they are programmed by our life experiences, and the programming they receive by those experiences then tells us how to interpret and receive our world through our emotional feelings and reactions.

Our limbic brain will be drawn toward those things it perceives to be life giving, and reactive against those things that it perceives to be life threatening.

As we shall see shortly all of this 'programming' is done through the synaptic connections in our brains, and then the subsequent encoding in our neural networks. Our developing system of 'wiring' begins to determine how we interpret and behave in our world.

Through the eyes of Joey

Growing up, Joey never felt good enough. He suffered from a learning disability and was the middle child in a troubled family. His mother routinely beat him and emotionally abused him. He struggled in school because of his disability, and came from a culture where there was great pressure to be successful. Because of his early experiences Joey's fear response system was encoded with the terror of abuse, and he began to see any authority figure through the eyes and emotions of that hurt child. He subsequently developed angry, impulsive, and combative behaviors that got him kicked out of several successive schools and institutions. By the time Joey was a teen he was in detention camp, then on the streets, and eventually addicted to alcohol and drugs.

Parts of Joey were terrified, and parts were longing for secure and healthy attachment and just wanted to be loved. He also had learned to protect himself by being angry and combative, or to numb the pain through addictive behaviors. Some of his reactions or 'programs' were subtler, like the ones that were insecure in school because he thought everyone was judging him, or the ones that felt threatened around any female merely for her gender.

Although Joey's experience may be more extreme than yours, we all have the same dynamics built into our brains and bodies that encode our response systems and shape our perceptions of reality. Moreover, these dynamics are being stored and released every moment of every day, many subconsciously, many very subtly. We all have vast amounts of information encoded in our response systems, and we literally cannot scan our environment without picking up something to which our response systems will attach meaning.

Joey's story will be briefly interspersed throughout the next several sections to help illustrate implicit memory storage and perception, as well as the subsequent development of adaptive behaviors

The 'data storage' centers of our brain

Deep in our emotional brain are three structures, the amygdala, the hippocampus and the anterior cingulate, that are associated with meaning making and emotional perception. These three structures, the amygdala in particular, are responsible for storing emotional or implicit memory. They are the seats of perception and the structures that help us attach meaning to circumstance in our lives. They are responsible for our non-conscious learned emotional knowledge throughout all of our life experience and become the way we make meaning out of current circumstance. And we may not even know it.

We spoke earlier about the foundational importance of the subconscious for our individual interpretations of the world. The amygdala is the seat of our subconscious. It stores, by way of our neural networks, almost unfathomable amounts of data all throughout our life experience. It stores major experiences, especially those that carry emotional content, but it is also constantly scanning our environment and storing everything it observes, sees, hears, smells etc. Moreover, it always stores what it observes in some emotional context. It really is like a programmable computer deep in our brain, and is most responsible for the inner nature of perception and what it means to be human.

Imagine what Joey's brain was programming him to believe about his self-worth. Imagine what he began to perceive about the safety of his female teachers. Imagine how he behaved in response. Imagine how he pulled the exact behavior out of his teachers that he was afraid of, just because of his expectations and his subconscious ways of drawing it in.

The amygdalae (there are two, one in each lobe of the brain) are the size and shape of an almond and are primarily responsible for how we make meaning of current circumstance. However, the meaning it provides does not come up as a conscious association with the past, it comes up as a felt sense for whatever is present for us at the moment. In other words, it is constantly scanning our environment, detecting broad clues of anything that has slightly resembled our past, appraising the significance, and causing emotional states consistent with that stored information. For example we may feel threat, anger, anxiety, joy, security, or happiness because our subconscious is telling us to either distrust or trust the moment, because something similar has either been threatening or helped us to flourish in the past.

The way this happens is any emotional event we experience, all throughout our lives, both large and small, carries with it a biochemical reaction consistent with that event. Biochemicals are chemicals all throughout our body and brain, and they tell our body what to do and how to feel. As we shall see later, our biochemical make up at any given point in time is largely responsible for how we feel, and how we see and make sense of our current circumstance.

We have strong biochemicals that are associated with emotion, and when we have an emotional experience, our biochemical reaction at the time tells our amygdala to make a corresponding memory of that event. The stronger the biochemical reaction during the original event, or events, the deeper the experience is encoded in these structures.

It is a pretty fair bet that Joey's cortisol levels were sky-high through the initial abuse, the other family struggles, and the trouble in school. The strong biochemical reactions associated with those emotional events wired them significantly in the cellular memory deep within his brain. The evaluation, or 'meaning making' centers of his brain processed the new events in school, or with new classmates, through the lens of his previous experience. He reacted in a combative way to deal with threat, insecurity, anxiety, and worry.

Implicit memory and the creation of perception

Life events are encoded deep in the neural networks of our brain. Remember, our neural networks are large groupings of brain cells that have formed a connection through past experience. The amygdala is subconscious so it is not stored as explicit or conscious memory (that happens in another part of the brain), so much as a feeling reaction, or implicit memory to guide our future actions and reactions. Implicit means that it is a hidden or embedded memory that carries with it a 'felt' reaction, without necessarily being fully connected or attributed to the original source as a conscious memory, although it certainly may be. It literally is our personal cellular programming that makes us 'us'. This process is called *memory consolidation.*

When an experience is interpreted as threatening or fearful in any way it is stored as part of the fear response system. It is encoded in our neural networks as an alarm system to be activated the next time anything looks remotely similar for the purposes of keeping us safe. It is like we are saying to our brain "wow, this is really scary, make a very strong imprint of this and activate these feelings anytime anything looks remotely similar, so I am never in this circumstance again!"

Again, this part of the brain is like an archaic computer, it can only store reaction patterns in broad categories or 'files'. When a current event or circumstance 'looks' even remotely like the original event, and it could be a subtle or as broad as a gesture, a tone of voice, a gender, its job is to release an all out alarm system in the form of an implicit, or emotionally felt reaction. *Joey felt insecurity in his new classroom. He felt threat from his new female teachers. He had no idea he perceived his new circumstances through the lens of his old; he just knew he felt very threatened by his current environment. It was an all-consuming bodily sense of fear that hijacked his ability to be grounded in any way.*

The amygdala is strongly connected to our brain stem and body proper by way of biochemical reactions, so when it gets activated it sends an all out alarm response in the way of a biochemical reaction that literally floods our whole body with an 'emotionally felt' response. This is when we feel angry, we feel scared, we feel threatened or we feel overwhelmed. It is less connected with the neocortex, so we may not even be aware that it is associated with the original event.

At this point our neocortex wants to make sense of it, so it attaches the emotional reaction to the current circumstance – whether it warrants it or not. *Joey really 'felt' that his female teacher might be as threatening as his mom had been, and reacted fittingly, even though her behavior did not warrant it.* Additionally, when the limbic brain and neocortex are presented with opposing information, and the emotional response is strong, the limbic brain wins. The emotional response feels so real we are convinced it is the true perception of current events.

This is because the neural connections leading from the limbic brain to the cortex are quicker, stronger and more numerous than those leading from the cortex to the limbic system. In other words, the flood of emotion going out is stronger than the reason coming in. These become our 'programming' or 'schemas' through which we look at and perceive the world. *Even when his new teacher, or new principal tried to reason with him, and told him that this was a completely new experience, Joey did not trust it because his emotional system told him otherwise.*

There are three very important points to remember here. One is that our systems were developed, and are activated, to keep us safe by giving us a strong emotional response to anything similar to that which has hurt us before. Another important piece of information is that the system gets activated if anything looks *remotely similar.* And the more threatening something has been in the past, the more our emotional system wants to protect us from harm, and therefore the more strongly it reacts and the less it needs to resemble the original impetus. Quite often however, our beautiful and protective emotional brains have far outlived their specific purpose, and it is time to give them more life-generating experiences through healing.

The last, and most important point at this juncture is that because our limbic brains will override our cortex – or reasoning - if the implicit reaction is strong, re-wiring our response systems through new experience is the answer. This is where the key to true healing lies. It is not effective to try and 'talk' ourselves out of harmful or destructive emotional response patterns or perceptions. The way to heal and calm chaotic and reactive fear response systems is to heal them at their source.

Trauma, woundedness, or what now may be harmful or degenerative emotional reactions are no longer in the event. Now where they are stored is in the neural networks deep within our amygdala and emotional brain. Until we re-program them with something different, we carry them constantly and perceive our whole world through their wiring. But the concept of neuroplasticity tells us that neural networks can be re-wired with new experience. In the words of Bruce Springsteen from his song *Living Proof*[6]:

> "You shot through my anger and rage
> to show me my prison was just an open cage
> there were no keys, no guards
> just one frightened man and some old shadows for bars"

When we can encode our emotional brain with healing and new experience, we break the connections of old patterns and establish new, life generating ones. A limbic system healed from its over-reactive fear response system can then allot its resources in new ways and allow its second drive to flourish – the drive for life-generating perceptions and behaviors. With a calm and balanced fear response system we can more effectively live a life directed by love, compassion, bonding, and relationship – to ourselves, others, our deepest potential and our Inner Being.

A boy and his mom

As an example of how the limbic system, and specifically the amygdala, provides meaning for our lives, Daniel Goleman, in his book Emotional Intelligence[7], tells the story of a young boy. This boy had severe epileptic seizures and it was believed that removing his amygdala would be the answer to controlling them. Unfortunately, at that time in our medical history we had no idea exactly how much the amygdala was involved in making meaning of our lives.

His mother was very involved and dedicated to her son and his medical issues, and was a constant companion through all of his medical troubles. After his amygdala was removed he was perfectly capable of rational thought, but he seemed to have lost all of his recognition of emotional feeling, or the ability to make meaning of his life. He was perfectly capable of conversation, but he no longer recognized close friends and relatives in a meaningful context, not even his mother. He could tell you what mother meant in a cognitive sense, but he no longer attached any significance or emotion to her specifically. The amygdala provides the emotional context for our lives, is responsible for determining emotional significance, and a life without an amygdala is stripped of personal meaning.

A person stripped of an amygdala cannot provide meaning to circumstance, but sometimes the amygdala will provide meaning to circumstance beyond our conscious awareness.

Somewhere we know

I have a funny experience with the subconscious nature of the amygdala and its anxiety or fear response system. The amygdala is very sensitive to smells, sights, and sounds and sometimes will react without conscious participation of the brain. I have a song that, for no apparent reason, makes me cry. It happens every time I hear it. It is a song from my childhood, yet I have no conscious memory of why the song would elicit such a strong reaction. It has even become a joke with my children and me. We will be driving in the car, and laughing, joking and having a great time. I take it as a personal challenge to be able to make it through the song and still be laughing. So we will play it. It is all very good-natured, and I want to prove to them that I can make it through without crying. I am wrong every time. I will start the whole process laughing and teasing, but invariably I am in tears by the end of the song – and I have no conscious reason why! The song seems to bring out profound feelings of loss and grief that I do not understand. I once even cried in the middle of a class I was teaching when a graduate student – who was old enough to remember the song – wanted to know what song it was. I told her. She sang it. I cried.

I recently had a conversation with my brother about this whole dynamic. He is 10 years older than I, and has much more conscious memories of when that song was first popular and likely was played on the radio a lot. He seemed to think the song was extremely popular when I was very young and my parents were having marital troubles. My dad had moved out for a few weeks and my siblings and I were very sad and feeling great loss. I only have very vague recollections of this time, but when he said that it made sense to me. The thought of the event brought up the same feelings the song always had. Once I had a context to understand why the song brought up such strong feelings, I no longer wanted to listen to the song in a joking context, but when I did listen to it, my reactions were tempered.

The song had nothing to do with the event, but that is the nature of the amygdala. The amygdala will attach seemingly random environmental cues to strong emotion to be either drawn toward, or repelled against certain circumstances. How many times has a certain smell brought you emotionally back to a space and time where you experienced that smell? Or how many times have you been completely transformed by hearing a song that is connected to certain emotional states, time periods, or events? These are all the function of the amygdala.

These may be more obvious instances. The key is to be able to decipher when the amygdala is at work in our everyday lives in larger and subtler ways. Some of the larger ways may have become predictable ways of reacting for us, and block any hope of a grounded way of being. Its job, when it is in its reactive state, is to convince us to believe its version of reality, whether or not it is warranted.

The meaning making centers of our brains are very strong, and very responsive. When they are chaotic, they are our greatest foe, when they are calm and grounded they are our greatest asset. We need not be at the mercy of our reactive brains. Understanding our programming, learning our triggers, and calming our systems are the first steps to inner transformation and developing a heartfully aware way of being in the world. Too, understanding that the process itself was originally protective in nature is the basis for a self-compassionate foundation from which to heal systems that are out of balance.

Review points

◊ Built deep into our emotional brain are two drives. One is a fear response system and one is a calm and connection system. Only one drive can be dominant at a time. To be able to effectively be grounded in, and connect with our own deepest potential or Inner Being, as well as other people, love, compassion and hope, we need to be able to calm the chaos and ground our fear response system. This is the state from which we flourish.

◊ Who we are, and how we see the world is largely a function of our neural wiring, or cellular memory from past experience. This is called implicit memory. The implicit memory of our fear response system is quicker and more overpowering than our calm and connection system.

◊ It is the job of our fear response system to evaluate and make meaning of our current circumstance through the wiring of past threat or trauma (large or small), and release an all out alarm system throughout our body.

◊ The reality is we have many, many implicit memories, or reaction patterns wired in our brain. These are the lenses through which we see the world. And they can be changed.

Our personal triggers

Heartful awareness cannot flourish when chaos is dominant. Understanding how implicit memory is stored, and consequently activated, is the first step in being able to heal these response patterns when they are out of balance, causing discord, or leaving us out of connection with a heartful way of being. We have done that.

The second step is being able to identify instances in our own lives where they might play out, and hold our selves in a state of heartful awareness in discerning when they are out of balance. We all have them; they may be more subtle and hidden, or you may be consciously aware that you have strong reactions to specific circumstances. However they are manifest, the nature of a reactive pattern is that it is designed to throw you off balance. Because when we are unstable we cannot begin to function from a state of heartful awareness, there is power in being able to identify, heartfully "hold", and take grounded responsibility for our own triggers. Heartful awareness directed back at our self fosters the necessary self-compassion to recognize and heal our own implicit patterns and triggers.

An important point about implicit or reactive patterns is that we tend to blame whatever situation is currently present for the emotional reaction we are having. In other words, we assume the situation 'in front of our face' rightly deserves the extent of our reaction, and quite often these triggers will re-cur or replay themselves in various circumstances. In other words, take notice if a reactive emotional pattern feels familiar, and may replay itself through different circumstances in your life. For example: "You are just like my former partner (or father, or mother, or sister, or brother)." "I always freeze up on important tests or interviews." "People are always criticizing me, or getting angry or disappointed with me." "Nobody really likes me." "I always end up alone." "Bad things always happen to me." Heartfully holding our response patterns with self-compassion and understanding helps us 'own' them without self-blame or shame, or blame for external circumstance; this, then, enables us to bring them into balance.

If the trigger often re-curs or replays itself in various circumstances there is a strong chance it is stored as implicit memory for you and may be a lens you see through and gets activated inappropriately or excessively at times. There are three strong possibilities for this recurrence:

1. A trigger within us is activated, and the current situation, while possibly uncomfortable, does not warrant the degree of reactivity we ascribe to it.

2. The situation is one that does need to be acted upon, but our own reactivity impairs our balance and severely inhibits our ability to perceive and react in a constructive or appropriate manner.

3. We sub-consciously draw situations or people into our lives because these circumstances evoke personal issues, or implicit patterns within us that we need to constructively deal with.

Too, sometimes these implicit memories manifest as behavior patterns. We may have typical response patterns of getting angry, withdrawing, feeling neglected, turning to food or other substances to numb the pain, etc.

Because our triggers are always colored by our own implicit memory patterns, it is very useful to be able to heartfully identify and name them when they happen. Again, because implicit memories or reactions are really our wiring from past experience, they are many and varied. I may have an implicit memory that triggers a sense of threat, I may have another implicit memory that triggers a sense of abandonment, and yet another that triggers a sense of being smothered. I may have one that causes me to react by getting angry; I may have one that causes me to react by withdrawing, etc.

I liken these to the puzzle pieces of our psyche. We have numerous pieces that represent different parts of our psyche and past experience that, in totality, comprise our perception of the world. And remember, somehow all of these were created from past experience to keep us psychologically protected. But none of these pieces alone are the total picture. And none of these pieces are 'us' when we are grounded in the center of our being. They are all implicit memory patterns that have been developed to keep us functioning, or safe in some way — and may have far outlived their purposefulness. They may have even become a problem in their own right. Bringing a heartfully aware posture to our triggers, and the dynamics that created them is the first step on the path to healing and re-balancing them.

I have a part of me that...

I find a very helpful language and way of looking at this phenomenon in the work of Richard Schwartz, and his description of 'parts' in Internal Family Systems therapy[8]. Although Schwartz's work is psychological and therapeutic in nature, I have my own physiological 'take' on the process. He basically uses the terminology 'parts' for those parts of our selves that have learned to either perceive the world in a certain way, or behave in response to that perception.

We will get deeper into Schwartz's work in subsequent chapters, but, for now, just the language of 'parts' helps us illustrate this point beautifully.

Say when I was young, one, or both of my parents abandoned me. I would have implicit memory patterns – basically cellular memory – that likely would reflect several things. I may have a part that would be continually lonely, a part that would feel abandoned at the least hint of neglect from other people in my life, a part that feels like I am imposing, or too dependent on other people anytime I needed or wanted connection. I may have a part that gets angry, or a part that disassociates at the smallest hint of rejection. These are just a few examples, and again, may be extremely varied depending on the initial psychological impact.

I may also have developed other parts to keep those more vulnerable parts psychologically protected. I may have a part that totally disengages, a part that gets distracted, or even a part that likes to sleep a lot. I may even have a part that hates all these behavioral parts and continually beats me up because I cannot function the way I think I should. Of course that part, then, requires so much attention I do not have to feel the more vulnerable parts.

From a physiological point of view, because we have been exposed to a variety of experiences in our life we have developed multiple implicit memory patterns associated with all of those experiences. As such, different aspects of our personality, reactivities, and behavior patterns have evolved from these cellular memories to protect us in some way. We have numerous implicit memory patterns, which contribute to many varied ways of perceiving, and they all work like interconnected puzzle pieces to protect the more vulnerable parts of ourselves.

One of my parts that I personally have worked hard on in my life is something I call my 'Niagara Falls' part. I am the youngest of five siblings and our age differences played a big factor in our growing up years. They were all very close in age, and were raised almost collectively as a group while I was much younger and raised, in a lot of ways, alone. I went to different schools, had different friends, was involved in different activities, etc.

We all have our own deeply held 'stories' that stem from this dynamic, but one of mine is that I never felt like I quite belonged. I had a 'part' that learned very well how to thrive in outside situations, but I had another 'part' that felt great despair when I was not being included with the group that I longed to be with. Although the instances were many, my most vivid memory of this dynamic was when we were in New York and they were all piling in the car to go to Niagara Falls. Because there were so many of us, I did not fit in the car. I, instead, went on a shopping trip with my grandmother, but felt great despair that I did not get to go with my brothers and sisters.

Although this is just one example, it has become a symbol for me of that 'part' of myself that gets triggered when I feel like I am being left behind. I feel the 'whoosh' of not being fully seen, or understood, or appreciated, and it carries its own physicality. When this part gets activated in me by similar circumstances I immediately notice that I cannot breathe, my chest tightens up and I feel a pit in my stomach. It also seems to carry this all over body ache of despair and frustration.

This is a part I have worked hard to heal and 're-program'. Now, most often, when I get even a slight feeling of the familiar 'whoosh', I can identify it as my Niagara Falls part, even laugh or be amused at it is tenacity, and look at the current situation through a clearer lens. Again, Niagara Falls is just the name I have given to identify, or name a much larger implicit memory pattern for me.

The above example shows a trigger, which I associate with a 'part', that I associate with some specific memories. It is important to know, however, that when identifying a trigger at this point you do not need to be able to associate it with a specific memory, or even a 'part'. Triggers are merely the things that throw us off emotional balance, feel chaotic, or color our perception of our current circumstance. They may be mild and they may be major.

At this point, learning to identify and name our own triggers from a posture of heartful awareness, without blame, shame or judgment, and without blaming them on the outside circumstances, is enough. Learning to identify the physicality that accompanies the trigger can also be an important tool. A trigger almost always carries its own associated physical reaction;

sometimes these are more obvious than the trigger itself. Again, the body is often more honest than the conscious mind.

Exercise and Reflection # 2 - Identifying your own triggers and associated physical reactions

◊   Honestly list and describe situations, events or conditions that you feel might be personal triggers for you. Again, a trigger is usually felt as a strong internal response to something that we are experiencing at the time. However, because of our own programming, the trigger carries an all-out physical and emotional response pattern, and, as such, we have a hard time seeing through a clear lens. The stronger the physicality, the greater the indication that it is a stored implicit memory pattern for us. In other words, it is a response system that has been wired in us due to our past experience.

Keep in mind these triggers carry their own physical reactions. Many times it is the physical feeling we are conscious of first. The first thing I notice when I am triggered is that I cannot breathe, my chest gets tight and I get a pit in my stomach. I have learned to use this as a guide-post that something in me is being triggered, and is engaging my own emotional memory – it is something I need to look at in myself.

If you are having trouble understanding this concept, just reflect on certain situations or circumstances that 'set you off', or make you feel emotionally unbalanced. If you look at times that you get set off in similar situations, it may be a good place to begin to examine your own reactivity. Remember, the point of this activity is to examine your own triggers, not blame external situations for your reactions. Be honest and authentic. Look for themes and patterns.

◊   Notice physical response patterns you may have in certain situations. Are there circumstances in your life that cause strong physical

of engaging the world, or the source of our deepest potential or Inner Being, we need to be able to calm the chaotic systems that are blocking us.

We have learned that the *process* of perception development – or our wiring in how we see and 'are' in the world – is a process designed to keep us safe and thriving; although time and past experience may have wired us in a way that is no longer serving us. Too, a large part of that wiring is subconscious in nature, so we may not even realize its impact on our life - we just do not feel like we are grounded in the way we would like.

We have also learned that our wiring and perceptions can change with healing, intentionality and new experience. First, however, we need to be able to recognize and reprogram our 'habits of reactivity' that are blocking us from accessing, and living from a state of heartful awareness.

Hopefully, throughout this process you have taken some time to reflect on how these dynamics play out for you in your own life. I also hope that you have taken the first steps to re-engage in a way that is truthful, and yet heartfully aware of yourself and your own processes. This is where healing a system that is out of balance takes place, and where true flourishing comes from.

In the next chapter we will see how our 'habits of being' adapt to more of the same. Through the cycle of adaptation or 'spiral of becoming' we shall see that we are continually becoming more of our life experience, and how profoundly transforming and healing new and heartful experience can be. Finally, we will begin to look at some concrete ways to break our habitual ways of being, and foster a greater connection to that which we know is possible.

3

The 'Spiral of Becoming'

Introduction – Moments of 'becoming' and the mindfulness / heartfulness whole

As long as we are human, and as long as we are living in these human bodies, we exist in beautifully designed systems of adaptation. It is the gift of being human. Our bodies, including our brains, body proper and all the interconnected systems that make us 'us' are designed to take care of us, and facilitate all the wonder that the human experience can give us. Our bodies are all-inclusive systems that allow us to think, feel, interpret, receive and perceive the universe we live in. They define for us what it means to be humanly alive. Even spiritual or mystical experience is facilitated through our human bodies. Life is truly an embodied phenomenon.

But they can only respond to, and grow from what they are exposed to. Although they facilitate all of what it means to be humanly alive, their adaptive process is dependent on our experience. They will continually adapt to any repeated experience, or internal state we expose them to. This is the cycle of adaptation, or 'spiral of becoming'. It can lead to continued states of stress, anxiety and reactivity, or it can lead us to heightened states of heartful awareness, and connection to our own deepest potential or Inner Being.

In the last chapter we learned how the amygdala and the subconscious brain allow us to make sense of, and perceive our world. We learned how important an understanding of perception is in learning to calm, or heal our reactive systems, and facilitate nurturing our life-generating systems.

However, understanding how our emotional evaluation system is programmed is only the first step.

The initial focus of this chapter is the second, very important piece to this whole conversation. That is how our reactive patterns, or life generating patterns begin to perpetuate themselves. When we look at the specific ways our various systems adapt to, and then facilitate more of our everyday experience, we can see the damage we are doing to ourselves when we are continually reactive and merely responding to life as it happens. We can also see the profound impact that healing, and intentionality have on who we are becoming. We can scientifically see how heartful awareness in the form of love, compassion, and other heartful ways of being profoundly change us, and our world. We can see that the 'spiral of becoming' can be one of life-generation or life-depletion.

A second focus of this chapter is on the cultivation of mindful awareness and fostering non-reactive ways of being. Once we have a firm understanding of our reactive processes, we can begin to take steps to reprogram them as they occur. Heartful awareness first requires a non-reactive, non-judgmental and accepting presence. We must be mindful before we can be heartful. Fostering a non-reactive, non-judgmental and fully accepting posture, and bringing that posture to the present moment, is the foundation of mindfulness. Its cultivation helps us calm a system in chaos and re-wire our reactive patterns as they occur. It is the first half of the mindfulness / heartfulness whole. This chapter shows us that every moment of every day we are adapting, and mindful awareness invited into these moments can significantly change their outcome. It also opens the space for an overtly intentional heartful shift.

Life is an embodied and adaptive experience

Our bodies and brains are systems of adaptation. Part of what it means to be human is that we filter all of our experience through our human bodies – including our brains, our biochemistry, and our hearts. Furthermore, our bodies are constantly adapting to any experience we give them. The beauty of the human body is that is constantly growing, changing and transforming through new experience. Adaptation basically means a responsive adjustment. Adaptation in physiology means that our bodies, brains, and hearts are responding to any experience, and adjusting its capabilities for more of the same experience.

As long as we are humanly alive, experience is a completely embodied phenomenon. Any experience we have is registered through, and can be measured in, various systems of our body. Without our bodies we cease to have the human experience. Again, this is not meant to be reductionist in any way. Even the most spiritual or mystical of experiences are registered in, and facilitated through our human bodies. This includes experiences when we feel we have transcended our bodies. There is actually a spot in our brain, and a biochemical state associated with that 'at one with the world' feeling. Again, those systems are not *creating* the feeling, but they are *reflecting* and *facilitating* the experience.

Experience is really how we live every moment of every day. Those are the experiences that comprise the totality of our lives. Those are the experiences that are being constantly recorded and processed through the system of our human body. Our brain, our biochemistry, our hearts and the systems of our whole body are continually working in concert to tell us what to believe, how to see our world, and the necessary changes we need to make. And it is all through physiological patterning.

Our human body is the instrument through which we experience life, and the instrument through which transformations are continually taking place. Most of us go through life completely unaware of this phenomenon, and, as such, fail to see one of the greatest tools of enlightenment at our disposal.

If we look at exercise as an example it is easy to see how our bodies adapt to experience. We know that when we exercise our body gets more fit, and better at doing it, through routine experience. If we begin to train for a marathon we run 1 mile, and then two, three, four and so on. Our body, then, begins to adapt and allows us to run further and further. With enough experience running, pretty soon we can run a full marathon of 26.2 miles.

It is the same thing with emotional experience, transformation and healing. Any emotional experience we routinely give our body and brain conditions us to be able to facilitate more of the same. We are constantly training our human systems through repeated experience – and most of the time, we do not even realize it. Worse, most of the time we are training it for a less than optimal existence.

Looking at life as a spiral and embodied phenomenon we can see how our neural, biochemical and electrical systems are adaptive in nature. We can see that merely reacting to our outside world, and the experiences that our outside world delivers, only cements reactive ways of being. We can also see how intentionally changing experience, and healing old patterns of traumatic experience, profoundly transforms us.

The 'Spiral of Becoming'

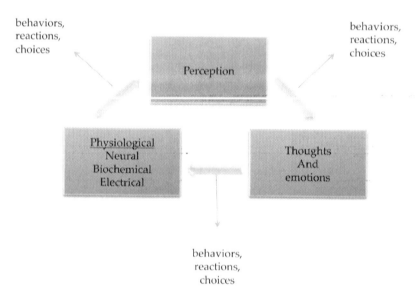

Fig. 3.1 - The Spiral of 'Becoming'

The 'spiral of becoming' model is a representation of how we are constantly transforming – for better or worse! We will use this as a foundation to explore how we become who we are in general, and as a tool to help our own adaptive processes. It is important to have a holistic view of how these three systems work together in concert to get a clear picture of how our body and brain are continually transforming through repeated experience. First, a general overview, then we will break down the components of the process, return to a story of representation, and, ultimately, look at our own patterns, and see how intentional transformation is possible.

If we look at the above chart we can see that when we have a perception we immediately have thoughts and feelings associated with that perception, which create physiological responses in our body and brain, which then go back and influence our perception! This process is a constant spiral, and this spiral can be adaptive and healthy, or maladaptive and destructive.

It is like anytime we have a physiological response from an emotional perception we actually put on the lens of that experience, and subsequently see everything through it. Like when we have a really bad day. We get up in the morning and something goes wrong that profoundly affects our mood. Then something else goes wrong, and then another thing. All the subsequent happenings of the day are making us a little more frustrated, and a little more upset. We begin to physiologically carry each of the previous events in our body and brain, and pretty soon we are beginning to perceive our whole day through the lens of how everything is falling apart.

Compare this to when we are first in love. Suddenly everything is rosy because we are in the physiological states consistent with love. The person that was making us mad yesterday is not quite so bad anymore, and even though most of our external events remain the same, our perception of those events is completely different. The sky is bluer, the trees never so green, and the world is a little brighter. Even frustrating events seem to roll off us like they are no big deal. We put on the lens of perception for any emotional state we are currently experiencing.

The neural, biochemical and electrical imprint of any experience becomes the lens through which we see reality.

As was stated earlier, physical, emotional, and, ultimately, behavioral responses are intimately related. The more intense the emotional response is, which stems from the original perception, the more intense the physical response will be. And, as we learned earlier, the severity of the physiological response, coupled with our past neural wiring, colors our perception of current and future circumstance.

In other words, our brain detects some, possibly remote, emotional match of our current circumstance with some past experience, and sends out an all-out alarm for our body to respond. Our body, then, responds, and sends additional messages to our brain about how to evaluate it and what to think about it. Our brain believes it, and releases further 'files' consistent with that belief. So goes the spiral.

When the initial response is reactive in nature we may have feelings of threat, fear, anxiety or terror. We then exhibit body impulses, or physiological reactions consistent with that emotional state, and have a drive to escape, freeze or fight. This is when we have that all over body 'whoosh!' These responses, then, go back and influence our further perception as one of greater threat. *It is important to remember that this is a physiological state of threat, and it is designed to throw us off-balance, give us a skewed version of reality, and cause us to react and react quickly. It is a system designed to keep us safe.* When we can truly grasp that this *process* is good, but our individual programming may no longer be healthy for us, and step back from its reactivity, we can begin to create the physiological states for healing.

Unfortunately, what typically happens when our perception is reactive, and it could be reacting to larger or smaller, even minute events, is that we begin to worry, catastrophize, or imagine all the things that could go wrong. Further, our brains do not know the difference between what is real and what is vividly imagined. Our 'brain chatter' takes off and we begin to have conversations in our head, or play the endless reel of possibly horrific scenarios. These both come from our subconscious programming, and they create more programming. Our brain and body begin to react as if this is the truth. Every time we play an imaginary conversation in our head or start to imagine all the things that might go wrong, or could go wrong, the cycle of reactivity, resulting adaptations, and the lens through which we see our current circumstance takes off all over again.

'Spiral of Becoming' - Overview

Let us look at how this plays out for us every moment of every day. Every moment we are experiencing life, and all our surroundings, and developing perceptions based on input from both our subconscious and conscious mind. A perception is basically the insight or evaluation that we give to each and every moment. Our subconscious and conscious mind works together in processing phenomenal amounts of information, and tells us what to think, how to feel, and how to interpret every moment. This is done in such an automatic and routine way that it is beyond our awareness. Basically we just interpret what we are fed and see our version of reality.

What the subconscious and conscious minds are filtering through is all a function of our past programming stored in our neural networks. Most of this is mundane, everyday experience, but we also have our own specific programming due to all of our emotional experiences that have been recorded throughout the whole of our life. In other words, when I have a new experience, my amygdala evaluates it and provides emotional meaning based on it is past experience. Again, our 'schemas' are very individual to us and are a result of all our non-conscious stored emotional knowledge. It generates behaviors, emotions and thoughts in response to current experience. What we perceive as reality is all filtered through the 'lens' of our personal data files.

As the spiral of becoming shows us, if our perception is one of reactivity, and it could be as mundane as seeing a dog on the street, or as dramatic as being exposed to something we perceive as especially threatening, we immediately have thoughts and emotional reactions consistent with what we perceive. Those thoughts and emotions then, conscious or not, cause a cascade of physiological reactions. Some of these responses are in our brain cells and our nervous system, some are in our biochemistry, literally affecting every cell and organ in our body, and some are in the electrical patterns of our heart. In reality, these responses can happen in less than a split-second and can literally hijack our body and brain. That is what we feel when we feel emotionally chaotic, and out-of-control.

The most important aspect of this is that these physiological states go back and influence our ongoing perception. These become the lenses through which we see the world. Also, because we have been programmed for survival, all throughout the spiral of becoming we also adopt behaviors, choices and response patterns that somehow have been developed to keep us psychologically protected.

Two important points are that, first, every time we perceive and respond in our habitual ways of reacting we just cement the spiral of becoming and become more of the same. Second, quite often our response patterns, or defense mechanisms grow far out of balance for what is currently appropriate, and those also get cemented. Our adaptive processes are literally going on every moment of every day, and continually shaping who we are becoming, and coloring the lens through which we see the world.

The good news is that, precisely because the body is a beautiful and complex system of adaptation, at any given moment in time we can begin to transform.

Let us see if we can break this down and make it a little more understandable.

Every moment of every day I am experiencing life. My body and brain are filtering everything in my internal and external world and telling me how to feel and what to think about it. Whatever I am feeling, experiencing and thinking is filtered through my body and my brain, which are establishing emotional tones and response patterns based on their past experience

My brain is filtering and telling me what to think and how to feel, both consciously and subconsciously, through its wiring system and past programming. As my brain filters experience, it sends emotional reactions associated with that experience all throughout my body by way of various biochemical reactions. The electrical patterns of my heart are reflecting the emotional tone of that experience and sending messages directly back to the subconscious part of my brain, and telling me how to further react.

Biochemicals are simply chemicals all throughout my body that assist with certain functions. Every cell and organ in my body is under the influence of various biochemicals and it is their responsibility to 'do something', or perform a specific function for my body. The chemicals associated with emotion and perception tell me how to feel and react, and are primarily responsible for that 'felt sense' that I associate with any emotional state. There are chemicals associated with threat, chemicals associated with anger, chemicals associated with overwhelm, chemicals associated with love, and so on.

There are also biochemicals that go back to my brain, and help my brain fire in perpetuating emotional patterns. The neural networks in my brain and the chemicals all throughout my body work together in responding loop patterns continually dictating perception and experience. In other words, this process goes on and on and tells me how to think and feel about any related experience. For example, if I perceive an experience to be threatening or overwhelming, my brain reflects that state and sends a message to my body to feel that overwhelm, and once I am consumed with the feeling of being overwhelmed, I begin to perceive everything else from that lens.

As well, the electrical impulses of my heart detect any emotional state I am currently experiencing, and make a pattern, or wave, consistent with that state. The pattern is perceived by my whole body, but most importantly travels up the vagal nerve and back into the deepest parts of my brain. Some of the neural connections go straight to the amygdala, which detects the patterning and further tells my subconscious brain how to proceed and further react. The electrical patterning of my heart profoundly impacts my emotional state at any given point in time.

Basically what this means is the wiring in my brain, the chemicals in my body, and the electrical patterns of my heart are reflecting any emotional experience I am having, and telling me how to feel as a result. And the more they do this, the better at it they get. Doing this routinely creates primary operating patterns that they function according to, and further dictates how I see the world and experience in general.

These three systems, my brain, biochemistry, and heart, work together in concert to literally hijack my body when I am in an emotionally reactive state, or ground and center my body when I am in a calm emotional state. Because these physiological systems are natural processes of the body, and the body will always adapt to any state it is constantly exposed to, we literally become more capable of every experience or perception that we routinely have. The next section will show more in depth how these adaptations occur in each of the separate systems.

The Spiral of 'Becoming' – In depth

Neural activity. Biochemistry. The electrical wave of our heart. What do all of these have to do with transformation? Any momentary experience carries with it an underlying and integrated physiological pattern that consumes our whole being. This pattern can show us how and why we perceive things the way we do, but also how those perceptions perpetuate themselves and become more of our lived experience.

As we saw from the spiral of becoming chart, there is a clear and perpetuating spiral from our original perception, to our thoughts and emotional reactions, to physiological responses consistent with those thoughts and emotions. This leads to the all-important arrow back to continued perception. This is how our systems adapt every moment of every day, and create who we are becoming. In this section we will break down the physiological response systems that reflect our thoughts and emotions. Remember, every moment of every day we are transforming, whether we know it or not, and whether we like it or not. These are the systems that are responsible for those adaptations and transformations. Once we have an in-depth understanding of how they work, we can begin to see how to be intentional about their transformative process through heartful awareness.

Neural patterning

In chapter 2 we learned all about neurons, how they transfer information, and how neural nets are systems of interconnected neurons. We discovered that these neural nets are responsible for transferring a thought, feeling, response pattern, or behavior, and they encode experience. Further, the more they fire in specific patterns, the more those patterns become a long-term way of being for us and create our individual life operating patterns. But they can be re-wired with new experience. Now it is time to put that information in the context of the spiral of becoming, so we can see how profoundly those dynamics affect who we are becoming at any moment in time. In other words, in chapter 2 we learned the neural dynamics of our initial programming, now we shift to how that programming perpetuates itself from repeated and daily experience.

It is important to remember that all the information encoded, or reality we experience in our day-to-day lives is made possible through the neural wiring of our brain. As long as we are living in our human bodies, it is the process of our neural networks, together with specific biochemicals, called neurotransmitters, that cause our synapses to fire and allow us to process information. Consciously and subconsciously, they create our version of reality.

Every moment of every day, our attention, associations, words, and thoughts wire more of the same. Through our neural networks we can see how subjective our interpretations may be sometimes, embrace how the phenomenon of our programming has actually been a protective mechanism, and, with intentionality, heal and reprogram to more grounded ways of being.

The following are some specific ways neural nets work, and are formed in everyday life. Understanding these concepts of wiring, and beginning to engage them in an intentional way is the first step to truly transforming our ways of being. This part of the chapter will focus on the concepts themselves, and at the end of the chapter we will see how we can use these concepts intentionally to engage in a different way of being.

The Power of Attention

Let us look at attention in terms of neural programming. *Anytime we place our attention on anything, be it a thing, a feeling, a thought, an impulse or a word, the neural networks in our brain fire in response and then record the experience.* Remember, our neural networks are really just the mechanisms of energy and information flow throughout our body[9]. Wherever our attention is directed determines the associated firing patterns. And remember, the more any pattern fires, the stronger it wires, and the more capable it becomes of firing that same pattern in the future.

When we do the same thing over and over again, including where we place our attention, we just get better at doing that thing, and this guides our further perceptions. And, of course, our perceptions, then, guide our further attention. Our attention at any given point in time is beginning to guide the way we see our present, and determine our future.

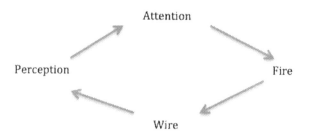

Fig. 3.2 Neural wiring cycle

If there are things in our present keeping us in emotional chaos, a change in the way our attention is focused is necessary to empower change or healing. This does not mean suppressing, pretending it does not exist, or 'thinking positive' when we really do not believe it. What it does mean is forming an understanding of the power of attention, especially when it is placed on things with emotional value. It also means discerning when we are driving our emotional attention by choice of focus, as opposed to our emotional attention driving us because something in our subconscious is nudging us for attention and begging to be healed.

In other words, sometimes my emotional attention is a choice. Sometimes I can just as easily be focused on all the things that are going right and finding ways to connect to the love, beauty, and compassion within and without me as I can the opposite. And my neural networks form to this way of being. Other times I may be experiencing an emotional response so strongly that I know it needs my healing attention. This is a different dynamic, and requires a different type of healing attention.

Both are powerful. Both are true. And neither are served by 'going down the drain' of self-flagellation, or undue catastrophizing. I have a tool called the HEAR scale that helps us make this discernment. It will be examined in depth in Chapters 4 and 5.

But for now, if we can understand that our emotional make up at any given point in time is largely a function of attention we can begin to truly understand what a precious resource our attention really is. It is not so much a function of trying to 'talk' ourselves out of a response, as much as it is authentically engaging our limbic system in a much more grounded way of being. Learning to engage in the love and beauty around us is a powerful tool. When we cannot, having self-compassion for the reasons that are holding us back is paramount.

Although we have talked about the cortex and the limbic, or emotional brain, as two separate systems, in reality they are intricately connected. There is energy and information flow constantly being transferred through the neural network connections of these two parts of the brain. What that means is that where we keep our conscious attention at any given point in time profoundly affects our emotional response and overall tone.

Further, the limbic system has very highly specific environmental adaptations. In other words, the limbic or emotional system is highly tuned to wiring, and re-wiring to specific experience and focused emotional attention. We can deeply change the functioning of our limbic system, but if we 'become' our old stories, suppress their existence, or take off with their re-activity, we do not allow them to change. What we 'share' with our limbic system, in an emotional context, becomes a reality. Become aware of the 'emotional content' of your attention. It may surprise you.

What this all means is that the stories we tell our limbic system through our focused conscious attention wires the system into believing those stories. That is, if I am constantly focused on all the things that could go wrong, are going wrong, or in my interpretation might possibly go wrong, my limbic system begins to believe those stories and responds with conforming assessment. Creating new 'stories' through attention, and healing, is the key to reprogramming our limbic system.

Lastly, focused conscious attention can be directed at our own reactivity, from an 'observers' point of view. If I can be aware that I am being triggered, without letting the trigger consume me, I am taking the first step in re-wiring my neural networks in a way other than continued chaos. This is called fostering non-reactivity. Much, much more will be said at the end of this chapter regarding ways to use awareness and attention to foster non-reactivity and for generative growth. For now, understanding that our conscious attention profoundly affects our neural wiring is enough.

The law of associative memory

The law of associative memory basically means that when we have a thought, experience, emotional reaction or perception it is reflected in certain neural networks. As those neural networks fire, they have connections with other thought patterns or other neural networks. That is, if I have one experience that commonly leads to another experience, those neural networks create associative patterns. For example, let us imagine I associate the word love with a specific person, and then my relationship with that person leads to betrayal, which leads to hurt. My experience and interpretation of the word love is going to be very different than somebody else's that has had a positive experience. Or let us say my parents said they loved me, but treated me horribly. My understanding of the concept of love will be heavily influenced by my past experience, and interpretation of what that feeling means.

Our associative memory networks connect feelings and concepts through experience that may or may not be appropriate, but they become a reality for us because of the associations we have. These associative memory networks become wired together and then become our operating pattern and the way we make sense of our world. These associative memory patterns can be obvious, subtle, or even subconscious. They quite often color our interpretations of the world without us even knowing it.

Our associative memory networks are intricately connected with our emotional system, and quite often elicit a very strong 'felt' reaction. They are also very connected to subtle and subconscious cues. A smell, a sound, a facial or verbal tone, a physical gesture etc. may all activate associative memory networks. They can be reactive, and harmful, or they can be life generating.

Marie felt like she was in heaven when she smelled the combination of spaghetti sauce and cigarette smoke. To most people the idea of this combination of smells may not sound very appealing, but for her it brought up the felt sense of deep love and security. When she was a child she would sit at her grandmothers feet as her grandmother cooked and smoked. This was a very wonderful time in my friends' life, and just that combination of smells could bring up a deep sense of connection for her. Although she could 'remember' from a cognitive sense, It was the emotional 'felt sense' that was most pronounced.

The reality is that our associative memory neural networks are at work every moment of every day. They are strongly connected to our two drives. Through their connections, they will typically react with either alert or calm. They are the networks that begin to establish meaning to circumstance for us, and repeat that 'felt sense' when we have a similar circumstance. They become our operating pattern and the way we make sense of our world.

State dependent recall

State dependent recall means that when we are in a specific mood or emotional state all the memories associated with that state will surface. It is similar to the law of associative memory, except with state dependent recall what surfaces are specific memories associated with that same state. It is like when you are in a fight with somebody. All of the sudden you can remember everything that they have ever done wrong for the last 20 years, and typically those instances do not bother you or are not in the forefront of your perception at all.

We store information in the neural networks of our brain with the associated emotional states that we were experiencing at the time. When those emotional states are activated, all of those memories come to the forefront and are very present for us. For example, if I suffer from test anxiety and I am nervous as I am sitting down to take a test, I may get flooded with memories of past failure. Academic anxiety, or pressure to perform will resurface and be in the forefront of my awareness.

Or, as in Sandy's case, if I have experienced a lot of grief, or separation in my life and a current circumstance brings up those feelings, my consciousness will be flooded with all my past memories of loss and probably tell me a story about my current situation.

Sandy's mom had a heart attack the week of Sandy's graduation. She always dreamed this would be one of the best times of her life; she and her mother had talked about it often. Instead, it was a challenging one. Because this memory carried both the disappointment of a lost dream, and the grief of losing someone close, she began to fear being happy and feeling accomplished. Every time a new circumstance surfaced where she might feel happy and proud of herself, she began to recall all the times throughout her life when she had been disappointed. Although she had many more events that went smoothly, because of her state dependent recall she honestly believed that "something always goes wrong, I am just not meant to succeed".

The examples are endless, but the idea is that specific memories, when they are related to certain emotional states, will resurface when we are in a similar emotional state.

Understanding these dynamics is incredibly important in retraining our neural networks to function from a grounded state. The laws of associative memory, or state dependent recall, are merely warning mechanisms designed to draw us toward, or repel us from that which has helped us or hurt us in the past. If we can see that they may or may not be appropriate for our current situation we can more easily not be overcome by their neural responses.

Conversely, letting the associations, or the memories take us away, or hijack us only further cements those response patterns and ways of being. Observing the process with awareness, non-reactivity, or maybe even curiosity at the dynamic begins to establish profoundly different response patterns for us. This allows us to see the current circumstance with much more clarity and self-compassion.

Furthermore, noticing which ones are especially strong may be a great tool in discerning which ones are nudging for healing.

The congruity of moods

When we are in a specific mood, feeling, or emotional state, we seem to only be able to feel more of that same state. This is a physiological truth. The congruity of moods is similar to, and may encompass state dependent recall, but is much more general in terms of it is emotional tone and the feelings it brings up. In other words, if I am depressed I look at the whole world through the lens of depression and everything looks dismal. Even the things in the past that have given me joy are now ineffective at doing so. We see everything through the colored lens of our current emotional state and react accordingly. I see current and past experience through the lens of my mood.

Our emotional systems are designed to react, and react strongly, so competing streams of input may actually overwhelm our systems[10]. Because there is a phenomenal amount of information stored in the emotional networks of our brain, some believe it is actually a psychological safety mechanism to only be able to feel 'like' emotional states at the same time. We can 'shift' emotional attention, and be able to change overall mood states, but unless that shift takes place, our entire world is colored by our current mood state.

Two really important points need to be addressed at this juncture. First, because the congruity of moods tells us that we perceive anything in our environment from the emotional state we are currently experiencing, we process our reality, make choices, and exhibit behaviors depending on what we are perceiving. If we are in a depressed or reactive state, our choices and behaviors reflect that state, and may be far out of balance for what is truly appropriate for the circumstance. And we may be sorry later. When we push to have a conversation, feel compelled to deal with something that is bothering us, or make large life decisions from that space they are almost always not the choices we would have made had we been in a balanced state.

The second point is that our neural networks, again, are firing to where our focused attention is. And, in doing so, perpetuating more of the same. If we remain in, or allow our mood state to completely color our reality or let it consume us far too long, we are hard-wiring that state of being. The answer is not to suppress, or pretend the mood state does not exist as much as it is to understand this dynamic and not let it dictate our reality. This is fostering non-reactivity. Finding some solid ground beyond the lens of the current 'mood' and re-engaging from a grounded state allows us more clarity and a clearer lens from which to see the world. Further, if we can do anything to authentically shift mood states, or re-ground ourselves, we have much greater access to our own intuition and inherent heartfulness.

In the next several chapters we will re-visit the idea of the congruity of moods and entertain ways to make it work for us instead of against us. For now, understanding the dynamic, and its power, is vital to not being controlled by it.

The neural networks in our brain are constantly wiring and rewiring to experience. This is the miracle of neuroplasticity. Associative memory, state dependent recall, and the congruity of moods, are a few of the brain dynamics responsible for how those neural networks process information and then *wire to further experience*. If we become consumed with the perceptions and reactions of destructively focused attention, in any of these neural states, that further wires our existence. Furthermore, our neural networks are a physiological system closely integrated with our biochemical responses. Our attention also determines our biochemical reality. Both work in concert in continually adaptive ways furthering the cycle.

Biochemical responses

The subconscious mind, and the conscious part of the limbic system – in other words, the emotions that we are aware of – are strongly connected to the body proper by our biochemical response system. Any time the subconscious, or both of our emotional brains are activated, they send an immediate message to the hypothalamus, which is like a chemical producing factory in our brain. The hypothalamus then sends a rainstorm of biochemicals throughout our body. These biochemicals very strongly affect how we feel at any given moment in time. This is the sense we get when we strongly feel something. It almost feels as if every cell in our body is affected. They are.

This is the mind / body connection of any emotional state, and shows us how the whole of our body is involved in our emotional lives. We can see how profoundly our two drives play out in our everyday lives, and how we hyper-react when faced with any threat. We can also see that when we are in a state of threat, it is virtually impossible to focus on states of heartful awareness including unconditional love, compassion and bonding. Furthermore, because it is the second, calmer drive that controls our receptivity to relationship and bonding, we can see that when we live from reactive states it is virtually impossible to create any deep state of heartful engagement with our own Inner Being.

Let us take a brief look at how this all works.

The endocrine and the nervous system work together in producing biochemicals that affect almost every cell and organ in our body. The biochemicals associated with emotion profoundly affect how we feel at any given point in time, and also have their own adaptive processes that further shape who we are becoming. The part of our brain that is involved in emotion is also the richest area in the brain in terms of biochemical production[11] and is intimately connected to our subconscious brain and somatic, or 'felt' emotional reactions; in other words, the ones we feel all throughout our body. They can drive our fear response system and cause our body to adapt to further states of stress. They can also drive our 'calm and connection' system to bond, create community, and form well grounded and heartful relationships with ourselves, our deeper potential or our Inner Being[12].

The way this works is every time we have a thought or a feeling or interpret something in which we attach meaning, we produce powerful chemicals that activate many cells and organs throughout our body. This biochemical reaction pattern can flood our whole body with chemicals consistent with that emotion. We have chemicals consistent with anger, chemicals consistent with threat, chemicals consistent with love, chemicals consistent with bonding, chemicals consistent with positive thoughts about the future, and so on. Basically any emotional state that we experience carries its own biochemical make up. It is like we have all these different internal IV bags and anytime we experience a specific emotion we squish the IV bag that has the biochemical reaction consistent with it.

These chemicals are sent throughout our body, including back to our brain, and are received by cells through receptor sites on their surface. Although biochemicals connect every part of our body, we also have nodal points of concentrated receptors all over our body. This gives us the specific bodily sensations that are intricately intertwined with feeling any emotional response. At the most basic level, the chemicals produced through our feeling states and emotional attention eventually dictates who we are by how we feel, interpret and respond, at any given moment in time.

Researchers typically measure our biochemical levels in our blood, saliva, or urine, and different biochimicals have different points of concentration.

They also all have different and lengths of time they are at maximum concentration. Some of the biochemical associated with emotion that you may have heard of are cortisol, oxytocin, serotonin, dopamine and endorphins. We will look at some of the primary effects of cortisol and oxytocin throughout this book, as cortisol is primarily linked to our threat response drive, and oxytocin is primarily linked to our calm and connection drive.

Neurotransmitters are specific types of biochemicals associated with the brain cell or neuron. These neurotransmitters facilitate the synapse to fire in the specific areas of the brain associated with that emotion. In other words, my brain reacts by responding with more of the same. There is kind of a 'feedback loop' between the biochemical reactions all throughout our body and the corresponding brain pattern associated with that emotion - which facilitates more chemical production and furthers the emotional spiral. The spiral can lead to chaos, stress and anxiety. The spiral can lead to love, compassion and clarity.

Our biochemical state and the state of what our neural nets are experiencing are intimately connected. In other words, our body and brain are acutely coupled in their response systems. Furthermore, the synaptic connections dictated by our biochemical response affects every aspect of our perception. That is, our brain will perceive through what our body is feeling. And we further adapt to the ongoing spiral. Every change in our perception, emotional state or attention, conscious or subconscious, carries its own physiological reaction patterns. These reaction patterns then go back to the brain creating different synaptic connections and further ways of perceiving or seeing our version of reality.

In chapter 2 we talked about reactivity, stress, and emotional chaos, and how when we are immersed in the states it is virtually impossible to get in touch with any grounded state or larger way of being. We can clearly see the 'spiral of becoming' at work when we look at how we biochemically react to these states. Let us look at how these responses play out in the integrated systems of our biochemistry and neural connections, and form further adaptations to this way of being.

To illustrate this, we will revisit the story of Joey and imagine how his brain and body may have reacted to a particular instance of stress, as an adult, and then look at how further adaptations would have been likely. This scenario is built on the background of his earlier story. However, even though we are using Joey's as a story of representation, this process is going on for each of us every time we are triggered by anything we perceive to be a threat.

Biochemistry in action - cortisol

Our conscious and subconscious minds are constantly working together to scan our lives for any potential threat, fear or danger. The data or 'life files' that we assess this danger with is what it has been programmed in our past experience. *Imagine Joey, as a young adult, in college, trying to make his way in the world with his past programming. He has 'files' that fear gender in authority; he has 'files' of feeling inadequate, he has 'files' of reacting in a combative way. And he has a particularly difficult woman professor who reminds him of his mother.*

Their first interaction is a difficult one, and Joey is immediately uncomfortable. He may not even know why, but his subconscious mind is making him feel very threatened and hyper alert. The moment this happens his amygdala sends a message to his hypothalamus to release a chemical called ACTH. Remember the amygdala is the organ that is responsible for scanning our environment for any emotional cues, and the hypothalamus, together with the pituitary, are the chemical producing organs in our brain. ACTH stands for adrenocorticotropic hormone, and it is the hormone that begins the stress process.

ACTH is released and sent down to his adrenal glands, which sit on top of his kidneys. ACTH tells his adrenal glands to release an all-out system of alert in the way of stress chemicals that invade his body. He is immediately on guard, reactive and hyper-vigilant in looking for any signs of threat. One of the stress chemicals released is cortisol. Cortisol is designed to mobilize energy sources to get us ready to fight or flee, and we need a certain amount of cortisol to get out of bed in the morning. However, in our current culture we do not usually need the extent of these resources to combat the stress to which we are exposed, and most of us live our lives in such a way that we have too much, too often, and suffer it is damaging effects.

Cortisol raises blood sugar and mobilizes fatty acids. It causes us to store more body fat, raises our blood pressure and floods the neurons in our brain. This 'brain flooding' is called cortical inhibition and it damages our ability to think, reason, and retrieve information that we know we know. It is why we cannot remember our phone number when we get in a car accident, or why we cannot recall things we are certain we know when we sit down to take a test. It is why our thinking seems 'fuzzy' during periods of prolonged stress. Cortisol's long-term effects have also been associated with premature aging, premature death, and a whole variety of stress-related health issues like high blood pressure, heart disease, diabetes, anxiety disorders, etc.

The cortisol in Joey's body and brain cause him to feel more nervous, he cannot think clearly and he perceives the situation as even worse than it really is. A large part of him is the threatened young boy fighting for his life. He is absolutely convinced, through his own subconscious perception, that she is the problem and he rightfully perceives her to be the monster he feels she is. This is regardless of the fact that most of the other students do not seem to have any issues with her.

Throughout his interaction with her his negative inner chatter is constant and creates a steady influx of what are called 'low grade cortisol baths'. Low grade cortisol baths are basically steady streams of cortisol all day long, and are primarily due to our thought process surrounding emotional issues, for example, the endless loop of negative things we say to ourselves, or the conversations we have in our head. These 'low grade cortisol baths' can be as damaging, or even worse than the event we perceive because we are exposing ourselves to a steady influx of the stress hormone all day long.

Cortisol has a 12 hour half-life which means after 12 hours it only takes one-half as much cortisol to get you back to the original level stemming from the stressful event. In other words, it stays in the body at fairly high levels for quite a long time. Further, any additional influx will have a cumulative effect in keeping levels up. *With all the 'cortisol baths' he is exposing himself to through his thought process and continuing reactivity, Joey is unknowingly keeping his cortisol levels sky high.*

Several important and harmful adaptations happen when cortisol levels remain elevated for extended periods of time. First, chronically elevated levels of ACTH promote a proliferation and growth of adrenocortical cells. What this means is high levels of ACTH signals our adrenal glands that we need to make more cortisol. The adrenal glands do this by actually making more cortisol producing cells. Further, as we learned earlier receptor sites in a cell membrane are what allow the biochemical to insert itself into the cell wall and activate the cell. These hormone receptors can increase or decrease in number in response to need, after which the hormone production will up-regulate or down-regulate in response to need.

What all this means, simply, is that our body adapts to chronic reactivity and stress by making more cells to make more cortisol, increasing the level of cortisol throughout our body, and making more receptor sites so more cortisol can perform functions within the cell itself. This whole process can actually stimulate the body to create even more cortisol and regard the elevated level as our new baseline. In essence, our cells may become addicted to the negative biochemical reactions taking place, produce more receptor sites for the specific hormones, and create a physiological and psychological need to feel those sites.

Joey does not realize his interpretation of events is colored by his past. Nor does he realize he has any control in his response patterns or the situation. He certainly does not realize that there is a possibility in re-wiring his neural record of the past and truly healing from its hold.

His ongoing reactivity and stress result in chronically elevated levels of cortisol and he suffers the resulting physiological and psychological consequences. All of these physiological changes go back and color Joey's ongoing perception of his life and life events.

Even though Joey's story is unique to Joey, we all have our own. And the adaptive processes that our bodies and brains go through are all very similar. Eventually we become our inner experience, and if everything stays the same nothing changes.

Epigenetic Influences

Our chronic biochemical states can be far reaching. Sometimes they can even promote changes within the cell nucleus[13]. We have always believed that our genetic make-up pre-determined certain aspects of our existence, that genes alone controlled our biology. However, now we are learning differently. Epigenetics show us how certain genes can be activated or deactivated by the biochemicals they are exposed to. That is, the DNA itself is not changed, but the way that gene expresses itself is. Because our biochemical make-up at any given point in time is largely a function of our emotional state, and our body's chemistry can actually effect our gene expression, we see how profoundly healing and intentionality can change us. All the way down to our genes.

SERT 5HTT is a beautiful example.

SERT is a 5HTT serotonin transporter gene. It was identified as a contributing factor, and possible identifier, of those who were prone to depression or anxiety disorders. Although it was an important finding, it seemed fatalistic for those who had the gene. It was as if they were predetermined to develop depression or anxiety and there was really nothing they could do about it. However a few subsequent findings showed that this was not the case.

First, these findings showed that there really needed to be a history of some significant life stressors for the gene to be expressed in that way. Some people were shown to have the gene and be living fine, while others became victims of anxiety disorders and depression. Specifically, it was the exposure to cortisol that determined whether the gene expressed itself in an anxious or depressive way. More importantly, it appeared to be activated primarily by chronic, low-grade 'cortisol baths'; not as much by 'things' that happened to us, as much as the emotional impact, and the way we 'held' those things. Still, if you had some traumatic life events, and were exposed to a certain amount of cortisol because of those events, the finding still seemed fatalistic. Worse, the personal blame for the cortisol baths, or mindset with the associated disorders perpetuated the whole occurrence.

The second series of findings, however, were hugely hopeful. They showed the gene was hyper-reactive in nature. In other words, the gene was hyper-reactive to the influx of cortisol and that is what caused it to express itself in an anxious or depressive way. However, because of its reactivity, if there were intervention techniques to reduce the cortisol, the gene actually recovered. Intervention techniques aimed at healing from trauma, or reducing

In other words, our heart transmits varying electrical impulses that carry messages throughout our body by the way they are patterned. Our body, being a phenomenal pattern detection system, picks up these patterns all throughout, especially in some very important and influential parts of our brain. These parts of our brain send an immediate message back to our body that releases a flood of chemicals, and tells us how to feel, how to react, and guides our further perceptions – which repeats the spiral all over again!

There are two further, even more important points. One is that our heart waves are intrinsically connected to the physiology of the rest of our body, and whether we 'feel' calm, or 'feel' chaotic it may be, in a large sense, due to the patterning of our heart. The second is that there are things we can do to intentionally engage and shift our heart wave pattern. By changing this electrical wave at the level of the heart, we can profoundly change our emotional state and outlook, reactivity, and ability to connect with others and generate a deep sense of heartful engagement.

The electrical patterning of our heart permeates our body, and it is intrinsically connected to our biochemical reactions and the neural responses in our brain. A change of heart can literally change our emotional state and the over all, and all-consuming response of our body. Simply, the functioning of our heart matters. And through practice it can be intentionally cultivated to nurture life-generating and sustaining states of being. Much more will be said about this in the next two chapters.

Conclusion to 'Spiral of Becoming'

When we look at the spiral of becoming it is a little like trying to figure out which came first the chicken or the egg. In other words, it is an ongoing cycle or spiral, and there really is no beginning or ending. The whole process is continually perpetuating itself. Our neural system, biochemical system, and electrical systems work in concert in reflecting any emotional state we are currently experiencing, and also adapting in their own specific ways to cultivate more of the same. What this means is we are constantly becoming more of any emotional state we are consistently experiencing – and seeing our world from that state. Too, this all goes back to how our personal and individual perceptions are created in the first place.

Let us look at how this may play out.

We all have perceptions stored in our subconscious from past experiences and relationships; parents, siblings, classmates, coworkers or friends for example. Someone in our present may do something similar, or even remotely similar, to a relationship in the past. It could be more overt, like a similar situation, or as simple as a facial expression, attitude, gesture or smell. Because of our associative memory patterns, if the original experience was stored with some strong emotional response, the new situation is likely to result in an anxiety filled reaction.

Our systems may be alerting us to true danger, but unless we can calm the emotional chaos surrounding it we will not be able to see the situation clearly. We, of course, feel the reaction, and since it is subconscious, we assume the current circumstance warrants the strength of our emotional response. We react as if today were yesterday; our adaptive systems kick in, and begin to 'hardwire' the same reaction for any future circumstance. Unaware, we perpetuate these reactive states, and this becomes the lens through which we see the world.

Our continuing behavior and attention furthers the cycle; every thought, choice of words, 'loops' of inner chatter, big response patterns as well as smaller response patterns are functions of this process.

The good news is we can break the cycle.

The good news is, with intentionality and healing we can re-wire implicit memory, and we can reverse the cycle of adaptation.

The way we can reprogram is to begin to shift and change our experience. Again our version of reality is basically what our bodies and brains have been programmed to have us believe reality is. It is all subjective interpretation from our original programming and our subsequent thoughts and reactions in regard to that programming. Breaking the spiral anywhere along the chain begins to make profound and foundational changes in the way we perceive and react in the world. Our life becomes a choice instead of a reaction. Unless we find ways to transform our habitual ways of perceiving and being in the world, we just perpetuate more of the same. Fostering non-reactivity through presence and non-judgmental awareness is the first step. And transformation is possible. Remember, neuroplasticity tells us that with intentionality to healing or a different way of being, we can change our synapses, grow new neurons, integrate brain regions, and create functional and structural changes throughout our body and brain. We can create and adapt to new ways of being and tap into the Larger Way of Living we know is possible.

Where we have been, where we are going

Let us review some of the things that we have learned so we can clearly see why and how a blue print for change and healing is possible.

We started this chapter looking at the fact that experience is an embodied phenomenon. In other words, as long as we are alive in our human bodies every experience we have is received through and reflected in our integrated physiological systems. Neural firing in the heart and brain are primary among these systems, and together with our endocrine system, tell us what to think and how to feel.

We also looked at the idea that our bodies are systems of adaptation and transform to any experience we routinely give them. This is where the hope for healing and transformation lies. Intentional experience, or directed attention, creates new and healing neural firing patterns, which then creates new ways of being, and transforms our life experience. The more repeated experiences are transformed the more the totality of our life is transformed.

When we looked at the parts of the brain in chapter 2 we learned that the functions of the cortex and the limbic system are very different – although the processing structures, namely the neurons and neural nets, are the same in each system. Here we learned the related hope and promise of neuroplasticity. We 'wire' to experience, but through new experience we can re-wire a faulty system.

We also learned that the limbic system is primarily in control of our emotional responses and carries two very strong drives. One of these drives is a fear response system that can hijack our whole body when it is out of balance. The other system is responsible for calm, connection and bonding, but cannot flourish if our fear response system is hyper-reactive. This drive is responsible for the feelings of being grounded and thrives on heartful awareness and engaged connection with our self, others, and our Inner Being.

So far we have taken a pretty in-depth look at how our human systems function, or how we 'are' in the world. Most of this has revolved around how we are formed, in a perceptual sense, and how we maintain our habitual ways of being through our integrated physiological systems. Interspersed, we have seen glimmers of hope of transformation, and healing, and truly cultivating a different way of being.

Now we will build on that foundation. We will look at ways we can 'reprogram our systems', if you will, through awareness, new and healing experience, and re-wiring the neural circuits in both our conscious and our subconscious brain. And through it all we will entertain the concept that a heartful way of engaging our world is not only possible, it is probable when true and foundational change and healing takes place.

Transformation is possible

Foundations for transformation and the building blocks of heartful awareness are embedded in these last two chapters. These are the bricks for the path of our metaphorical labyrinth. They will all at once provide the foundation, and pave the path to healing, transformation and provide the skills for us to make heartful awareness a lived reality.

Review points

◊ Our original 'programming' or implicit memory patterns were formed from past experience, and our response patterns were first developed to keep us safe or protected in some way. *Refraining from judging, and conversely appreciating or holding our implicit memory patterns with non-reactive self-love or compassion is the first step to healing.*

◊ Because our implicit memory patterns, or programming, carry an inherent emotional response (felt, but not necessarily consciously known), they create subjectivity in the way we see our current world. We subconsciously see our reality relative to all of our past experience, primarily unbeknownst to us.

◊ Memory is malleable. In other words, *all past programming is now a function of wiring and chemistry. And those can change, heal and transform.*

◊ *Our mind, spirit, and soul are not our brain, although our brain registers and reflects activities from these wonders. As such, we can use intentional engagement of them to retrain and profoundly transform who we are, and how we are in the world.*

However, the word transformation itself means 'to move beyond our current form'. To truly be different we need to be different. In other words, we need to take action to change, or everything remains the same.

These next several chapters introduce new ways of being. The rest of this chapter will focus on the power of awareness and non-reactivity, characteristics generally associated with mindfulness. Subsequent chapters will focus on intentional heartful engagement, or the development of our second drive; the drive to flourish, love, and connect with both our inner and outer worlds. We will also focus on healing what may be blocking us. These concepts progressively build, and in truth, are not separate from each other. And all are built on the science, and art, of heartful transformation.

Cultivating Mindful Awareness

Cultivating awareness basically means that we are using our conscious attention to be mindful of our circumstance. This mindfulness is directed both at our internal environment as well as our external environment. It is based on a 'non-reactive' way of 'observing' or being with, and in, the present moment without engaging in thought or interpretation about it. We are just 'present with' without evaluating or placing judgments. When we can observe our response, but disengage from its reactivity, we can more easily maintain a grounded way of being. This, then, begins to shift and re-shape all of our typical response patterns.

Because our usual way of behaving is to immediately process thought from wherever our attention is, cultivating 'mindful awareness' or attention helps us break the neural chains of associative memory and behaving and reacting in our typical ways. In other words, we are aware of what is going on, internally and externally, with out immediately responding with our pre-programmed responses. An intentional breath helps. And thus begins the re-wiring process.

As we learned when we looked at the neural aspects of the cycle of adaptation, the brain is always wiring to experience. When we can be aware, or mindful of an external or internal situation without responding in our typical ways, we are creating new response patterns. There is a concept called 'new mind' or 'beginners mind' that illustrates this point beautifully. The more moments in my day I can respond with a 'new mind' the fewer I am responding with my pre-programmed patterns.

When we can respond in this way, we also temper our mood congruency, and greatly reduce our state dependent recall. We quiet our resulting brain chatter. In essence, we stay in the moment instead of subconsciously reverting to past struggles or interpretations of life. We see through a clearer lens.

Cultivating awareness basically uses the prefrontal cortex of the brain to pay attention, without evaluating or appraising. We use it to see, but not to judge. People usually think of the prefrontal cortex as the part of the brain that is responsible for thought and analysis, but it is also responsible for taking in data through our body's senses, mediating conflicting thoughts, and regulating behavior[16]. In other words, it is sensing how we are feeling and choosing how to respond.

As this part 'mediates' the tendencies of each side of the brain, it promotes brain integration which has been argued to create a much more balanced way of seeing and being in the world.[17] Research has also shown that these types of practices actually grow new fibers between the hemispheres of the brain. This is called across hemispheric advantage, or AHA, and is believed to help us integrate thought and meaning in a much more valuable way in our lives.

The prefrontal cortex is also extensively connected with limbic structures.[18] This means it is both related to sensing what is going on for us emotionally, as well as stimulating emotional responses from things it is focused on. In other words, it is receiving messages from our emotional brain about how we are feeling, but also sending messages to our emotional brain about how to respond, by where our attention is focused.

Awareness practices can be done alone, or, as we shall see in the next several chapters, be the first step in practices that intentionally engage the limbic system or emotion in a grounded and healing way.

Let us look at attention focused outward first.

Paying Attention

Paying attention to where our attention is breaks the chain of associative memory that we typically function from all day long. When we can be aware of where we place our attention, without immediately responding, we break our habitual ways of seeing and reacting. The more we do this, the more we form new ways of being. Nerve cells that no longer fire together, no longer wire together. Too, the choice of where we place our attention profoundly affects the development of our consciousness.

If we literally see what we pay attention to, as was demonstrated with the in-attentional blindness idea, we can see what we are fostering, or cultivating as our routine experience. Again, this can be referred to as paying attention to which 'seeds of consciousness' we are planting, and then nurturing them to grow. Remember, anytime we have our attention focused on something our neural nets are firing in response to that attention, and cultivating the capabilities of more of the same. Our ongoing experience is really a function of which neural nets are firing, and with focused attention we can begin to choose those neural nets.

While we should never suppress internal or external conditions that need our attention and need to be healed, sometimes it really is a function of where our attention is placed. The HEAR scale in the next chapter will help you make that discernment. It will help you determine which responses in you are nudging for healing, and which are habits of attention.

Pay attention throughout the day to where your attention is. Put a Post-it note on your mirror at home, put a Post-it note on your rearview mirror in your car, pay attention every time your hand is on a doorknob, as these usually represent transitional moments in your day. Find creative ways all day to stop and pay attention. Remember, every moment of every day you are creating your neural programming. I actually have a bracelet that buzzes every 90 minutes to remind me to stop and notice.

Pay attention throughout the day to where your attention is. Sometimes I can just as easily be focused on everything that is going right, as I can on everything that is going wrong. Quite often, both stories are true. This does not mean I am suppressing the things that are bothering me, but if the things that I pay attention to are the things that show up for me, and determine the neurophysiological state I carry through the day, I might be a little more careful about where I place that attention. Your attention does have power. Be careful how you use it.

Fostering non-reactivity

There was a Native American grandfather encouraging his grandson to pay attention to the two 'Wolves' battling inside of him. One was associated with reactive ways of being, for example anger, hate, greed or jealousy, the other was associated with more grounded ways of being, for example calm, love, and compassion. The young Indian boy asked his grandfather "which one wins?" The grandfather answered, "The one you feed".

Fostering non-reactivity is a concept that primarily focuses on the idea of using attention or awareness to be more in touch with our own reactivity, and then genuinely cultivating a different way to be. It is quite often used in its own right, and also used as the first step in other types of practices.

In other words, if I can notice or just 'be with' without 'thinking about' or evaluating, I am significantly changing my emotional response to the situation. Using our awareness like this kind of creates a 'middle-ground'. What I mean by this is we are not taking off with the thinking, or left side of our brain, but we are also not being consumed by our limbic connected right brain. This is fostering non-reactivity.

First, however let us look at our standard way of reacting.

We typically have three responses to our reactive states. First, we may let the process just totally hijack us. We think our perceptions or reactivity are totally warranted, and respond from an emotionally chaotic state. We become immersed in the trigger, and triggered state, believing that 'I have a right to feel this, so I am going to!'

Letting ourselves be hijacked, whether the situation warrants it or not, only cements our reactive patterns all the more. The truth is, this is also about self-care. Even if the situation does warrant action on our part, being totally consumed by a reactive state is not healthy for us. It is only perpetuating our reactivity. It is much better to deal with what needs to be dealt with from a grounded way of being without the chaotic charge.

Second, we may understand that letting the process hijack us is harmful, but we think the answer is suppressing, either by pretending it does not exist or thinking that we can actually talk ourselves out of it. We try to 'think positive', but, in reality, fundamentally do not believe it.

As we learned, this approach is ineffective because our subconscious and limbic brain is so powerful. This way of responding just allocates stronger reactions to the subconscious to be activated later, and does little to heal or reprogram our limiting patterns. Further, when two parts of our brain are in direct opposition in what they believe, it creates dissonance or brain 'dis-integration[19]' in other words our left brain is trying to reason us into another way of thinking, and our limbic connected right brain fundamentally believes something different. Dissonance or 'dis-integration' is when both halves of our brain are working independently, and each is working very hard to have us believe its own contrasting versions of reality; this kind of disagreement within one organ creates even more stress and reactivity!

Third, we may know there is a better way to handle our stress reactivity, but just cannot seem to get there. We then blame, shame or judge ourselves for not having the strength or wherewithal. We have not been shown the tools and we just feel like failures in being able to truly embody a different way of being. The blame, shame, and judgment exacerbate the whole process, because then they get programmed into our way of being!

There is a fourth possibility.

We can learn to be aware of our feelings with out being swallowed up by them. We can stay mindful and present with what is happening inside, without being totally hijacked by our response and then letting that response take us away. We are not suppressing it, or our reaction; we are just not letting it consume us. Neither is there blame, shame or judgment in our emotional response; we are just being with 'what is'. We are disengaged from the emotional reactivity without being disengaged from the emotion itself.

Sometimes you hear this referred to as 'cultivating the witness', or 'being the observer'. The idea is that if we can observe our own reactivity, as if from a third person point of view, we can stop, or at least lessen the impact of being flooded with the chaotic emotional response. Sometimes we can even disengage from the intensity enough to foster a little curiosity, or even humor. The more we can stop ourselves from either taking off or being flooded with the chaotic emotional response, the more we are 'patterning' another way of responding.

I believe very strongly that understanding how the whole process of Implicit, or subconscious programming is cultivated is the first step in not letting it hijack us. We can understand, and embrace the beauty of our fear response system without having to surrender to its high-intensity alarm every time it is activated. We can even learn to appreciate and love our emotional response for the way it has protected us in the past, at the same time realizing that it may no longer be serving us.

When we become fully present in the moment we are not hijacked by programmed reactions from the past, nor worries about the future. When we ground ourselves in the present, and foster non-reactive, non-judgmental ways of being, we break the chain of our typical response patterns and begin to re-wire a new paradigm of presence. We are no longer consumed by the hold of our threat response system and the present moment offers new opportunity.

Mindfulness in the moment

Typically people think contemplative practice requires a specific length of time and appropriate space in which to do it. Because reactivity can happen in any moment of any given day, and what typically happens is that a person is carried away by that reactivity, only solidifying it is destructiveness, there is a great benefit to practices designed to be done right in the moment.

Practices done right in the moment of reactivity begin to break the associative memory neural nets that usually carry us away from one reaction to the next, quite often resulting in full blown psychophysiological chaos (mental, emotional, and physical). Breaking the chain of reactivity, then, begins to re-wire a different way of responding to life's triggers, and establish more grounded response patterns. Additionally, practices done right in the moment can profoundly change or stabilize our biochemical response. With a more grounded system, we are able to perceive and react with more calm and clarity. Fostering non-reactivity, and 'In the moment' practices are the first steps in beginning to re-formulate the 'spiral of becoming'.

The first activity builds on the practice of chapter 2 'the Power of Pause'. The Power of Pause, or being able to pause right in the middle of reactivity, cannot be understated. Although it was presented in Chapter 2 as a way to respond to our triggers, it can, and should, be practiced any time when we are caught off-guard. Most times, when we are in a highly reactive state, it is the reactivity that determines the outcome of the situation rather than the initial event.

Exercise and Reflection # 3 - The Power of Pause

List many situations in your own life, big and small, where you might benefit from taking a moment to pause before you react. You might also reflect on how the outcome could possibly change if you are able to react differently. Too, it is important to anticipate the situations before they happen so you can be mindful of pausing and actually do it when you are feeling reactive. Brainstorm ways to keep the 'pause' in your awareness so you are more likely to employ its help when needed. Reflect in ways that are appropriate for you.

Exercise and Reflection # 4 - Paying attention to attention

◊ What can you do to stop at several points during the day, and pay attention to where your attention is?

◊ Where is your typical attention throughout the day?

◊ Where are your thoughts?

◊ What are you doing during the day that is cementing your habitual ways of being?

◊ What stories are you telling about your current circumstance throughout your day?

◊ What else could be true?

◊ Process and reflect in a way that is appropriate for you.

Conclusion – Claiming the foundation

Awareness practices and ways of being can be done in their own right, or be the first step in practices that intentionally engage another way of being. As we are learning, being mindfully aware is the first, and necessary step to being heartfully aware.

Throughout this chapter we have seen that the 'spiral of becoming' is playing out in our lives every moment of every day. We are constantly transforming through the interconnectedness of our brain, body and heart, and all the momentary experiences we give them. We have seen how our perception, at any given moment in time, is filtered through these three bodily systems and further cements the spiral in the emotional direction it is heading. We have seen the power of the moment. We have also seen how being mindfully aware of our processes, and the presence we bring to each moment, can shift the texture of that moment, and subsequent moments. We have learned what it means to be mindfully aware, and we have learned the power of pausing in the moment of reactivity.

This is the necessary and solid foundation from which heartful awareness is constructed. In the next several chapters we will focus on intentionally and heartfully engaging the limbic system through love, compassion, clarity, calm, etc., and developing our drive to connect and thrive. We will learn the foundational importance of active engagement. We will look at the profound and transformative powers of heartful awareness and how we might embody them in our everyday life. We will take the journey from mindfulness to heartfulness, and then entertain what it means to heal.

4

From Mindfulness to Heartfulness

The force of deep love, compassion and other heartfelt emotions can literally unite our brain, our heart, and all of the cells in our body. By experiencing what these heartfelt states are like inside of us we can then activate the dormant impulses, cultivate them, and embody them in an integrated way of being. This union feels harmonious and expansive; like we are all at once in touch with the depths of our being, and connected to a much larger way of living. Done intentionally and routinely they form an even greater union, become our primary way of operating, and profoundly change our world and us.

Approaching Heartfulness

From the last two chapters we learned that there is an inextricable relationship of mind, body and spirit. We also examined the concept that whatever we feed this mind, body, and spirit dynamic, as the 'seeds of consciousness' are what we end up harvesting. In other words, any state of being we continually experience, especially ones that are deeply, or routinely felt, become our 'operating system' or the way we perceive and function in the world. The next obvious question then, becomes how do we begin to take this knowledge and have it work for us instead of against us?

Relationality, deep love, compassion, gratitude, purpose, clarity, a sense of being grounded in our Inner Being… We know that these states change us, but why? And how do we be intentional about creating them? How do we – more often than not – live from this place in our everyday lives?

This chapter is about intentionally cultivating and practicing the conditions of these life-generating states of being. As we saw in chapter 1, I believe that these are best described as heartful awareness. These are the states where we most fully experience, and are guided by love, compassion, a sense of purpose, and a larger way of living. With understanding, intentionality, and heartfully engaged awareness, we can begin to more fully incorporate these ways of being in our every day lives and have them emerge as our standard way of living.

However, at the outset, it is very important to understand the depth of what heartful awareness really is. Because words like love, compassion, clarity, or expansiveness are often glossed over, overused, or diminished from their true depth, I feel it is important to understand the essence of what this chapter is offering. Heartful awareness is a choice of full presence – body, mind and soul. It is a continual and intentional sense of full presence, and heartfelt communion, with our self, our surroundings, and others. And, as we shall see, it can profoundly change us, in all areas of our lives. As Ticht Nhat Hanh says, "There is no greater gift, than the gift of your presence".

This sense of presence leads to an expansive way of seeing, and being in the world. It allows us to see the deepest purpose, and fullest potential of every moment. It creates whole system integration in our bodies, brains and psyches, and is far beyond an un-grounded emotional sense of just feeling good, or grasping at something we are infatuated with. Heartful awareness allows us to flourish. It allows us clarity. Its cultivation is appropriate for deep thriving in all aspects of our life, from the deepest of intimate relationships, steeped through workplace ethics and vocational life, all the way to our everyday involvements and those we may not even know. It is the momentary choice, moment after moment, to let our truest sense emerge into our lived reality and intersect with the outside world. It allows us to be the best that we can be, in whatever we do.

As we begin to explore the profound potential and possibilities of heartful awareness, we will look at the power of our daily attention, begin to feel the texture of what heartful awareness is, and reclaim the role that grounded and deep emotion may play in it. With heartful awareness in mind, we will provide an alternative definition of rationality, consider a blueprint for our own awareness, and look out how heartfulness, embodied, profoundly changes us. As well, we will take concrete and specific steps to develop heartful awareness in our own lives, and the lives of those around us.

Lastly, as we will see in this chapter and the next, living from these states needs to be in deep truth. In other words, no matter how hard we try we cannot 'talk' ourselves into feeling something we genuinely do not. Sincere transformation through heartful awareness is only possible if it is steeped in truth. Accordingly, we will look at how we cultivate these states of being in an authentic way and examine how our own blocks or triggers may be responsible if we cannot. We will also consider how we might more effectively address our 'nudgings for healing' by directing heartful awareness back at our self.

The power of emotional attention

Heartful awareness is profoundly connected to how we embody, or the sense of presence we bring to every moment of every day. In other words, we know when we are 'on purpose' or not, and this sense bleeds into all other areas of our lives. We basically have two ways of being in the world, and in emotion, and we have seen how life begins to be a reciprocal system of adaptation to any state we are routinely in. We seem either to be consumed by reactivity, in difficult or distracted emotional spaces, or grounded in generative or life enhancing emotion with a greater connection to both our outer world and Inner Being. A great percentage of this is determined by the focus of our attention or awareness moment after moment, day after day.

Throughout this chapter we will journey deep into what it means to be heartfully aware, and specific ways we might do that, but first it is important to have a first hand experience of the power of attention, both in our own focused attention as well as in engagement with others. For where we have our emotional attention, whether by choice or by circumstance, profoundly affects the way we feel at any given point in time. When our attention and awareness are consumed in states of reactivity it is physiologically impossible to connect to the heartful awareness all around us. Our attention, perceptions, and the resulting impact on our physical and emotional experience cannot be separated.

The following exercise is designed to help you grasp this concept and a deeper level than you would experience from just reading about it. It is important to engage it at a meaningful level, and write about personal experiences that carried a significant amount of feeling response for you.

Exercise and Reflection # 5 - The feeling states of awareness

Get out three pieces of blank paper, and do each of the below sections on a separate piece of paper. This will help you more freely focus on each section as it is intended.

Part 1 – 'Felt states of stress'

Vividly write about a time you felt particularly stressed, or in emotional chaos. It does not have to be the most severe time in your life, although it can be if that is what you choose to write about. It can be a smaller event that happened recently. The key is to choose a time where you really experienced and 'felt' emotional uneasiness or chaos, and describe the event in as much detail as possible. Give some time and thought to the exercise, and make sure you write in the specific steps the exercise suggests. Write within the following guidelines:

Describe in as much detail as you can the specifics of the event. Share what happened, where you were, what was going on, etc.

◊ Describe how you generally felt psychologically during this event or time period. (e.g., overwhelmed, tired, anxious, etc.)

◊ Describe any specific physical sensations you felt during this event or time period (e.g: headache, racing heart, pit in stomach etc.)

◊ How do you physically feel right now, recalling the event? (not looking back on the event in retrospect).

STOP- Pause a moment, process and reflect

Part 2 – 'Felt states of joy'

Take a few deep breaths, get out a new sheet of paper and try and clear your thought process from the previous writing. Now write about a time where you felt particularly happy, 'in the zone', or grounded in your essence. Again, this does not have to be the most impactful time of your life, although it can be if you choose it to be. The time you write about should be one where you truly felt the sensations of happiness or coherence in yourself and the situation. Write within the exact same guidelines as described above.

STOP - Pause a moment, process and reflect

If at all possible, re-tell both of the events to another person, in an intimate and engaging atmosphere.

Part 3 - Review

Personal writing – Reflect, summarize and process the exercise, the questions, and what resonated with you most throughout this experience.

◊   What was this whole experience like for you? How easy was it for you to think of something to write about and how enthusiastically did you begin writing during each event?

◊   Did you re-experience the same feelings as you re-lived the experience? As you re-told the experience?

◊   If you re-told the experience how did you feel? If you listened to someone else re-telling their experience how did you relate to their re-telling?

◊   The theme of this exercise was to pay attention to our psychological and physiological demeanor as a response to where we choose to put our emotional attention.

◊   Is there a lesson in this anywhere for you?

The 'feeling' states of awareness

This is one of the most powerful exercises I do when I conduct workshops. It is significant because it illustrates, in a very experiential way, the concept that our bodies and psyches are not only profoundly affected by our experiences, but reliving those experiences often evokes a similar reaction as the initial event. The experience of this exercise underscores the fundamental concept that where we choose to place our emotional attention, every minute of every day, eventually becomes who we are.

When I ask participants to describe the stressful event or series of events, they are typically very eager to begin. They write with energy; they write with determination; many times they write with anger, frustration or a sense of defeat. I am fascinated by the body language and non-verbal communication being displayed as they write. Many of the participants are clutching their pens so tight their knuckles are turning white, some are angrily tapping the floor with their feet and others have their head in their hand as they write. I am very often curious about the amount of pressure their pens are exerting on the paper, as it looks excessive and the collective energy in the room begins to plummet.

I ask if someone would be willing to share any or all of their story. Usually there is a slight pause but very shortly someone raises their hand and begins to share. Many more participants volunteer to share; it is almost like they are trying to outdo each other in how challenging their stories are.

At this point the stories have ranged from horrific life events to being stressed about more mundane things, but the re-telling of the story, more often than not, begins to evoke emotional, psychological and physical reactions similar to the initial event. I have had people cry, express anger, break their pencil, tighten their shoulders in knots, grit their teeth and slump in their chair from despair. I usually have to cut the stories short because so many want to share.

As we begin to process the experience, and as participants are sharing their stories, I am writing on the board descriptive words of their general experience. I quite often get words or phrases like overwhelmed, anxious, tired, frustrated, tense, "I felt like crying," totally spent, angry and many more of the same essence. When they describe specifically how it felt physically, I get responses like my heart was racing, I could not eat, I got a headache, I could not sleep, I was anxious and tense all over, I had a stomach ache, or an upset stomach, my neck hurt, I was exhausted. Unfortunately the list goes on and on.

At this point I usually pause and simply ask one of the participants who has just shared how they are feeling at the current moment; the moment when they are re-telling their story. The vast majority say they are feeling angry, stressed or anxious all over again. Many feel like they have re-experienced the event, physically and psychologically.

The energy in the room has plummeted and as I look around I see many anxious, stressed, frustrated and unhappy faces, complete with the body language to match. I ask the participants to just look around and observe the room and absorb the energy. I give a pause of silence to reflect.

When I ask the participants to write about a time where they felt particularly happy, 'in the zone' or as if everything was flowing effortlessly, what is immediately apparent is the participants' reluctance or inability to write. Some sit there as if they cannot think of anything to write about. Others write a sentence or two and then stop as if nothing will flow, and a few remark that they truly cannot allow themselves to write about anything good. Some even exhibit a nervous laugh.

After several minutes most begin to write. The process of allowing themselves to focus vividly on a time when they really felt good comes slow, but gradually the majority seems to shift and begins to focus. A few still struggle with what to write about.

As the participants get more involved in their writing their body language beings to shift. Some sit taller, some do not grip the pen so tight, and some actually begin to smile and become quite engaged. The whole energy in the room seems to shift, but I keep quiet about what I am observing. The participants continue writing.

At the end of this process I ask the participants again if anyone is willing to share their story or any part of the writing activity. Typically they are much more reluctant during this phase of the activity; it is almost as if they are not culturally allowed to admit to times of feeling good. Some seem like they want to share, but are embarrassed to acknowledge to the others in the group that have had experiences that they felt positive about; it is so much more comfortable to share their negative experiences.

Eventually someone volunteers, and if the story is an engaging one, or if the other participants can relate, the story seems to generate a collective shift in energy. Once one person has shared and the atmosphere in the room becomes lighter, there are many more volunteers. The people listening are usually quite engaged, and the story-telling becomes infectious. Participants are smiling, laughing, and truly absorbed in each other's stories.

The typical general description of what they experienced is similar to " I felt light", "I felt like everything was flowing", invincible, happy, clam, transcendent. Quite often the re-telling of the story will elicit a genuine smile, a complete shift in body language, and a visible transformation of attitude.

After several stories, or one or two very meaningful stories, the atmosphere of the room has undergone a complete shift and participants are now aware of the shift; some verbally express disbelief in what they are feeling. "I would never have believed this shift was possible if you had just told us about it. I came in with a horrible headache, but now I feel really happy." Something very important has happened through our experience, and it would never have been possible without the actual experience of genuinely engaging in the activity.

The lessons learned through this activity exist on many different levels of awareness. The first, and most obvious lesson is how events in our lives, whether they are joyful or stressful, carry with them a profound and definite physical and psychological reaction. We feel the emotional experience in our bodies in a very noticeable and definite way. This reaction underscores a very important point of this book, that chaotic and anxious, or conversely, heartfelt times, carry with them a whole cascade of psychological and physiological reactions that invade our bodies, change our perceptions and transform who we are at that moment, whether generative or not.

A second lesson arises when I point out how enthusiastically the participants were willing to engage in writing about a stressful or unhappy time in their lives and almost unable to write about a time when they felt happy. I point out how they grabbed their pens and pencils tightly and began to write about the stressful event before I even finished giving directions. I also call attention to their reluctance, looking around, pausing after one sentence, and general feeling of discomfort as I asked them to share a happy or coherent time. The participants usually nod or laugh in agreement of that realization, as they are beginning to realize the depth of the lessons they have just experienced.

A third, and very important lesson comes when we focus on their engaged attention. This is when I share what I observed in body language, feet tapping angrily, pencils breaking, general scowls etc. and, of course, the collective environment of the room as they were writing their stressful stories. A few will laugh out loud as they realize they were a prime example of this. Then, of course, I share the collective shift in non-verbal behavior, some verbal comments and a seeming transformation of attitudes as they wrote about their life-generating events. This brings the experience to a much deeper level, and illustrates another, all-important, lesson of this activity.

Something else has happened. During the telling of the stories we were heartfully engaged with one another. This heartful engagement provided support for the difficult stories, and shared enjoyment for the joyful stories. I ask the participants to focus on that dynamic and share what they experienced. More often than not, even when a student shared a difficult time, the 'witnessing' from the other students provided something of a healing factor. Too, those that were deeply listening, when engaged compassionately, felt the physiological shift of heartfelt engagement in themselves.

They begin to look back half in disbelief and half in genuine recognition of the fact that they have just experienced an intense feeling of, and shift in emotional behavior; complete with all the profound psychological and physiological shifts.

My query usually goes something like this: "What has changed? We are still in the same seats, with the same pieces of paper and pen or pencils we were an hour ago. All I did was ask you to participate in an activity where you chose to focus your emotional attention on a specific event. By focusing your emotional attention on these events many of you felt like you re-lived that event at a psychological and physiological level, complete with mood, perception, and environmental shifts to match. That shift happened through a stressful recollection as well as a happy re-collection. Too, when we were heartfully engaged with one another we 'felt' each other's stories, and the shared experiences created resonance in the room. We collectively feel like we have been all over the place emotionally yet here we are sitting in the same seats, in the same room."

After a deliberate pause, the depth of this lesson begins to become clear. Although through the activity I directed their emotional attention to specific events, the first piece of this profound lesson is that we unconsciously do this to ourselves all-day, every day, 24-7. Where we choose to place our emotional attention, every moment of every day, profoundly affects our psychological outlook, our physiological reaction patterns, how we feel, and our perception of the world we live in.

The second important piece of this lesson is that we are both changed when we choose to heartfully engage with another.

Focused attention profoundly affects how we feel any given moment of every day. Experiencing this shift first hand demonstrates the empowering lesson that, for a large part of the time, we have control. During this activity we deeply experienced the shift of emotional states by choosing to focus our emotional attention. Further, when we are in an ungrounded or emotionally chaotic space, catastrophizing, constant and turbulent mental chatter, or our willingness to focus on chaos rather than heartfulness just creates more of the same.

If we can understand the damage of being continually possessed or hijacked by chaotic emotional states, the hope of paying attention to the ones nudging to be healed, the power of heartful awareness and engagement with others, and the unbounded joy of heartful engagement with ourselves, we are much more motivated to change. What facilitates that change is a continuum of intentionally creating heartful awareness when we are capable, and healing what may be blocking it when we are not…. for our self, and others.

While the previous activity demonstrates well the power of attention, the underlying message is absolutely not one of just trying to "think positive" all of the time, or to pretend to be engaged when we are not. This activity was not meant in any way to judge or be-little the difficult circumstances in our lives. As we saw from the 'spiral of becoming' in the previous chapter, we continually adapt to our perceptions, thoughts and emotions, and physiological responses, and then create new, resulting perceptions. However, this cycle is a result of the deep truth that we feel at any given point in time. Our bodies will always know, and reflect the truth.

Another very important message is determining when our attention is a choice or when our soul is nudging to be healed. If deep and generative affect or heartfulness heals us, but it needs to be our deep truth, we need to find the best route to authentically create that truth. Can we authentically create a deep truth of love, compassion or gratitude? Or is there something in us that needs to be healed first? Do we fix what is wrong? Or do we intentionally create what is right? The answer is both. The answer is also that deep within you, somewhere you know.

As we shall shortly see I have a tool called the HEAR scale, or continuum of healing, that will help you make the discernment.

The next chapter is all about healing. If, in the previous writing reflection you chose to focus on an especially difficult event or dynamic in your life that is blocking you from authentic heartfulness, know that a foundational piece of true transformation is embracing that healing from a state of heartful awareness for ourselves, from a state of self-love, or compassion, and will be addressed shortly. For now, the focus is on the transformational power of heartful awareness in the form of intentional engagement in the choice to love, feel compassion, gratitude or any other state of heartfulness that rings true for you. And it can be intentionally cultivated from where you are, right now.

What heartful awareness is and how it changes us

It may be easier to understand what heartful awareness is if we have a better grasp on what it is not. I was once struggling with an issue in my life that I felt deeply about. I was talking to a friend about my struggle and he asked me if it was coming from my 'shallow heart' or my 'deep heart'. I knew immediately what he was talking about. Although I might not have been able to explain it in words, or clearly define it, I knew he was questioning whether it was motivated by a deep sense of heartfulness, or an ungrounded grasp of emotional appeal.

When we are in the state of heartful awareness we are changed. Our biochemicals are bathing the cells in our body in the hormones of love and compassion[20], our brain is being activated to greater states of calm and reduced stress, and our hearts are responding with a corresponding, coherent wavelength[21]. When we are in a state of heartful awareness in contact with another person there is brain synchrony and a shared heartfelt way of being[22]. There is system integration in our humanness and we experience it as an expansive way of being in the world.[23]

Heartful awareness, then, is a place of non-reactive awareness where our own heartfulness is allowed to emerge, and connect to that of the people around us. It is grounded in non-reactivity, awareness and attention, as was outlined in the previous chapter, but it is also grounded in intentional love, connection, compassion, purpose and clarity. It is grounded in the intention to create, and reside in these spaces more often than not.

There is power in intentionally generating life-affirming ways of being. Heartful awareness be-friends and calms our limbic, or emotional system, and creates body and brain integration. In other words, we can use the conscious part of our brain that is responsible for awareness and attention, to help us generate sincere and healing emotion, by how we choose to engage every moment. And, as we have seen, the more we are in any emotional state the more we cultivate more of the same. Actively engaging in love, compassion and gratitude begets more of those life-generating states, and intentional moments of heartful awareness profoundly change us.

Too, because perception is dependent on our own emotional state, when we are in a state of heartful awareness ourselves, it naturally flows out to those around us; we see, and then behave from greater states of expansiveness and resonance. Heartful awareness is both our connection to our own inner being, and a quality expressed in our outer world. It also holds for us a sense of deep resonance, meaning that we cannot fake it. It needs to be a truth, within us, and with others.

We begin, then, to be able to look at the whole of life through the lens of love, compassion, healing, and life generating emotions. This remolds our brain, reformulates our blood, changes the waves of our heart, and we begin to function from greater states of clarity. All this happens through the dynamics of memory reconsolidation, neural re-wiring, the biochemistry of heart-based emotions, and the brain integration of heartful awareness. Our nervous system remolds itself to match our heartfelt state[24], and we begin to operate more routinely from our calm and connection system versus our fear response system.

Our limbic system calms, our brain integrates, and we better distinguish between emotional chaos and heartfelt truth. The physiological realities that are apparent when we experience 'the zone', the 'flow state', feel on purpose, or grounded in our center, adapt to more of the same. All this results in the feeling of being in a larger or more expansive way in the world, and a greater connection to our truest self, purpose and potential. And all this can be cultivated. It has a heavy emotional component, but only in the most deep-seated and grounded way of being. And by emotion I mean something that is deeply felt in our inner experience.

Because heartfulness inherently includes a deeply emotional component, I feel it would be helpful to distinguish what exactly it is I mean by emotion. In my opinion it is time to reclaim and celebrate the fact that there is a part of us that deeply feels, and when it is grounded, may be the greatest asset we have.

Reclaiming emotion

Love. Compassion. Care. Connection. Awe. Wonder. Resting in the ineffable. How do we accurately define those things that are so deeply felt? How do we convey a universal experience of something so subjective? And how do we begin to understand its place in the context of what it means to truly thrive? Emotion, in my opinion, has gotten a bad rap. In our cognitively driven society, emotion is often seen as a weakness, an obstacle to rational functioning. It also inherently includes a gender bias. Women, on the whole, are seen as too emotional, and men as their rational counterpart.

There is a fundamental problem with this line of thinking, however, because the denial of emotion also means the denial of life generating emotion. As destructive as persisting in chaotic emotion can be, what would our lives be like without love, connection or compassion? Too, when understood or embraced in the context of implicit memory, even difficult emotion can be seen as a path to healing. The parts of our brain that are involved in emotion are the parts of the brain that provide meaning for our lives. Removed of emotion we have no capacity for deep meaning. The focus should be less on whether or not emotion is a good thing, and more on the quality and context of our emotional lives. We should be looking at how they may or may not lead to a larger way of being in the world.

But what exactly is emotion? How can we use one term to describe the deepest of love in the worst of hate? Unfortunately, there has never been any clear agreement, among philosophers, scientists, or anyone else, about what this term means. And how can we begin to use it objectively if we cannot agree on the meaning? The perpetual discussion about what we should 'do' with emotion will be convoluted at best until we can find some common ground on what it means.

Still, it is beyond my intention for this book to engage in an academic debate about what emotion is or is not. At some level, I do not even find it a useful conversation because it does not change the dynamic. And the dynamic, or truth of it all, is that whatever physiological state we are routinely in, we are cultivating as a long-term way of being. We are different people when we are grounded in heartful awareness, for instance love, compassion, our deepest potential or our Inner Being, and this way of existing automatically leads to very tangible, and larger or more expansive ways of being in the world.

What I am proposing here is that there are certain deeply felt states of being, states of deep affect, that are profoundly transforming. Limiting and chaotic emotional states are decidedly different from these expansive and grounded emotional states; and have physiological implications to match. Furthermore, these states, which I am choosing to call heartful awareness, can be cultivated – both through active intentionality, and through healing when they are blocked.

Neil McNaughton in *Biology and Emotion* offers a biological approach to defining emotions and identifying clusters of emotional patterns that lead to specific reactions or general principles[25]. In other words, which ones are life-generating and which ones are not. An embodied, scientific approach to emotion clearly shows that there are grounding, nurturing and life-sustaining emotional states, and there are those that are chaotic, de-stabilizing and destructive if allowed to remain too long.

Our emotional lives in a large sense determine our biochemical lives. In chapters 2 and 3 we had an in depth look at how our biochemistry, at any given point in time, determines our perception, our attention, how we feel, and the behavioral choices we make. From a biological point of view, emotion matters profoundly.

We saw the power of our limbic, or emotional system, we saw the power of our biochemistry, and we saw the fact that no amount of reason, or denial of these systems, will work in calming or healing them when they are out of balance. We saw how implicit memory is developed and how it provides meaning and feeling to our lives through its continual perception. We have also seen the importance of attention and the brain synapse patterns that are a result of where attention is placed. We have seen how our synapse patterns, enabled by biochemical neurotransmitters, literally become who we are.

To engage our limbic system in life generating ways, or heal it when is out of balance, takes direct engagement. And that takes embracing life-generating emotion. It takes honoring and intentionally cultivating the emotions that lead to life; it takes paying attention to the emotions that are out of balance and need healing attention. And it takes awareness and heartfulness to balance our brain in an integrated sense to achieve all of this. According to Rhawn Joseph, man, and woman remain creatures of emotional being[26]. It is time to acknowledge, celebrate and employ that fact in transformational ways for our self, and our world.

We are feeling beings; we should be working with that fact, celebrating it, and cultivating it in its most grounded and generative form. We feel love, we feel compassion; we feel the presence of God. Heartful awareness is a term I have chosen to describe connection to the deepest space within ourselves; that expansive place of calm, clarity, connection, love and compassion. It is not shallow, or fleeting, or impulsive. Heartful awareness invites us into active engagement with those emotional states, which, by their very definition, are life-generating, expansive and stabilizing.

This is the place that holds for us the deepest of affect and life generating ways of being. It is full of purpose and potential, and it is ineffable. We may not be able to describe it, but we know it when we feel it. And actively engaging in it profoundly changes us. Heartful awareness, then, is being able to get in touch with, and operate from, that ineffable state deep within each and every one of us. It is that deeply felt sense that gives meaning to our lives. It may be in relation to others, our outside world, or our selves. And our lives are changed in very measurable and tangible ways because of it.

Intentionality and active engagement

If we look at our lives from the perspective of neurobiology there is no question that some emotional states are life generating, and others, if left unchecked or allowed to fester for too long, are degenerative or destructive – most often a cry for help. Yet most of the time we live our lives in states of constant reactivity, not heeding the cry, nor embracing heartful ways of being. We are routinely responding to, or perceiving life through a lens that is decidedly different from heartful awareness. Now the question is what do we do with this knowledge? How do we make heartful awareness our truth?

There are three important pieces that can help us shed further light on our path. First, are the lessons that we can learn from the intersection of positive psychology and neurobiology. In other words, how these two disciplines overlap to show us we are foundationally changed by intention, and active engagement, and can use them to create and live from heartful awareness. Second, it is important to understand some vital dynamics in brain science. These show us that developing the drive that leads to calm, connection and expansiveness requires devoted attention to develop it fully. That is, because our fear response system, neurally, is quicker and stronger, and will override the calm and connection system when activated, we need overt intention to cultivate and strengthen the fewer neurons in our drive to connect. In other words, while our fear response system is immediate and reactive, it takes awareness and dedication to fully develop heartful ways of being. And, again, our calm and connection system is both in regard to others, as well as the deepest parts of our self.

Lastly, we need to be able to discern when heartful awareness can flourish naturally, or where there are implicit patterns in us that are blocking its emergence and need healing attention. This is when our re-activities are so ingrained, or active, they require some healing attention before we can turn outward.

This section will address those important pieces, incorporate an activity called heartful awareness charting, and a tool called HEAR yourself, a continuum of healing versus attention discernment. These tools are designed to help you process the material at an individual level and take meaningful action in your own life, for it is only movement, internal and external, that transforms us.

At the intersection of neurobiology and positive psychology

While I tend to shy away from words like positive and negative, hoping to preclude any inherent judgment of times when we are feeling less than optimal, there is a lot that we can learn from the discipline of positive psychology. Even more, we can learn from where the disciplines of neurobiology and positive psychology intersect. As we have seen throughout this book, the field of neurobiology tells us that any state of being we routinely experience becomes our 'operating system', or the way we function in our world. The field of positive psychology shows us that to create high levels of well-being, or in our case, heartful awareness, we need to be intentional about it. In other words, the focus of just 'not being sick' does not necessarily lead to 'being well'.

The continuum of wellness

Need for healing   High sense of wellbeing

"OK enough"

Fig. 4.1 The continuum of wellness

Historically, research in the field of psychology primarily focused on the need for psychological healing. The idea was that if we could heal 'what is wrong', it would necessarily lead to the creation of 'what is right'. Focus on the need for psychological healing was, obviously, profoundly important for those in need of that healing. But what we found was that people were only getting to where they felt 'okay enough'. The field of positive psychology's message is to "...remind our field that psychology is not just the study of pathology, weakness, and damage; it is also the study of strength and virtue. Treatment is not just fixing what is broken; it is nurturing what is best[27]." And one does not automatically lead to the other.

Other research in the area showed that positive and negative aspects of experience are actually two separate psychological systems as is evidenced by our two basic drives. This research showed that to develop the positive we needed to focus on the positive. This research also showed that intervention through generative psychological focus was an important avenue for developing emotional resilience, and leads to positive affect shift overall.

What this all means, basically, is that we adapt to the things most present in our inner experience. If our inner experience is one of psychological damage that is crying for healing, that healing needs attention. If we are existing at the level of 'okay enough', yearning for a deeper sense of heartfulness, that also requires intentional focus. The truth is, we all have many individual continuums, this concept will be addressed shortly when we focus on the HEAR yourself scale of emotional reactivity. But, for now, the important point is that intentionality of inner experience creates more of the same. If we want to function from, and have deeper levels of heartfulness in our life, we need intentional focus on the creation of those states.

When we look at the field of neurobiology this all makes perfect sense. If we are constantly adapting to inner experience, finding ways to authentically create that inner experience as one of deep heartfulness profoundly changes us. The question of 'do we fix what is wrong' or 'do we create what is right' is a false dichotomy. When addressed from the state of heartful awareness it is all true. Heartful awareness can, and should be, intentionally cultivated everywhere along the continuum. However, as we shall see in the next section, the drive to nurture, bond, and connect, with others, our Inner Being, and ourselves requires overt and intentional focus for greater development and thriving. It takes a lot of intentionality for the highway of love to override the freeway of fear.

The freeway of fear versus the highway of love

In chapters 2 and 3 we learned, quite in-depth, the power of our fear response system. We learned that to keep us surviving as a species our fear response system had to be quick and strong. We also learned that besides our fear response drive, we also have a drive to bond and connect. Because to keep us surviving as a species we had to be more quickly reactive to fear, then drawn to life enhancing environments, our brain is wired to be reactive.

In other words, our fear response system is more analogous to a freeway, whereas our drive to connect and bond is more analogous to a two-lane highway. What this all means is it takes far more intentionality to create and nurture the neural systems of our drive to bond and connect. We have to 'work out' those neural systems to see greater levels of fitness in them. We have to be far more intentional about nurturing the drive we want, rather than running away from the drive we do not want. It takes choice and intention to love, be compassionate, be grateful, and be grounded in a more expansive way of being. And, to see true change, it takes making that choice far more often than the choice to be reactive.

Exercise and reflection # 6 - Heartfully engaged awareness charting, and reflection

The premise of this book is that the embodiment of heartfully engaged awareness profoundly affects our lives and the lives of those around us. Where we keep our emotional attention, or level of heartfulness, every moment of every day determines who we are becoming. There are enormous psychological and physiological differences between deep states of heartful awareness and extreme states of reactivity. Feeling deep love, compassion or clarity from our core is vastly different than being consumed by hatred, wrought with anxiety, overcome by guilt or shame, or profoundly depressed. The neural, biochemical and electrical states produced by these diverse feelings are also immensely different. As McNaughton suggested, maybe the best way to define these states is by the biological response they generate. If we define emotions by the type of biological response they generate, in other words how *you feel* when you experience them, a clear-cut distinction emerges.

Use the following chart to brainstorm.

Above the line write emotional states that you would define as a deep state of heartful awareness. The states should reflect heartful awareness for yourself, as well as personal awareness directed outward. These states should carry for you a 'felt sense' rightness, resonance, or coherence. Remember, heartfulness is not fleeting, it is not shallow, nor is it grasping or inauthentic. It is a deep state of expansiveness and connection, and is grounded in the radiance of our Inner Being. List those states.

Below the line write states that, for you, are reactive, or that block you from a state of heartfulness. These, also, should carry a 'felt sense', but one of uneasiness, agitation, anxiety or disconnection.

Brainstorm, and list words or phrases all over the page. List those states that elicit the most generative feelings for you highest on the paper and the most harmful for you at the lowest level. For instance, above the line I might write love, compassion, connection, Inner contact, serenity, gratitude, etc. Below the line, I might list disconnection, worry, anxiety, fear, insecurity, guilt, and so on. I would rank them in some sort of hierarchy based on how they affect me and what kind of deep 'felt sense' they evoke in me; the most generative at the top, the most degenerative at the bottom.

There are no right and wrong answers.

When we learn emotional words and terms, they are completely subjective to our emotional experience as we learned what that word meant. In other words, what one state may mean to me may be completely different than what it means to somebody else. For instance, while one person may put forgiveness above the line, somebody else who still carries significant hurt, does not feel ready to forgive, or feels more reactive than heartful when they hear the term, may put the word below the line. This chart needs to reflect Your Truth.

Exercise - Heartful awareness chart

Process and reflect – personal writing

Process and reflect on what you wrote. Look at the states that you listed below the line and process how these states block you from a deep state of heartfulness. Look at what you wrote above the line. Process and reflect on why these states hold importance for you, what they mean to you, and how you can work to intentionally nurture more of them in your life. Write in a 'stream of consciousness' manner, and engage this exercise at a deep level, as these 'felt states' will be re-visited often through out our journey.

There is a lot to be learned from this chart and throughout the next chapters we will re-visit it often.

Life-generating or adaptive, versus
life-depleting or maladaptive

Any degree of heartfulness, whether deeply engaged, and reflected by those at the top of the chart, or lack of, highly reactive, cut off, and reflected by those at the bottom of the chart, cultivates more of the same. However, it is not so simple as "those at the top are good", and "those at the bottom are bad". As we shall examine much more in depth in the next chapter there is a lot to be learned from the bottom of the chart as well. Those at the bottom of the chart should never be judged, suppressed, or denied, and are, most often, when seen in the context of emotional or implicit memory, behaviors or feelings associated with our past "threat wiring". And through neuroplasticity they can be rewired. They are maladaptive when we are submersed in them and they are experienced long-term. However, it is important to remember that initially they were formed as some sort of protective mechanism – and probably now are nudging to be healed. Holding these in the place of self-understanding sheds a whole new light on how we might deal with these reactivities.

We will return to the "nudgings for healing" in the next chapter, but for now let us look at the intention for direct heartful awareness.

When we look at the chart, the words that you listed above the line, just by definition of the way I asked you to write them down, are life generating. In other words, all the physiological responses that we would gain from resting in those states, more often than not, create physiological adaptations that lead to deeper states of heartfulness, deeper psychological and physiological resonance, and strengthen our drive for connection and life. When we look at both levels of the chart there is no question, from a physiological or adaptation standpoint, that some are adaptive, or life generating, and some are maladaptive, or life depleting. Intentionally creating times and spaces in our lives to focus on those states that we listed above the line profoundly change us.

Engaging change

When we look at how profoundly heartfully engaged awareness can transform us, we can look at it both from a neurobiological point of view, in other words how it affects our bodies and our brains, and also from the behavioral point of view. The behavioral point of view shows us how the day-to-day choices we make literally cause us to see, behave, react, and live in our world differently. Heartfulness begets heartfulness, and we are profoundly changed people when we can live in this state more often than not. The question is how do we do that?

If we go back to the heartful awareness chart, those that you listed above the line are the ones that carry the biochemical, neural, or electrical changes associated with generative transformation. Those neurobiological components are the aspects of us that adapt and transform us to higher states of being. Choosing to intentionally cultivate those states, then, begins to transform our humanness, or the way we exist in our human bodies. Again, our bodies may be the best spiritual tool we have.

Cultivating day-to-day awareness

So what does that specifically mean in terms of our day-to-day life? Barbara Fredrickson has done some great work on the impact of positive emotions.[28] Although I tend to shy away from the labels of positive and negative, I am convinced that what she's describing as positivity, or love, is contained in what I am describing as heartfulness. In our respective work we are both describing a place of deep expansiveness, connection, and authenticity or resonance.

3:1 ratio

Fredrickson's research on the influence of positive emotion shows that our sense of self actually expands to include others in greater degrees the more often we can live from those states. Our awareness seems to expand from 'me' to 'we', and it is all the little moments that add up. Her research shows that a 3:1 ratio of positive moments to negative moments can make a profound difference in our transformational process. She also says that 4:1 or 5:1 gains even greater benefits, but 3:1 is really the critical tipping point.

I find this ratio such a helpful and tangible tool because it makes the whole idea of intentional transformation 'doable'. In other words, it is not human nature, nor emotionally honest to try to be in heartful states 100 percent of the time. This ratio gives us the idea that if we can just tip the scales of our emotional attention, and be intentional about creating more life generative moments than not, big shifts can take place in our emotional lives. Also, it is based on research on real people, in real life, making significant transformations.

Authentic moments

There are three very important components of this idea when we look at how it might be implemented. The first is that they need to be *authentic* moments of positive emotion. Our bodies, and their adaptations, know the truth. We cannot convince ourselves to feel something that we truly do not. Our subconscious mind knows the truth, and will send that message to our body, which will adapt accordingly. *But we can invite into our awareness those things that carry a true sense of heartfulness for us.* Authenticity is key. Being able to discern when our emotional awareness is a choice, or when it is something calling to be healed, is an important consideration. The HEAR yourself scale for discernment, presented shortly, will help you do that.

Intentionality is vital

The second important component is that they can be intentionally cultivated. We spend most of our time reacting to the outside world as if we have no choice. Intentionally created moments of heartfulness change our biochemistry, our neural nets, and the electrical patterns of our heart, and, done repeatedly, radically change our 'operating systems'. It is not about pretending we feel something we do not; it is about finding spaces and times, when we can, to shift into moments of authentic heartfulness. Authentically and routinely finding heartful spaces in our days, and our lives, profoundly changes us. It is kind of like every moment of every day we have a 'budget of awareness'. If we can 'bank' more moments of heartful awareness than moments of 'status quo', we begin to naturally transform into that larger, and more heartful way of living we know is possible.

Micro moments of shift

The third component is very connected to the second, in that intentionally crafting spaces and times to be in heartful awareness changes us. However, Fredrickson's research has also shown that they can be what she calls 'micro moments' interspersed throughout our day. Micro moments are exactly as they sound. They are those momentary instances scattered throughout our day that give us ample opportunity to practice heartful awareness. And they add up. Perhaps a moment of genuine connection, an authentic smile with eye contact, a hug, kiss, or "I love you" to someone for whom we genuinely mean it, or a moment of compassion to someone we may not even know. The opportunities for micro moments of heartful awareness are almost endless, but, again, they need to be authentic. And they need to be in full presence. Routine, or perfunctory behavior, without heartful presence will not do it. It is not just the moments in the day that and up, it is how we bring ourselves to every moment.

Heartful presence

The moments, situations and opportunities for heartful presence are endless. We may even experience micro moments of heartfulness for ourselves; possibly a momentary pause to feel loving-kindness, appreciation, or self-compassion for all that we are, and all that we do, even throughout our struggles. Every time we choose to bring that attention into our awareness, even in the small moments of the day, we give ourselves a physiological shot of transformation. Remember, physiologically, we get more of what we experience. By choosing to authentically cultivate heartful presence in micro moments, or larger moments in our lives, we become increasingly more capable of living from deeper states. And it does not take a huge conversion experience.

In the world of neuroscience, little shifts add up

When I was teaching the concepts of transformation in a course at the University, one of my students, who was very excited about the concepts overall, asked, "So how do I just do this, how do I just began to shift to another way of being?" It was as if she felt overwhelmed with the idea of needing to be totally different, and no idea how to begin. When I presented her with the idea of momentary shifts of heartful awareness, and their great cumulative effect, she immediately realized this was something she could do.

In the world of neuroscience, little changes add up. As Joe Dispenza clearly shows in *Breaking the Habit of Being Yourself*, little shifts, or changes in routine, break the neural nets of our typical functioning[29]. Continual internal shifts, and the quantity of generative moments add up. Modest, heartfully aware choices, day after day, break the status quo or habit, and create a new baseline way of being in the world. And every day is full of moments of opportunity.

Charting opportunity

I find it very helpful to use the 3:1 ratio in conjunction with my heartful awareness chart. In other words, when we can authentically create, or reside in the felt states that are above the line, and make an intention to do so, we see deep change. It also helps to see the visual, and know that we do not have to be there all the time. There is no blame, shame, or judgment, for where we are momentarily falling on the chart. However, understanding the power of engaging in genuine heartful opportunities all throughout our day can be truly transforming. Making an overt intention to engage in deeply felt heartful states, like those you listed above the line, create the momentary shifts that eventually become our standard way of operating. Driving to work, walking the dog, in conversation with another, in line at the grocery store; these are all ample opportunities to practice moments of heartful awareness.

HEAR yourself when you are reactive

But what happens when some 'felt state' at the bottom of the chart is present for us? How do we know if it is an authentic shift or not?

The heartful awareness chart is meant to show you the power of physiological states of being. However, blame, shame, judgment, or even denial of emotional states below the line only perpetuates reactive states of being. The next chapter will specifically focus on the power of embracing and healing emotional states below the line from a place of self-love and understanding; or heartful awareness for our self. But how do we know? How do we know when our emotional state, if it is below the line, is basically a choice of awareness, or something that is truly nudging to be healed? How do we measure our reactivity? I truly believe that somewhere we know, and if we can get in touch with the deepest parts of our inner being, it will tell us. Below is what I call the HEAR yourself scale of emotional healing.

Heartfully Engaged Awareness Reactivity scale

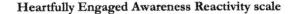

Heartful Healing		Heartful Awareness
0% engagement	25% 50% 75%	100% engagement

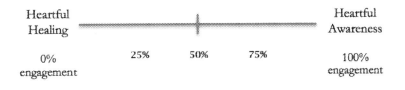

Fig. 4.2 HEAR yourself scale

The idea of the scale is a visual continuum to assess your own reactivity. It is to be used any moment of the day, or when struggling with a specific issue. To use it, rest in your deepest intuitive sense, and tune into the truth of our body. See if you can foster non-reactivity as presented in the last chapter. After a few calming breaths imagine where you might fall on the continuum. *Basically, if you can authentically shift to a state of heartful awareness do so,* but if your reactivity is coming up strong, and you cannot genuinely shift, acknowledge that as well.

Chances are, if you are between 0 – 25% on the scale, something is nudging for your healing attention. Give it heartfully aware attention directed back at your self, and what is yearning for your healing attention, as soon as possible. Twenty five – 50% could go either way. Sit with it. Rest in a few intentional breaths, and your deep heart. If you can shift, do, but promise yourself you will go back and address what ever is asking for your attention when you are in a more grounded state. Promise yourself you will give it the voice it is requesting. If you cannot shift, offer yourself, and your soul, healing attention as soon as you can. Fifty – 75% is probably OK for now, but may be something you need to go back and deal with at some point to more fully flourish in heartful awareness. Conversely, remember the congruity of moods, and state dependent recall. It may be the current lens you are looking through, and you just need to ground yourself to see clearer, and return to a more authentic and heartfully aware space. Somewhere you know. If you are 75 – 100% on the scale, bask in your deep state of heartful awareness and cement it in your cells. When we give focused awareness to ourselves when we are in a deep state of heartful awareness already, we cement those ways of being in our primary operating patterns.

A few examples my help illustrate this point.

It was the day that we wrote about the feeling states of awareness as presented at the beginning of the chapter. José, a participant in the workshop, was very agitated after the first writing exercise. He had chosen to write about all the little stresses that presented themselves while trying to prepare and travel to the workshop. Typically, these would send him into a feedback loop of stress and anxiety, which he would allow himself to be engulfed by, and he could feel that coming on in full force.

When I asked the participants to write about a time period or event they felt joy or appreciation for, he was very reluctant. Somehow the stress and anxiety, although uncomfortable, was a familiar way for him to be, and that is how he 'saw' himself. However, he allowed himself to go with the activity, and chose to write about the time where he and his wife first fell in love. As he was writing his demeanor, body language, and facial expressions - were completely transformed. He literally became that young man in love again.

He chose to share his story with the group, and when he did, not only was he transformed but everybody that was engaged in his re-telling was as well. The shift was palpable. He was as surprised as everyone else in the major shift in his heartful engagement, and he ended his time with, "I feel like I am in love all over again!"

On the HEAR scale of reactivity José was able to make an authentic shift where his inner being was able to connect with the love that he felt for his wife. Jose shifted from below 50% on the scale to almost 100% by deep and focused attention to the love he had for her.

Many times we have multiple 'stories' going on at once. Often, I come home from a very full, and demanding day at work, to a very full and demanding, and quite often messy, household. I am carrying the stresses of the day, and of writing, and it seems like I have left one environment where I was spread way too thin, and walked into another. And then I look around. My children, and quite often their friends, and my husband surround me. It dawns on me that these are moments that I will never get back, and even in the chaos, a wave of love and appreciation comes over me. Both stories are true. While it is important to go back and re-visit the dynamic of our household from a grounded state, the 'story' I choose to give my emotional attention to in the moment has the power to transform my evening. In this example, my HEAR scale is a little closer to the middle, and to make an authentic shift to heartful engagement I also need to be heartfully aware of my own needs, which I will address at an appropriate time. With this inner assurance I can make a genuine heartful shift to a higher percentage on the scale and bask in the love surrounding me.

These are examples of being able to *authentically* make the switch to heartful engagement. But what happens when we cannot? What happens when those 'felt states' that we listed below the line on the heartful awareness chart need some attention? In other words, what do we do if we are overcome with reactions of anger, shame, threat or fear etc., and we cannot authentically feel anything above the line? And why is it so important not to blame, shame, or judge ourselves if we seem to be spending more time below the line then above the line?

Is there a part of you that needs loving attention?

The work of Richard Schwartz[30], and his concept of parts has been mentioned earlier and will be examined in the next chapter as well, but a piece of his work is pertinent here. See if you can look at what is below the line on the chart for you and conceptualize those as parts of you, but not your deepest self. In other words, I have a part of me that gets angry, or I have a part of me that feels shame, or I have a part of me that feels anxious, but they are not really who I am at my core.

Any moment of any day, or when you are feeling reactive, tune in to those 'parts' of you that may be monopolizing your awareness. See if you can distance yourself from their reactivity and they will be calm enough for you to engage in awareness and heartfulness; in other words, if you can rest in your deepest self or Inner Being. Cultivate a state of heartful awareness if you can. If you cannot, hold that part of you in a place of self-love and understanding until you can work on healing it. Essentially, hold that 'part' of you in a state of heartful awareness. Basically this means cultivating life-generative states when we can, healing states when we cannot, and engaging it all heartfully.

Remember, even when we can shift to heartful awareness we may need to give some attention to what is bothering us. This is absolutely not about suppressing things that are present for us, and requiring attention. When you use the tool above, make a special note to yourself of the things you may need to go back and deal with when you are grounded, and it is an appropriate time. And then follow through.

It may also be important in the moment of reactivity to identify your own personal needs that may be nudging for attention. Many times our reactivities are actually our un-met needs in disguise. Examining your own needs, and then meeting them, or promising yourself you will meet them at an appropriate time, may free you up to once again shift to a heartful way of being. What are your inner needs? What do you need to offer yourself before you can authentically engage with others?

How we are changed

How are we changed from heartful awareness?

The *awareness* part of heartful awareness means our conscious mind enters the network and creates whole system integration. Because heartfulness is a trainable emotional state, a heartfully integrated way of being creates perceptual, behavioral, functional and structural changes in our being. In other words, we see foundational changes in the way we see our world, and the way we choose to behave in it. We see changes in the way our human systems function in the moment, but we also see deep, and long-term structural changes in our make-up. In essence, we become different people.

Research has shown that we see more 'free flowing choice' in our world[31], and have greater distance from reactivity. While, when we are in a reactive state, even our best friend can seem remote or separate from us, states of heartful awareness increase our sense of connectivity to all that is around us.[32] Our sense of self actually expands to include others in greater degrees.[33] We begin to experience memory reconsolidation, which is the re-wiring of implicit memory, and we begin to 're-program' our 'operating system' of perception, and the way we see the world. In other words, the 'charge' is taken out of our reactivity, and we begin to see opportunity instead of threat. Every change in our perception causes changes in our physiological state, but then every change in our physiological state goes back and furthers our perception. When we begin to live from states of heartful awareness this cycle is a life-generating one instead of a destructive one. We behave and make choices from our new way of being, and our 'spiral of becoming' is one of heartful awareness for ourselves, and all those around us.

Our congruity of moods, and the way we see every moment of every day, begins to reflect that of heartful awareness. In other words, we literally put on the 'lens' of a different mood state from which we see the world. Too, our state dependent recall functions from a more expansive way of being, and the resultant memories that are most present with us are those that lead to more life-generating choices. Because our amygdala is only capable of resting in one drive at a time[34] either our fear response drive, or our drive to love, bond and connect, through heartful awareness it is calming, re-consolidating, and rewiring our subconscious. Furthermore, because only one half of the amygdala is associated with the drive to love, bond, and connect, and both sides of the amygdala are associated with the fear drive, intentionality begins to strengthen what was previously a slower, and less responsive system.

When we genuinely and intentionally, feel love, compassion, or other deeply felt heartful ways of being we 'light up' our whole brain. In other words, we experience brain integration, meaning several different parts of our brain are in resonance and working as a coherent whole. The more we do this, the more those neural nets are wired, and the more this becomes our typical way of being. When our brain is working together as an integrated whole, in other words, the two hemispheres are better connected through the neural wiring, we can better attach meaning to reason and we see more effective solutions, and make better choices. This way of being, I would argue, should re-define what it means to be rational.

Through the phenomenal research on the brain, we have learned that the frontal cortex, or thinking part of the brain, functions much better when we practice intentionally cultivating heartful ways of being. For those who have put significant time into training states of compassion, the connection between the frontal and emotional regions of the brain became stronger. In other words, mental training can alter connections between the thinking and emotional parts of the brain, and we see clearer decisions as well as heightened empathy and love[35]. And the dynamic carries out in all aspects of our lives. When I presented this concept to one of my graduate classes, a student came up with the following equation:

Compassionate Thinking = Smarter Thinking

Because an integrated brain leads to clarity, and meaningful thought, cultivating mindful awareness is being rapidly promoted as the new business paradigm. I believe heartful awareness will be the new frontier. When we are more resonant within ourselves, and with others, we operate at a higher potential. Further, heartful engagement calms the cortisol that so often floods our brain. The cortical inhibition, or reduced brain functioning associated with flooded levels of cortisol, begins to dissipate and we can think more effectively and perform better. We see solutions that may have been clouded, we can better access stored information or knowledge, and we are more open to intuitive insight.

We change both our neural and chemical 'scripts'. Our neural nets change with new patterns of wiring, and our neuro-associations, meaning the emotion that we attach to circumstance, changes with new experience. Our biochemical 'blueprints' change as well, and where cortisol was dominant, oxytocin begins to replace it.

The power of oxytocin

I love oxytocin.

In a lot of ways I think that oxytocin is my life's blood.

Oxytocin is a neuropeptide, or type of biochemical associated with feelings of love, compassion, trust, bonding, care and other heartful ways of being. Physiologically, it calms our fear response drive and encourages our drive to connect. While it is not exactly the opposite of cortisol, in many ways it acts like an 'anti-cortisol' and performs many opposing functions; it even reduces cortisol in the body and many of its damaging effects. Oxytocin has a profound impact on our perceptions, physiology, behavior and choices. Some claim that we need oxytocin for emotional sustenance just like a healthy body needs food for hunger, and we intensely long for it if we do not have it. Through heartful awareness oxytocin can be intentionally cultivated.

Oxytocin is associated with a countless number of behaviors and perceptions linked to our calm and connection system. It provides us with feelings of security and closeness, and is responsible for our ability to bond with others, both in intimate pairing and with trusted others. It gives us that secure feeling of being 'held' by another – both literally and figuratively. It lights up our social circuits, helps us through stressful social situations, leads us to positive social situations, and helps us more effectively appraise others' feelings and motivations[36]. And, it is reciprocal. In other words, it both nurtures these behaviors and perceptions, and is a result of experiencing them. It helps us feel the expansiveness of being grounded in our core, and it is what provides for us the visceral experience of being loved and being held. It also gives us that warm and fuzzy feeling we associate with a particular person.

Physiologically, oxytocin calms the amygdala and reduces ACTH and cortisol, the two hormones primarily responsible for anxiety and stress. And it calms other systems throughout our body. It reduces negativity and dampens the effects of our fear response. It helps create biochemical synchrony between people in close connection. Oxytocin is produced in our gastrointestinal system, and may be the reason we reach for comfort food when we are feeling lonely, or why we feel bonded when we share a business lunch or a family meal. Oxytocin reduces blood pressure, increases longevity, activates the parasympathetic nervous system which is responsible for calming us down, and is associated with decreased pain. Because it is connected with other physiological systems throughout our body, it creates a 'feedback loop' of calm and resonance. It is closely connected with other neuro-chemicals like serotonin, dopamine and endorphins, which all help us to see, and act in the world in more heartful and hopeful ways.

When we re-visit the idea that what it means to be human is that we are systems of adaptation, or, as Barbara Fredrickson so succinctly states[37], our bodies are not nouns, but verbs, we can see that oxytocin is both a result of our behavior and constantly contributing to who we are becoming.[38] Heartfully engaged awareness changes us, and oxytocin is one of the reasons why. So what are some of the ways that oxytocin can be intentionally cultivated in our lives?

Eye contact; a genuine smile; a heartfelt connection[39].

There are many and varied ways to include oxytocin generation in the moments of our lives.

Oxytocin levels rise through authentic love, compassion, care, and connection, for our self, a specific person, or as a global way of being. Oxytocin is a result of authentic trust and bonding, close companionship, and selfless giving to a trusted and loved other. That choice to trust and love the other can be for another we know, or someone we do not. It can be created through a sense of gratitude, caring touch, moments of deep connection, time in nature, massage, meditation, prayer, implicit or explicit memories steeped in heartfulness, music, imagery, and creativity that touches our soul. For females, it is produced through childbirth, and nursing our young.

It is the hormone that binds couples, sometimes for life, and is responsible for making another the sole choice for partnership. While it is often termed the love, or cuddle hormone, it has also been dubbed by researchers as the molecule of monogamy[40]. It is responsible for the feeling of loving and being in love. It is produced in large quantities through heartful and trusting physical connections, including kissing, intercourse, and orgasm. It builds lasting love resources. In couples it can also be cultivated through nurturing affection, quiet time together, close companionship, micro-moments of love, and selfless giving. But, as a love relationship is also a verb, it takes routine and intentional re-cultivation. Oxytocin is a fleeting hormone, physiologically speaking, and it takes continual attention, and intention, to keep it flourishing. In other words, to keep our love thriving we need to keep priming the oxytocin 'i.v. drip'.

For people engaging in sex and orgasm in a trusting and loving environment, either alone or with another, oxytocin is produced in large amounts; however, if there is threat this is not the case. Also, oxytocin is designed to create a sense of bonding, and if that bonding does not take place competing biochemicals can cause feelings of emptiness, loneliness, loss or depression. In other words, sex does not automatically lead to an oxytocin rush. If that sex is threatening because it is unwanted, or unfamiliar, or does not culminate in a sense of bonding, competing biochemicals can actually produce the opposite effect. I wish all of my college students knew this. Although 'hooking up' may seem fun and engaging at the time, if it is not done in a trusting and bonding environment, it may actually produce feelings of separateness and depression.

Lastly, oxytocin heals.

The oxytocin response system is initially produced through mother / child bonding. If, for whatever reason, e.g., trauma, separation, abuse, etc., that response system is not fully developed, it can be healed later in life. Nurturing adult relationships can create the biochemical circumstances for bonding and trust to heal and reprogram a damaged oxytocin response system. Healing therapies[41], conscious and intentional nurturing behaviors[42], and loving and trusting adult relationships may be especially beneficial for people with a less than optimal parent / child relationship. Through new and trusting attachments, a healthy oxytocin response system can be fully developed and healed.

And oxytocin can be intentionally produced.

For our lives to be better steeped in our calm and connection system, oxytocin can, and should, be cultivated by intentional awareness and behavior. In other words, the choices in behavior I make, moment after moment, day after day, profoundly affect my oxytocin levels at any given point in time. I can turn on the oxytocin drip, if you will, by intentional engagement and heartfully based behaviors. Little choices of engagement, every day, add up. Lastly, oxytocin is a kind of use it, lose it, or long for it hormone[13]. Finding ways to continually cultivate it is mandatory to engage its lasting effects.

Intentionality is crucial

Again, because our bodies are verbs, not nouns, what we expose them to on a routine basis is what we are continually becoming. To 'be' different, or transform, we need different experience. If nothing changes, everything stays the same. If we are constantly reacting to our outside world through all our past-programmed perceptions, as if they were the only truth, then that is what we are cultivating more of. To build a world based on heartfully engaged awareness, it takes intentionality. Through intentionality we can create different inner experience and truly transform our lives. It takes intentionality to create, and re-create the circumstances for heartful awareness to flourish.

Throughout this chapter we saw, and experienced, the power of our own attention. We saw the power of intentional heartful awareness. We saw the power, and necessity, of intentionally cultivating our calm and connection system. We saw the power of intentional love, compassion, care and connection, and we saw the role oxytocin plays in it all. We saw how we are profoundly changed by these states of being, for our self, and others. We looked at what, for you, are life-generating patterns of being, and we saw a formula for how to simply apply them in your life. We learned a tool to assess our awareness in any moment, including moments of reactivity, and the importance of healing attention when our heartfulness seems to be blocked. We saw how intentional moments and activities, day after day, add up. We saw that it might be the simple intentional choices, or micro-moments of heartfulness that change us the most. And we saw how 'doable' it all is. But intention takes action.

Beginner's heart

Recall the concept of beginner's mind. This concept basically encourages a way of being present in each moment, fully aware of all the possibilities it brings. It is a non-reactive way of being fully present. When we are present in this way, we are not consumed with perceptions of the past, or fears of the future. It is a moment full of potential. It is as if everything is new, and we are seeing it for the first time.

I would like to take beginners mind one-step further and suggest a way of being as Beginner's Heart. Imagine how we, and the world would be different if we were able to live each moment with a beginner's heart; to be able to live, more often than not, from a non-reactive way of being fully present, aware, and pregnant with the possibilities of love, compassion, care and connection all around us. Beginner's heart may be a way of living one moment at a time, each full of heartful potential.

"The gorilla was my girlfriend"

Jon, student in one of my classes, had a profound experience of seeing routine things in a 'new' light. It was the day I showed the in-attentional blindness video I spoke about in chapter 1. Again, this video shows groups of people weaving in and out and throwing basketballs. I so focus the students attention on the weaving and basketball throwing that most fail to see a gorilla walk right through the middle of the group of players, and stop in the middle to pound on its chest. Most are shocked when I re-show it and point out the gorilla.

As in the exercise in chapter 1, the writing assignment they do immediately after is titled "what are the gorillas in your life?" The idea being that we have beautiful things that are present for us right in front of our face every day, and we fail to see them because we are so focused on other things. Jon started tearing up as he was writing. After the writing I asked if someone would like to share, and he raised his hand and said his girlfriend, he realized, was his gorilla.

At the end of the quarter they write about their most transformative moments in the course. He wrote about the gorilla. When he realized that he was no longer 'seeing' his girlfriend, he began to make small shifts to see her in a 'new' light. The small moments of seeing her 'new again' completely transformed their relationship. The spiral of their connection became one of newness and re-birth, and he reported that he felt like he was falling in love all over again. And it was all by choice of attention.

When we approach each moment with beginner's heart, life is full of possibility. Typically we go through life, with all its promises and setbacks, in reaction to what it is offering us. We may go through generative cycles, or degenerative cycles, however they are primarily dependent on outside circumstance. When something seems especially promising for us we may go through a 'honeymoon period' complete with perceptions, choices and behaviors consistent with that promise, but, most people will tell you, the honeymoon period is doomed to end. However, at the intersection of beginner's heart, and intentionality, we may have a whole new definition of what is possible with the honeymoon period.

The myth of the honeymoon period

I believe, in a large part, that the 'honeymoon period' is a myth. The honeymoon period is often referred to, in all walks of life, including spirituality, as that period when something is novel, or new, and we are emotionally and biochemically alive with the promise of potential. Thus, we make certain life-affirming choices and behave in life-affirming ways. And we make time to intentionally cultivate the circumstances that reflect our perception, and further it is growth. These choices and behaviors, then, create corresponding biochemical and neural states, and we feel like we are flourishing. But, in a large part, we are still reacting to the outside world. Most of the time this reaction is in gratitude for something new and wonderful in our lives.

As we have learned, life is a reciprocal spiral of perception, choice and behavior, complete with the physiological adaptations to match. What most often happens, however, when the novelty wears off we stop making those choices and exhibiting those behaviors. In other words, when something becomes familiar we no longer invest the time, attention, or intention in the way we did in its earlier state. Thus, we, *unintentionally*, stop the spiral of flourishing. We think the chemistry has waned, and the honeymoon is over. However, it is really the cessation of the intentional choices and behaviors that change our biochemistry and resulting perceptions, rather than the other way around. This sheds a whole new light on the concept of 'keeping it new'.

What if we could approach life with the beginner's heart, *and* keep all the deep and sincere appreciation for all that we have gained through time? What if we could, more often than not, create an intention to be heartfully aware, all at once through new eyes, and in appreciation for all that is and has been? What if we could allow ourselves to behave, make choices, and keep the spiral of intentionality flourishing by investing time and energy to do so? With heartfully engaged awareness, beginner's heart, intentionality, and gratitude for the wonderful things that already exist, every moment is pregnant with the potential of new life.

Heartful awareness takes intention. And intention takes action. If nothing changes, nothing changes. The following are some specific concepts and suggestions for how to incorporate heartfully engaged ways of being in your life. They are based on the physiological principles shared throughout this chapter. They are only suggestions. The truest engagement of heartful awareness is what rings true for you at the depths of your own inner being.

A blueprint for change

Behavior change theorists tell us that we are much more likely to change if we have specific ideas about what that change might look like. The following are suggestions for specific tangible ways you might implement heartful awareness into your everyday life. Remember, it is the implementation, or action that changes us.

◊ As was laid out in depth than the previous chapter, pay attention to attention. Stop and pause several moments during the day and just notice where your attention is. Make an overt intention, when you are authentically capable, to become heartfully engaged with yourself, your surroundings, or others.

◊ Look for, and create opportunities for heartful engagement. Remember, in-attentional blindness means that what we pay attention to shows up for us. Pay attention to the 'seeds of consciousness' you are planting every moment of every day. Are you planting 'weeds' or 'flowers'? Continually look for new opportunities.

◊ Remember the 3 to 1 ratio. And remember heartful awareness only works when it is authentic. We do not need to be there all the time, and we cannot fake it. Intentionally creating moments of heartful awareness begins to tip the scale.

◊ Savor what you already have.[14] The 'spiral of becoming' shows us that we physiologically change to any state we are routinely in. When we are already in states of heartful engagement, focused attention and awareness to 'cement' these states further imprints them in our cellular memory.

◊ Micro-moments add up! Momentary choices of engagement make profound shifts. They re-wire our neural nets and habitual ways of being, create oxytocin-rich changes in our blood chemistry, as well as dopamine and serotonin the hopeful outlook neurotransmitters, and foundationally change our perception to one of expansiveness and possibility.

◊ When you are feeling less than optimal imagine the HEAR scale of reactivity. Cultivate heartful awareness when you are able, if you are not, determine what you need, what you may need to deal with, or what 'parts' may need attention.

◊ Continually tap into the deepest sense of who you are and let that lead. The more moments we spend resting in our deepest potential or connected to our Inner Being, the more they become our primary 'operating system'. Pay attention, and shift when you can. When you cannot, hold yourself in a place of loving-kindness and awareness, and promise those 'parts' healing attention when you are able. Offer the love and support to yourself, as you would a best friend.

◊ Use as a constant query: "is this good for my soul?" If it is not, and you can opt out, do so. If it is not easy to opt out, see if you can find something about the situation to refocus your emotional attention so that it is authentically and heartfully engaged. Is there something about the situation you can genuinely appreciate?

◊ Creating a plan and vision of how these shifts might be manifest is the first step in taking action.

Exercise and Reflection # 7 - Heartful Awareness in daily life

Taking into account the blueprint for change above, and whatever else rings true for you, write and reflect on the following questions. They are designed to help you process specific and tangible ways that you might engage heartful awareness in your daily life. Remember the questions are not meant to be answered verbatim, as much as just guide your thinking. They are meant to guide a 'stream of consciousness' style of writing that is true for you.

◊ Refer back to heartful awareness chart. What can you do for the next several minutes, hours, or day that will heartfully engage you in some of the 'felt states' on the top of the chart? Remember, more generative moments in a day leads to more generative days, years, and life in general.

◊ What can you do, either today or routinely, to get yourself into an integrated state of body, mind and spirit – the space where generative emotions are more likely? How can you schedule more heartfully aware moments in your days and years?

◊ What can you do to remind yourself to 'go there' often throughout the day, so you can begin to 'be there' most of the day?

◊ Pick at least three or four of the bulleted points above and write a specific action plan for how you will implement them in your life.

◊ Refer back to the heartful awareness chart. Create a list of images that bring up the 'felt states' that you listed above the line on the chart. Keep this list handy, as we will use it more in the next chapter. Also, pick two or three of the images that you listed and write a few paragraphs about what it is about those images that bring up the sense of heartful awareness for you.

Practice: HEARTful Breathing

While mindfulness practices typically foster non-reactivity through awareness of the moment, other types of practices actively engage the limbic system directly. In other words, they actively and intentionally engage with a life-generating emotion. Actively engaging the limbic system in a specific state trains it to better operate from that state. Compassion, love, gratitude, clarity, and confidence, for example, are all trainable states.

HEARTful Breathing uses the concept of heartful awareness to create the biochemical shifts associated with a desired 'felt state'. In other words, it jumps in at the physiological level of the 'spiral of becoming'. It uses the concept that the brain does not know the difference between something that is imagined, or deeply felt, and something that is going on in present time. The shift to breathing a 'felt sense' of a desired outlook actually shifts our biochemical state to one consistent with that outlook, and thus changes our perception, and, ultimately, creates that outlook.

1. Notice and disengage from the reactivity of the moment and, from an observer or witnessing state, discern its emotional component.
2. Refocus your eyes, and shoulders and bring your awareness to your breath. Establish a relaxed breathing pattern.
3. Nurture what a more desirable, and heartfully engaged outlook would be. Again, this heartfully engaged outlook might be heartful awareness of your own personal needs.
4. Calmly breathe the 'felt sense' of that outlook. If an image helps you hold that felt sense, hold the image, but remember it is the felt sense that is most important. In other words, if confidence is the outlook you'd like to create, see if you can breathe what it feels like to be confident. If an image, either of you or someone else, helps you bring up the outlook then hold the image in your minds eye as

you breathe. Breathe the sensation, or 'felt sense' of whatever outlook you would like to create for yourself, and 'feel' it soaking every cell in your body. As you transition out of the practice, pause and bring your conscious awareness to how you are feeling. This awareness will help you cement this state of being so you can more easily access it with only a few breaths at a later time.

Conclusion – Making the shift

The shift from mindfulness to heartfulness invites us into active engagement with that which is life generating. Heartful awareness builds on the foundation of the non-reactive, non-judgmental, fully accepting momentary presence of mindful awareness, but then actively seeks, and engages. It actively seeks out life-generating connections with the deepest parts of others, our outside world, or our selves.

Heartful awareness invites us to see every moment as a moment of opportunity for heartful presence. It invites us to look for, and intentionally connect to the deep and grounded spaces to be found in all the moments of our lives. It is a full and non-reactive presence that looks for, and engages in whatever heartful opportunity that moment may offer. It can be found in all the moments of our day, little changes of heartfulness add up, and micro-moments of love, compassion and connection can be intentionally cultivated. It is found in our external existence, and in the deepest places within ourselves.

Heartful awareness does not blame, shame, judge or coerce if we are feeling less than heartful. It holds it all in a loving and compassionate state. Heartful awareness, embodied, shows us that there are clearly life-generating emotional states, and those that are not. It invites us to actively embrace life. Every moment offers the opportunity to seek, and actively engage in deep love, compassion, gratitude, or joy, internally or externally. And, if we cannot find it, it invites us into heartful awareness for ourselves, and a compassionate 'holding' of our past programming to clear those blocks.

Routine practice and engagement in sustained and predictable ways solidifies it as a primary way of operating for us. And, if it is elusive, heartful awareness directed back at ourselves in deep and intentional ways offer us a chance to heal. Such are foci of the next chapter. And our journey continues.

5

Live and Heal with HEART

We began our journey to heartful awareness as if it were a labyrinth. We followed a specified path. On the outskirts, we learned what it looks like – from an embodied perspective – when we operate from 'status quo' or merely reacting to what the outside world offers us. We looked at how our perception, or reactivities are stored as implicit memory, and how they perpetuate our reality unless we offer them a different experience. We determined that it takes intentionality to cultivate our calm and connection system and subdue our fear response system. We discovered that it is our calm and connection system that facilitates connection to others, as well as our own Inner Being. And we saw that it is within this system that the place of reduced stress and anxiety, healing, and inner potential lies.

We took a look at mindful, or present moment awareness, the Power of Pause, and the importance of fostering non-reactivity.

In the last chapter we experienced the power of intentional heartful ways of being. We saw how they can profoundly change us and we learned specific ways to engage them in our everyday lives. We also saw that the degree to which we are able to heartfully engage, may be directly related to the degree to which we are able to tap into our inner potential, and experience transformation in our lives. And we saw that it is experience that is the key to change.

Now, we are nearing the center of our metaphorical labyrinth. With the idea that our lives become the sum total of our experience, the question still remains: How do we maximize our routine experience of resting in our calm

155

and connection system, and use that as a path to transformation? How do we most effectively employ everything we have learned to heighten and deepen our transformative process?

The degree of intentionality is key. The total time and depth of experience is key. And when we are locked out by our own reactivity, or ingrained implicit programming, intentional healing may be the exact thing that unlocks the door to the center. That is what this chapter is about. And we are now at the heart of our labyrinth.

Intentional Experience

Length and depth of experience are what change us most. As we have seen, being able to intentionally cultivate moment-to-moment, day-to-day heartful awareness is foundational to our transformative experience. So too, are deeply intentional, and sustained ways of being. The deeper, and more often, we 'go there', the more likely we are to 'live there'. Additionally, the more often we are able to replace reactive ways of being, right in the moment of reactivity, the more we are able to permanently replace those patterns. In other words, overt practices of heartfully engaging our reactivity when it happens, and time spent with the experience of deep and intentional heartful awareness, may be what change us most.

In this chapter are tools to do just that. They are tools, or practices, that have been developed, with all the scientific and physiological bases presented in this book, and with our western culture in mind, to be most effective. In other words, they are designed to be simple, and 'doable' within the context of our every day lives. And yet, even though simple and doable, they are based on the scientific truths.

They are designed to get us to honestly engage in experiential ways of being that can truly transform us. They are designed to be done in, and transform, our moment of reactivity. They are designed as sustained practices to cultivate deeper ways of being. And they are designed to help us heal. They are like pushing the 're-program' button, if you will, to get us re-connected and rooted in our Inner Being, or deepest inner potential, and have that reflected in our external experience.

Heartfully Engaged Awareness Reprogramming Tools (HEART)

The HEART techniques are a set of contemplative practices designed to cultivate heartful awareness in our everyday lives. Contemplative practices are mental, emotional, or spiritual exercises typically involving focus on the breath, intentionality, and reflection. It is a sustained and deliberate time of turning inward, and resting our awareness or attention on a specific inner-directed process. Research has shown phenomenal and foundational changes in our mind, body and spirit – indeed the way we are in the world – from routine engagement in various practices. Contemplative practice has the potential to quiet our fear response system, and allow our calm and connection system to flourish. Consistent and regular engagement creates the time in, and depth of experience the changes us most.

HEART are a set of practices that intentionally cultivate heartful awareness often enough and deeply enough, that it becomes our operating pattern. Heartful awareness becomes our 'new programming' from which to engage the world physiologically, psychologically and spiritually. With regular, and sustained practice they can transform our baseline level of functioning, and help us find a larger, more expansive way of being in the world. We can change the spiral of reactivity and be overtly intentional about change through the embodied science of transformation.

These practices are deceptively simple. They are built on both the scientific concepts of 'becoming' as presented in this book, and concepts from various wisdom traditions. They are packaged in a way to make them accessible and 'doable' for many of us in Western culture. They are intended to be simple enough to encourage routine and consistent engagement, as it is 'experience of' not 'knowledge about' that leads us to true transformation. Again, the more often, longer, and deeper we engage in any experiential way of being the more it becomes the operating pattern of our life.

We have seen throughout this book how damaging life's experiences can be when they are dictated by our fear response system. We have seen how the intentional cultivation of our calm and connection system leads to expansiveness, inner potential, clarity and a larger way of living in the world. These practices are a way of consciously developing our calm and connection system. They are our 'exercise program' for developing heartful fitness and thriving, and they are based on the physiological foundations presented throughout this book.

HEART are comprised of six different practices, that when practiced in everyday life may overlap, or intersect. HEARTful breathing was presented in the last chapter, however the specific steps embedded in all the HEART practices are presented in much more depth here. HEART in the Moment is meant to be done right in the moment of reactivity. It is a tool designed to foster non-reactivity and replace our typical ways of responding with heartfully engaged responses. Changing our response patterns right in the moment begins to rewire them at their source and re-program our reactive systems overall. In short, we transform the ways in which we habitually respond.

Sustained HEART is done for a specific period of time to lengthen and deepen the time we spend in heartful awareness. The longer and more deeply we engage in a sustained practice, the more we re-wire our whole system. HEART for Clarity and Sacred HEART are versions of Sustained HEART, in other words they are practiced for a specific period of time. However, they have their own overt focus, and will be presented in later chapters. HEART for Healing is a sustained practice, but also engages an explicit intention to heal and re-program unbalanced implicit memory patterns. It is designed to heal past trauma, or problematic perceptions that may be clouding our current functioning. It is presented later in this chapter.

The appendix includes a diagram of all the practices presented in this book conceptualizing how and when they might be used. It also includes a summary of all the practices, a record log to record your use of the various practices, and a link to audio recordings of them. As you begin to implement the practices into your every day life, it can be extremely useful to record your experiences. I urge you to spend some time with the appendix for a full grasp of the power and implementation of the various practices.

HEART are easy to remember and implement. They are designed to induce functional and structural changes in our brain, biochemistry, and electrical patterns in our heart. They create momentary, as well as long-term changes that lead to greater clarity, coherence, and connection, and change our perceptions and behaviors. And as our internal lives change, so do our external lives.

Most of the time, when we are in the status quo, our attention and intention is unknowingly in a chaotic emotional state. As we have seen, these states eventually become who we are. The HEART practices offer an alternative experience. They offer us an opportunity to intentionally create, and sustain deeper ways of being.

All of the HEART practices are based on three basic steps and should be modified depending on the circumstances in which they are used.

HEART Basics

The three simple steps are:

Notice

Refocus

Nurture

They are intentionally simple so they can be practiced anytime, anywhere, and be used as a core daily practice. They are simple so you can keep them in mind and practice them regularly. They are simple to remind you that your level of authentic heartful engagement, at any moment in time, powerfully determines what is being nurtured inside of you. And they are simple to encourage you to set up a daily practice to cement heartful ways of being into the depths of your physiology, psychology, and soul. And, even though they are simple, the physiological, psychological and spiritual impacts of routinely practicing them can be profound.

As we journey into what the tools would 'look like' in practice, first we will take a brief overview of each of the steps and how to do them.

Then we will delve much deeper to entertain the background, rationale and physiological implications of each step. Lastly we will look at how they are engaged, and the nuances of the steps in each of the separate practices.

The recurring nature of how they are presented is designed to give you a firm grasp of the steps themselves, as well as an understanding of how each step plays out in the various practices.

HEART overview

Notice – **This step invites us to pause, turn inward, and begin to notice what is present for us.**

Notice any reactivity coming up for you and take a few intentional breaths. Try and disengage from the reactivity's charge, observe and witness your response rather than being hijacked by it. Notice your thoughts, feelings, and any emotional responses without engaging them. Attempt to foster non-reactivity, ground yourself in your breath and Inner Being if possible.

Refocus – **This step calms our system and creates receptivity to a heartful shift.**

Establish an intentional, calm and natural breathing pattern. Focus on your eyes and intentionally let go of all the tension or stress in the tiny little muscles all around them and throughout your eye sockets. Let go of all the tension in your shoulders and release into your breath. Bring your awareness to your torso where it feels right for you as a place to focus on your breath. With all your awareness on your breath, breathe slowly and deeply, but most of all comfortably and naturally. You can silently repeat the word 'release' to yourself on the out breath if it helps. See if you can begin to create a 'felt sense' of openness.

Nurture – **This step nurtures a heartful way of being, and responding, which transforms us overall.**

Intentionally engage in an emotional shift to heartful awareness. It could be something about the situation you can generally appreciate, or an emotional shift to focus on something in your life for which you are truly grateful. It could be an intentional state of being that you would like to create, or it could be a state of self-understanding or self-compassion for any difficulty you are experiencing. The key is that it needs to be a genuine shift to a heartful state of being. And it needs to be felt.

I think of the notice, refocus, nurture steps of HEART as the integration of the mind, body, spirit dynamic; or as an embodied journey from mindfulness to heartfulness. The notice step is primarily about cultivating mindful awareness, fostering non-reactivity, and disengaging from the reactivity's hold. The refocus step is designed to engage the body physiologically to induce states of calm and connection, and cultivate receptivity. The nurture step engages the spirit, or soul. Its purpose is to intentionally engage in heartful ways of responding, and cultivate them as a long-term way of being. They are a step-by-step process to the full embodiment of heartful awareness.

Philosophical and Physiological Steps to HEART

What follows, are the basic philosophical and physiological foundations of each specific step. Again, the dynamics of each step may vary depending on the particular practice, and those variations will be highlighted as each practice is introduced further in the chapter.

Notice – from a nonreactive, or observing state of awareness:
   Notice your mental activity – disengage from its hold
   Notice your physical responses – disengage from their hold
   Notice your emotional responses – disengage from their hold
   Rest in your center and Breathe

This step is about training yourself to become acutely aware when you are having an emotionally chaotic reaction, and disengaging from the 'hold' of that reaction. It is most similar to the process of mindful awareness as presented in Chapter 3. And, again, it is quite often referred to as 'becoming the observer' or 'cultivating the witness'. It is not suppressing the reaction, nor is it letting it hijack you. It is training yourself to develop a keen awareness of when mental, emotional, or physical stimuli are throwing you off balance. It is the release button from our system's reactive grip.

It may be our mental activity that is throwing us off balance, the constant inner chatter, catastrophizing, inner conversations, or the endless reels of 'internal perception and evaluation' that captivate a large part of our day. It may be an emotionally chaotic response that is consuming us, whether or not we are aware. Or it may be a 'felt sense' of uneasiness we carry in our body, and all the possible physical manifestations inherent in it. It may be a combination of all three.

This step is about training yourself to identify these things the moment they happen, and noticing the potential for all three levels of reactivity. Mental, physical or emotional reactivity may be an indication that there is something going on in our implicit memory, or perception patterns, that is throwing us off balance. And they may not be overtly conscious. In other words, it may require our awareness to realize we are having reactivity. Remember, too, that our body may reflect all three levels. Again, our body may be more honest than our conscious mind, and most often will reflect both our mental and emotional processes. Many times, it holds the truth.

When our emotional reactions are manifest as physical responses they may show up as a racing heart, tight chest, sweaty palms, a pit in the stomach etc. Being able to tune into that truth is an important tool in gauging our emotional reactivity. For example, I know my own physically reactive patterns involve tightness in my chest, shortness of breath, sometimes a slightly nauseous feeling in my solar plexus, or a general feeling of threat. I notice the physical response first, and it is then I realize something is throwing me emotionally off balance and needs attention.

Stopping and tuning into your mental, emotional and physical activity may surprise you. It is fairly constant, and most of the time we are unaware. One of my sons has learned to identify his typical set of reactions as 'that feeling.' He has been able to train himself to recognize and identify it before he cognitively even begins to process what is happening to him. "Mom, I am getting *that feeling* again," he says to me. Also, the stimulus may be external, meaning something that is going on in our environment, or it may be internal, just something that we are thinking about. It is a process of 'being with' a response instead of being 'consumed by' it.

The second piece to the notice step is disengaging from the reactivity. Again, disengaging from the 'hold' is very different than suppressing it. If we can recognize it as an implicit memory pattern, or our programmed and stored perceptions, but not really 'us', and also remember the destructive spiral if we let it hijack us, we can begin to ground ourselves in the here and now.

Resting your attention in your torso, wherever feels comfortable for you, helps take the focus off the inner chatter. Because the inner chatter comes from a very specific part in your brain, just bringing your awareness down to the center mass of your body - the heart, the solar plexus, or deeper in the belly – will help quiet the chatter. To help take your attention 'off' one thing (the chatter), you put it 'on' another thing (a focused spot in your torso). A few intentional, releasing breaths help calm and center your awareness, and help you gain distance from the reactivity.

Chapter 3 documented many of the physiological changes we experience when we foster non-reactivity. Basically, these include breaking the chain of associative memory patterns, re-wiring or reprogramming new response patterns, stopping the spiral of state dependent recall, and starting to balance both hemispheres of our brain. In other words, we can stay in the present, see things more clearly, and react with calm.

Refocus – establish an intentional, calm, and natural breathing pattern and:
  Refocus your eyes
  Refocus your shoulders
  Bring your attention to a comfortable spot in your torso
  Deepen and sustain your breathing pattern, focus on 'releasing' with the out breath and cultivate a feeling of openness

The refocus step is primarily about engaging your body at the physiological level to automatically calm it down and make it more receptive to a heartful, or sincerely felt shift.

The first part of the refocus step is to establish an intentional, calm, and natural breathing pattern. If it feels comfortable to do so, you can deepen it and slow it down a little bit, but this should not be forced.

After establishing a comfortable breath, we refocus our attention to specific areas of our body that are directly connected to our emotional system. The first of these, and most important, are the eyes. We carry stress and anxiety all throughout our eyes, and the structures around our eyes, including all the tiny little muscles in the eye sockets. Further, our eyes are directly connected to our limbic, or emotional system, and it is a two way street; straight from the deepest parts of our emotional brain to our eyes, and back again. You often hear terms like "Look into his eyes, you can see if he's lying", or "The eyes are the window of the soul". You can lie with your smile, but you cannot lie with your eyes.

Just by relaxing all of the tiny little muscles surrounding the eyes and behind the eye sockets we begin to send an automatic, and very strong message to the deepest parts of our emotional system to calm down. Those parts of our brain sense the shift in our eyes, and send a message throughout our body to shift from a state of alertness to one of calm. The 'felt shift' can be quite dramatic, and we automatically begin to get grounded. Relaxing the shoulders carries many of the same responses relaxing the eyes does, and further calms our system.

Bringing our attention back down to a spot in our torso that feels comfortable for us, and focusing on the breath as it fills and empties that space, kicks in an additional set of physiological response patterns that affect our whole body and make it more receptive to an emotional shift. I like to think of a ladder of release, stepping down from the eyes, to the shoulders, to the torso. Our parasympathetic nervous system, which responsible for the relaxation response, becomes dominant, and this release is further reflected in our physiological response. We feel calmer. We feel more receptive. And we begin to sense more clarity.

We see biochemical shifts in the reduction of cortisol, higher production of oxytocin and the associative neurotransmitters responsible for feelings of connection and positive outlook. Our bodies, and brains, begin to quiet. Too, we see the patterns of our heart wave becoming smoother and more coherent. They travel through the vagal nerve, back to the amygdala. The amygdala, then, sends a system-wide message throughout our body to further activate our calm and connection system, and our receptivity to a genuine, heartfully engaged shift.

Nurture – While sustaining your breathing, shift your emotional attention to a 'felt state' of heartful engagement. Some possibilities might be:
Something in your life you love, appreciate, or have compassion for
Any image that brings up a sense of heartful awareness
Something about the situation you can appreciate
A sense of self-love or compassion for any difficulty you may feel

The nurture step involves intentionally shifting to a heartfully engaged, or deeply felt way of being. It is a conscious shift of our emotional attention to a life-generating state as opposed to a life depleting state. It could be a state of love, compassion, gratitude, or anything that for you is a generative emotional state. It is a shift to a state above the line of the heartful awareness chart, if you will, instead of sinking below the line. Simply put, we focus on something that is meaningful to us.

But, again, it needs to be an authentic or genuine shift. And it needs to be deeply felt. It could be something about the situation you can appreciate, something in your life you are grateful for, a posture you would like to create, or a state of self understanding, or self compassion for whatever difficulty may be coming up. The key is to feel it, and breathe it, as deeply as possible.

The nurture step is the most variable of the steps depending on which HEART practice you are using at the moment. The specifics of the nurture step for each practice follow under the heading of that specific practice. The idea, however, is to make an intentional emotional shift to one that facilitates a more expansive way of being or responding. It is a genuine 'felt shift' to a sincerely felt, and life generating emotion.

The way we engage in the nurture step, or intentionally engage heartfulness, is to tap in to the experiential nature of a life-generating emotion. We are either recalling a conscious memory, or a 'felt sense' of a known emotion; it is far different than 'positive thinking' because it needs to be a genuine shift. You cannot lie to your body. When I can vividly recall, and let myself feel, a significant heartfully engaged emotion, my body and brain respond to that experience with a life-generating reaction. That reaction in turn changes my perception and possibly my behavior. I am creating my own internal experience, and that experience changes me. When I routinely do this, I not only bring about immediate changes in my brain, body, and perceptions, but I also begin to establish long-term reaction patterns that are strengthened by repeated experience.

We are using the cognitive part of our brain that is responsible for awareness, to shift our attention and engage our limbic brain in an intentional healing experience. What happens, then, is our neural networks break the chain of our typical response patterns, and create new response patterns from the fresh experience. Our brains, through the different areas that are being stimulated, become much more integrated, our biochemistry further shifts to reflect the genuine state of heartful engagement, and the electrical patterns that connect our heart and our brain become much more coherent. Routine experience begins to cement these changes as a long-term way of being.

From all we have seen so far, we know that new experience can induce change in brain regions involved with regulating emotion. These changes are formed in both the function, and structure of the neural networks. In other words, how they function in the moment, but also long-term changes, which become our core way of functioning. Instead of reacting to life in the status quo, we begin to use the process of attention, or explicit memory to activate our emotion neural networks in life generating, and more expansive ways of being. In other words, we use conscious thought, feeling and memory to stimulate unconscious emotional healing patterns. Essentially, we are training our bodies and brains to function in more heartfully aware ways of being. The more we can effectively do this, the more these types of experiences become our primary 'operating pattern' in our neural circuitry, and biochemical reality.

When I do this, I am in the physiological state of healing and rewiring, and I am establishing this as my primary operating pattern. Love begets love, compassion begets compassion, and the more we can feel any of these states the more they become our primary ways of being. The nurture step in the HEART practices is the conscious training of our calm and connection system, and it is done through the willingness to authentically engage in heartful ways of being. And, as we shall see when we look at the various practices, the shift may be in the moment of reactivity, it may be in an intentional and sustained practice of engaging heartfulness, or it may be in holding ourselves in a healing state of self compassion or self-love, even through difficulty.

HEART made easy

All of the heart practices are based on these three easy steps. Each practice varies depending on its intention, but these three easy steps serve as the foundation for all. Learning the basics will help you more fully incorporate them into your everyday life, and understand the dynamics of each separate practice.

Notice – from a nonreactive, or observing state of awareness:

    Notice your mental activity – disengage from its hold

    Notice your physical responses – disengage from their hold

    Notice your emotional responses – disengage from their hold

    Rest in your center, and Breathe

Refocus – establish an intentional, calm, and natural breathing pattern

    Refocus your eyes

    Refocus your shoulders

    Bring your attention to a comfortable spot in your torso

    Deepen and sustain your breathing pattern, focusing on 'relaxing' through the out breath and cultivating a feeling of openness

Nurture – While sustaining your breathing, shift your emotional attention to a 'felt state' of heartful engagement. Some possibilities might be:

    Something in your life you love, appreciate or have compassion for

    Any image that brings up a sense of heartful awareness

    Something about the situation you can appreciate

    A sense of self-love or compassion for any difficulty you may feel

HEART in the Moment

HEART in the Moment is a practice primarily to be done in a moment of reactivity, although it can be done any moment of the day to cultivate and cement grounded, more expansive ways of being. In it, we notice any reactivity we are having, refocus our physicality to a state of calm, and nurture a heartful engagement; usually by focusing on an image or 'felt sense' of something that will ground us in our center. Following are Michelle's words describing her experience with HEART in the Moment:

"Heart in the Moment was very successful for me. At first I thought it would be easy, but to do it right you cannot trick yourself into feeling a certain way. I used my dog's image mostly. Her smiling face and her unconditional love for me are able to trigger feelings of happiness. I could feel the changes in my body that changed my perceptions. The first time it happened was such a trip. You can actually feel when you do it right. It was so weird, I could actually feel it all through my body. I would describe it as a feeling of elation.

I used it a lot in different situations, and the time that stands out most was during a bad fight with my husband. I let him know I was going to my 'happy place' for a moment. Of course he laughed, but it really worked. I actually came up smiling. I tried it before a presentation one day and it helped me get centered. I think it worked so well for me because it is so in the moment."

In chapter 3 we looked at the power of practices done right in the moment of reactivity. Again, these practices are designed to disrupt, and reprogram, our chaotic response patterns as they occur. If done routinely, they break the associative memory neural nets that usually carry us away from one reaction to the next, those reactions that, if left unchecked, lead us into full-blown emotional chaos. Breaking this chain, then, re-wires a different way of responding.

Too, they profoundly change and stabilize our biochemical response, which, in turn, changes the clarity we bring to every moment. This level of clarity determines our behavior and the choices we make in that moment. How many times have you over-reacted in a moment you wish you could have reacted to differently? How significantly could the outcome have been changed? How often is this your typical way of responding?

It is the moments, and momentary reactions of our lives, that determine who we are becoming. Being able to break the chain of reactivity and re-wire response patterns in the moment is fundamental to developing a heartfully engaged way of being.

HEART in the Moment is designed to do just this.

Practice: HEART in the Moment

HEART in the Moment is similar to the Power of Pause, in that it can be done in any moment of the day. It is meant to be done in moments of reactivity, as well as any other moment you would like to cement a heartfully engaged way of being into your physiological makeup. It takes the Power of Pause one step further, in that it intentionally engages in an emotional shift. This emotional shift further intensifies the biochemical shift from chaos to calm, and potentially furthers your clarity and expands your perception. In other words, we are not just *pausing* from our typical reaction; we are *creating* another one.

The steps follow:

- Notice – Bring your awareness any reactivity you may be having

  Notice your mental activity

  Notice your emotional activity

  Notice your physical response

  Ground yourself in your breath

- Refocus – While becoming more intentional about a natural, and calming breath

  Refocus, and release the tension around your eyes

  Refocus, and release the tension around your shoulders

  Bring your awareness down to your torso, and rest in your breath

  Become very intentional about a slower deeper but mostly natural breathing pattern

- Nurture – Nurture a state that, for you, is more life-generative.
  It may involve holding an image of something that creates feelings
  of heartfulness, or a 'felt state' that facilitates an emotional shift.
  Nurture and sustain this feeling as long as it is possible, or appropriate

---

Shortly, we will do an exercise looking at how you might specifically cultivate this practice in your own life, but first let us look at a scenario of how this might play out.

HEART in the Moment in action

Imagine I am in a heated conflict with a co-worker, and in the past this has caused me problems. I know it is in my best interest to behave from a clear-headed and emotionally coherent state, but I notice I am beginning to get upset and anxious. I remember HEART in the Moment, so I notice and tune into my physical reactions in my body. I notice that my chest has tightened, my breathing has become much shallower, and I have a 'pit' in my stomach and a general sense of threat. I make a conscious decision to disengage from the emotional hijack; I 'cultivate the witness' or 'become the observer.' I do not blame, or shame myself for the reaction; neither do I let it hijack me. I just remain with my reaction, as I would a best friend having a difficulty. I refocus my physical attention from that reactive pattern right in that moment by relaxing the tension around my eyes, relaxing my shoulders, bringing my conscious attention to a place that feels comfortable in my torso, and I begin to breathe slowly and deeply, but most of all very comfortably.

I now begin to notice my body and mind calming down and I make a conscious effort to intentionally engage in a heartful shift. From my brainstorming on the heartful awareness chart I recall that the feeling of a sacred connection, love, or compassion are generative states for me, and I intentionally nurture one of those feelings. I remember that on my list of images that bring up those feelings is rafting down the quiet and still river in Yosemite as one of the most profound feelings of the sacred I have ever experienced.

I continue to keep my eyes and shoulders relaxed, my attention in my torso area and keep breathing deeply and comfortably. I now hold an image of myself on the raft in the sun, on the peaceful river floating amidst the beauty of Yosemite Valley including Half Dome and El Capitan. Just the image of really letting myself feel that memory invokes a whole body response of relaxation, peacefulness and clear and coherent thinking. My neural patterns in my brain change; because of the profound effect the changes in my breathing patterns elicit, my whole body beings to relax and the genuine heartful engagement creates profound biochemical shifts in my body.

Imagine all of this has happened in less than a minute while I am still in the same place and in the same discussion; but I am fundamentally different in my body, my brain, my behavior, and the way I respond.

Now imagine being able to make this shift when you are in the middle of a difficulty with a loved one. Imagine being able to make the shift when you are nervous because of a job interview or a speech. How about when you are in traffic? Or a car accident? Or with too much to do and too little time to do it?

The situations will vary and the benefits will increase exponentially the more you make a conscious effort to cultivate this type of internal experience. Too, intentional heartful awareness is effective not only under stressful or anxious conditions, but also at times when you just want to perform or behave at your best; when you want to rest in your inner potential.

It can also be used during the wonderful moments of our lives. We can train ourselves to notice when things are right. We can teach ourselves to take notice when we are experiencing a sense of elation or joyfulness in our mind, emotions or physical state of being. We can refocus our physicality to be even more receptive to the moment, and intentionally commit that moment to cellular memory. Too, when we bring conscious awareness to an emotional shift, we better cement that shift in our primary way of being.

It is before sunup and my husband and I are driving in a convertible on a road along the ocean in Hawaii. This specific place, a lesser-developed side of Maui, is my spiritual home. My soul feels nurtured in its deepest sense, and this is the place, more than any other, where my mind, body and spirit feel completely united. Every cell in my body feels completely alive. We are listening to one of our favorite songs, there seems to be a million stars in the sky. I have this profound feeling of 'rightness.' I want to cement this moment forever in my cells, so I take a few moments to notice how deeply impactful it is, to re-focus my body to be even more receptive to the moment, and nurture an intentional willingness to fully absorb the experience.

I have said many times, and I will repeat, that it is the repeated experience of anything that creates and strengthens our neural networks and biochemical reaction patterns. These techniques are no different. To gain the benefits these techniques have to offer they must be practiced, routinely and often. This will change, and break the cycle of destructive reactive patterns and create new, life-generating ones.

However, they must be experienced; it is the experience that produces change, not just the knowledge of how they work. The following is an exercise and reflection to help you process how you might engage HEART in the Moment in your own life.

Exercise and Reflection # 8 - HEART in the Moment

Two important aspects of HEART in the Moment are remembering in the moment of reactivity to actually make the shift, and knowing what feelings or images may bring you to a state of heartful awareness.

1) Brainstorm and list many situations that would be beneficial for you to heartfully engage in an emotional shift right in the moment of reactivity.

2) From the situations that you listed in the question above, are there specific heartful states appropriate for a particular situation? In other words, is there something about a certain situation that would determine the heartful response, for example, something about the situation that you can feel grateful for, have compassion for, or develop a sense of love towards?

3) Refer back to the heartful awareness chart and recall those states you wrote above the line. Are there any you would like to add? Which ones are the most important to you?

4) Make a list of images, or feelings, e.g., various people, places, experiences, animals, thoughts, etc. that would elicit a state of heartful awareness for you. These images do not have to be real. It could be a fictitious place where you feel especially secure or

comforted, etc. They merely need to be something that prompts a heartful shift for you. These can serve as your personal 'data base' of images to facilitate a heartful shift in the moment of reactivity.

5) How will you remind your self to practice HEART in the Moment in the middle of reactivity?

6) HEART in the Moment can also be used during all moments of the day. We can use it to shift our emotional attention at any time, to better establish heartfulness as our primary way of being. Too, it can be used during especially meaningful instances to further cement those response patterns in our core make up. What situations or events in your life can you use HEART in the Moment to cement already heartfully engaged ways of being?

HEART in the Moment review

The basic idea of HEART in the Moment is that we can shift in the moment of reactivity, or any other moment of the day, to a place of heartful awareness. And, when we do, we completely shift our physiological state of being. In other words, we intentionally shift to a state of clarity, calm, and coherence. It is not about suppressing, or denying emotion. It is about self-care, in any moment of the day, to get us operating from our fullest inner potential. It is from there that we most directly see, and behave in more expansive ways of being.

Also, to most effectively facilitate the shift, we typically use an image, or 'felt sense' of something that will genuinely engage our heart. It could be real, it could be imagined, or it could be a sense of self-love or self-compassion in the face of difficulty. Again, it is not the 'thing' that is important, it is the genuine shift of heartful engagement.

Lastly, different circumstances will determine which images might be most appropriate. In other words, if I am in a highly upsetting, stressful or negative emotional circumstance, it will probably be hard to shift to a state of deep love. At this point I may need to shift to the feeling of unconditional love that my dog has for me. It is simple and quick, and when I hold an image of her face I can usually shift to a feeling of gratitude for the love she has for me. When I am in a less chaotic state it might be easier for me to shift to deep feelings I have for the loved ones in my life, or images of places that are sacred to me. It is the shift that is most important; the image is just a tool to get us there.

Remember, this is really about self-care. The best way I can take care of my self is to be settled in my own internal reactions, not from a place of denial or suppression, or from a place of chaos, but from a place of love, acceptance and gratitude. Then, from that heartfully engaged state, I can make clear, coherent and grounded choices, rather than emotionally reactive ones. One phrase I think is valuable to commit to memory is "drop to your HEART" and breathe. If, when you begin to feel reactive, you can remember this phrase, it will remind you, in the moment, to begin to make a heartfully engaged shift. That shift, then, carries with it all the possibilities and potential of transforming that moment, and all the subsequent moments of our life.

Sustained HEART

A sustained practice is exactly as it sounds: a practice that you hold for a sustained period of time to lengthen and deepen the heartfully engaged meditative experience. While 'in the moment' practices rewire our moments of reactivity, or cement moments of joy, sustained practices create foundational changes in our baseline emotional makeup. It is a designated space and time in which you intentionally cultivate an inner focus, and nurture a heartful way of being. After becoming aware, and fostering non-reactivity, you involve the breath, the body, and the heart in an experience of deep and sustained heart felt states. Bryan's responses to Sustained HEART:

"Immediately, I knew Sustained HEART would be beneficial for me. The combination of my workload and outside responsibilities became overwhelming.

I had known for a long time that I must do something about this, but I just constantly seemed to be reacting to what life was dealing me. Sustained HEART kept me sane at a time I should have been quite insane. It is amazing to me how little time it takes to feel so much better. I ended up feeling calmer, and more focused about the rest of my day after every session. I feel like I am becoming a different person"

Rationale of sustained practice

If experience creates and strengthens neural networks and biochemical response patterns, and repeated experience exaggerates this process, what we routinely and consistently do has a profound effect on who we are becoming at any point in time. Sustained practice of HEART provides the routine and consistent experience necessary for long-term change.

This sustained practice is built on the concept that the longer and more routinely we expose our self to any physiological, psychological, or emotional state, the more likely our bodies are to adapt to that state, and create it as our primary operating system. If we routinely and consistently create an internal experience, complete with the neural and biochemical shifts of authentic heartful engagement, our bodies adapt to that state and change in function and structure. That is, how we function in the moment, and who we are becoming long-term. This concept works just like exercise does.

When you routinely and consistently exercise, your body undergoes a complete overhaul of the way it functions in the moment, and its long-term way of being. Muscles change, enzymes change, you cardiorespiratory system changes, and your use of blood sugar changes. If you have problems with high blood pressure, exercise may reduce it. Even your bones change. And these are only a few of the physiological changes that take place. In short, routine and consistent exercise completely transforms a body. The same is true of sustained mental and emotional practice.

But again, just as exercise must be experienced, so any form of contemplative practice must be. It is not something we can 'know about' to reap the foundational changes it offers. It needs to be truly and routinely engaged and experienced. Once again, it is experience that changes us. Sustained and routine practice of HEART will create fundamental changes in the operating system of our body and brain. As research has shown us, the more one practices, the more profound the changes. The following are just a few comments from workshop participants:

"I was able to focus on life"; "I had reduced worries"; "I had a profound feeling of peace"; "I felt a sense of joy"; "I was clear"; "I felt calm"; "Today's session felt strangely spiritual".

The specific steps of sustained heart will be presented shortly, but first let us look at how you might set up a routine practice.

Cultivating practice

Research has shown over and over again profound and foundational changes from various contemplative practices. What it has also shown, however, is getting people to set up, or follow through with a program of practice is not always so easy.

Because regular engagement is an important part of sustained practice, it is important to set up a routine that you are likely to stick to. As you will read in the next chapter, any avenues of behavior change are more likely to be successful if they are planned for, and built into your schedule.

Routine, consistency, and prolonged practice are what produce change. What does all this mean in practical terms? Five to fifteen minutes a day will produce some positive changes. Twenty to thirty minutes once or twice a day will produce even greater benefits. When people are first beginning, unless they are very committed to creating a more serious practice, I suggest twenty minutes a day, as most people will perceive this amount of time as doable.

Where and when you practice is, in a large sense, the result of time and space availability. In other words, some people have a dedicated space, complete with a personal altar, and a specified time every day to practice. Others, either because of a busy life or less personal space, will invent both creative spaces and times in which to practice. My first practice space was in a transformed closet. I often tell my workshop participants, or students, that even five minutes in a parked car can do a world of good.

Anytime, any place you can practice is beneficial. You can practice in a parked car, in a waiting room, under a tree, any time you have a moment, want to calm down, think clearer, or rest in a larger way of being. The main message here, is that even if you do not have obvious space and time availability, there are ways to build it into your day and have it make a profound difference in your life. Somehow, somewhere, if you are motivated, you will find the space. And, the more it is scheduled in, the more likely you are to be successful at maintaining it. Be creative. Find what works for you.

Also, some prefer to do a sustained practice silently, some prefer ambient music, and some prefer a guided practice. In the appendix is a resource to access audio recordings of the guided practices.

Once you have created an appropriate environment for you, sit in a comfortable position, or lay down with your back straight to give your diaphragm room to breathe. Your diaphragm is a muscle that cuts across your chest cavity, almost like a pancake. It is responsible, by its up and down movement, for creating pressure differences in your lungs that cause them to inflate and deflate. If your diaphragm does not have room to move, your lungs cannot inflate sufficiently and a full and natural breath, which is foundational to any sustained practice, is impaired.

Whether you sit up or lay down seems to be a personal preference. I personally have found that if I am being guided through, lying down is fine. If I am doing a silent meditation by myself, I need to sit up to keep my mind from wandering, as it is too much like sleeping. Again, find what works for you. Once you have created a supportive environment and allotted an appropriate amount of time, follow the HEART steps with the following adaptations. In sustained practice, because we have more time and focused attention to contribute to the process, the steps should be deliberate with full emotional attention paid to each step.

Notice - Thoughts. Emotions. Body sensations. Disengage from hold.
The notice step in Sustained HEART is similar to HEART in the Moment, however you might not be having an obvious reactivity. The notice step in this practice asks you to take a brief inventory of the mental, emotional, and physical states of your body.

Take a few intentional breaths, and begin to establish a natural and calm breathing pattern.

From the point of view of the witness, or observer, notice any thoughts you might be having. Again, you are not letting the thoughts take you away, nor are you engaging in them, as much as you are witnessing or observing their activity. Then notice your emotional activity. Your emotional activity may, or may or not be associated with your thoughts. Are there any feelings that stand out? Are your emotions harbored in a different spot in your body then your thoughts? Again, you are just noticing, or observing your emotional activity, and its nuances, without letting it consume you. You are not 'thinking about' as much as you are just 'being with.'

Notice the physical sensations in your body. Are your shoulders or any other areas of your body tight? Do you feel anxious? Scan your body. How does it feel? Are any areas harboring stress or tightness? If you feel stress, tension or tightness anywhere in your body make a conscious effort to release it. If it feels right, you can also begin to repeat the word 'release' silently on the out breath and imagine yourself releasing all the tension from your body.

Refocus - Eyes. Shoulders. Torso. Breathe.

As you continue to ground yourself in your breath, focus your attention on your eyes, and release all the tiny little muscles all around the eyes, and the eyes sockets. It almost feels as if you are losing the expression on your face. Again, you can continue to repeat the word 'release' on the out breath if it feels comfortable to do so. If you are repeating the word release, physically feel the sensation of release throughout your body every time you repeat the word. Now release any tension, tightness, or stress in your shoulders. With every out breath, physically feel the sensation of release a little bit more acutely. Now bring all your awareness to an area in your torso that feels comfortable for you. It could be your heart, it could be your solar plexus, which is right below the heart, or it could be deep in your belly.

The purpose of the refocus step is to refocus the physical attributes of your body to bring you deeper into the experience and make you more receptive to the next step. The two main parts are, first, refocusing and releasing through the eyes, the shoulders and the torso, and, second, resting in the breath.

When you are at the breathing step of Sustained HEART, your conscious attention is keenly focused in an area of your torso that feels comfortable for you, and on the process of breathing. Again, this is where some people really find it helpful to focus on the word 'release' on every out breath, and vividly feel the sensation of releasing throughout the body. Some contemplative traditions recommend you count each breath. In Sustained HEART, you might find it helpful to count the breaths in the refocus step to further ready yourself and be receptive to what comes after.

Count each in-and-out cycle as one breath. Many people count from 1 to 10 and then go back to one, while others count from 10 down to one and then go back to 10. The idea is not to count how many breaths you are taking, for example ending at 565, it is to engage your mind just enough, not have it on a hundred other things, and have it begin to settle on your body. Counting your breaths is just a tool to keep your awareness focused on your interior process. Again, if your attention is keenly focused on your breathing, it will not be on anything else.

The main concepts to remember in the refocus step are that we are physiologically readying ourselves, and making ourselves more receptive to deeply engaging in a heartful way of being. We are doing this through incorporating physiological practices that will directly impact our calm and connection system, as well as intentionally engaging our awareness in the experience of our breath. The importance of breath, and re-focusing our physicality, cannot be understated. Do what feels comfortable and natural for you, and remember that it is this step, that, when deeply absorbed is what creates the receptivity for heartful engagement.

Nurture

After several breathing cycles you will probably begin to feel a deep adjustment in both your physiological and psychological feeling states. Once you begin to feel the deepening, make a conscious and intentional shift to a heartfully engaged way of being. The main goal of this practice is that you maintain a heartfully engaged emotional shift long enough, and deep enough that you begin to make foundational shifts in your physiology. It cannot be faked. It cannot be forced. Sincerely felt heartful engagement creates physiological, biochemical, and neural response patterns that are very real, very powerful, and create profound change if practiced regularly.

While keeping an intentional breath somewhere in the background of your awareness, shift your attention to something that engages your heart. This could be an image that you listed in the last exercise, something that sincerely generates 'felt states' above the line on the heartful awareness chart, or something that is currently more heartfully present for you. It could be a sense of communing with some sacred presence, or it could be a feeling of self-love or self-compassion for some difficulty. Bask in this felt state while continuing your breathing pattern, as if it were soaking every cell in your body. If your mind wanders, just gently bring it back to this heartfully engaged state.

The main goal of this practice is to maintain, and genuinely bask in a state of genuine heartfulness for a period of time. If using an image helps you to create or maintain this engaged state, it is a good tool to use. However, it is important to remember that the image is just a tool, and a genuine heartful focus is the important aspect of this practice. Occasionally I have participants that, theoretically, have something above the line that they think should bring up heartfully aware feelings; however, in reality they do not. If you find yourself becoming saddened, angered or frustrated by an image, or if you find yourself shifting from image to image, try to settle in on an image that brings up authentic heartful states for you. Do not think about it too much. Let the practice guide you. It is the sincere engagement that is most important. Also, remember that some people are not image based. In other words, just resting in the 'felt sense' of a heartful emotion may be a more effective practice.

Practice: Sustained HEART

Notice-

◊ How you feel mentally, emotionally and physically - scan your body and make a conscious attempt to relax any area that is tight, stressed or anxious.

◊ Intentionally disengage from the reactive hold of whatever is present. Hold it from an observing or witnessing point of view.

◊ Begin to establish a comfortable breathing pattern

Refocus-

◊ Check your eyes and your shoulders and intentionally relax, 'release' on the out breath if it helps.

◊ Bring your awareness to your heart, solar plexus or deep in your belly

◊ Breathe- slowly and deeply, but most of all comfortably. Sustain this breathing. If you want, use counting tools to keep your attention keenly focused on the experience of your breath. Vividly feel the sensation of release.

Nurture

◊ When you begin to feel your body release, make an intentional shift to a heartfully engaged state and 'feel' this state. Use an image if it helps to make the shift.

◊ Sustain the relaxed breathing and focused emotional state for approximately 15 minutes or more.

◊ If you find your mind wandering, gently bring your attention back and continue. Try to not get too caught up in the thought process and instead try and intentionally cultivate a non-conscious feeling state of a heartful engagement.

◊ Sustain and breathe.

Exercise and Reflection # 9 - Sustained HEART practice

The benefits of this type of practice cannot be overstated. Routine and consistent practice changes us at the cellular level, the neural level, and all of our behaviors, perceptions, and actions follow from there. Reflect and process whether this is an appropriate practice for you, and if it is, how you can incorporate some form of this practice into your daily life. Be specific,

181

be creative, and do what works for you. You might find it helpful to address the following questions:

1) How would it best work for you, given the current state of your life, to establish a sustained practice?

2) How could you best create space and time in your schedule?

3) How could you make it a habit or priority to routinely practice?

4) Do you think it would be easiest to do a silent practice, one with ambient music, or one that leads you through by a guided audio?

5) What kind of support might you need?

6) Would you be interested in finding a local group that engages in similar types of practice?

7) Write a few paragraphs on what you believe would be the best plan of implementation for you. Be specific.

Sustained HEART is the core practice in which HEART for Clarity, and Sacred HEART are built. They are presented later in this book. It is also the core practice underlying HEART for Healing, which is presented next.

HEART for Healing

The transformative ideas thus far in this book have focused on directly developing the calm and connection system. They have looked at direct heartful engagement as a path to reprogramming our inner experience, and thus, our outer lives. HEART for Healing engages what might be blocking us. It looks at deeply ingrained and obstructing implicit memories, in other words, our embedded perceptions and reactions that may be barring us from authentic heartful engagement. It invites us into heartful engagement for our self. It invites us to look at our implicit programming, or ingrained reactions from a place of self-understanding, self-compassion, and even appreciation. Only then can we rewire the deep-seated programming that may be keeping us blocked.

How we heal

What happens when it is not working? What happens when authentic heartful engagement seems impossible? What happens when, no matter how hard we try to shift, something below the line on the heartful awareness chart is so present for us, it is demanding our attention? What happens when we are on the low end of the HEAR scale?

Sometimes our soul needs to heal. Sometimes implicit memory patterns, or their adaptive behaviors, choices, or reactivities are so out of balance they are demanding our attention. And sometimes, until we give them the attention they need, we will remain in feedback loops of the fear response system, continually a casualty of this process. Sometimes we need to heal the implicit memory or reactivity at its source.

What does all this mean? It means sometimes we have such ingrained traumatic memory, behaviors, response systems, or wired reactivities that they need intervention before we can balance our system. They need additional attention before we can reverse the 'spiral of becoming' from the fear response system to one of calm and connection. In the language of parts: a 'part' of us is present, and active, and until we can give it the attention it needs our system will remain completely out of balance. And we cannot do that by merely ignoring it, blaming or shaming ourselves for having it, or pretending it does not exist. Sometimes our fear response system is so ingrained, and so in control it needs to be unlocked.

Her mother abandoned Kendra when she was young. Although her father was around, he was angry, and for the most part emotionally unavailable. Her grandparents raised her. When she was a teenager, her grandfather, who she was especially close to, passed away. She had an enduring sense of loneliness and abandonment, although, in reality, there were many close relatives and friends around her that loved her deeply. She also had many other wonderful things in her life. Nonetheless, because her perceptions were so colored by her implicit memory, her ingrained protective mechanisms would not let anybody close, or any other sense of happiness in, for fear of being abandoned again.

Let us look at what is happening physiologically when we are caught in a spiral of reactivity, and our fear response system is keeping us out of balance.

Along the way most of us have had life's experiences that have carried significantly challenging emotional impact. These instances of impact can range all the way from repeated patterns or situations that were emotionally upsetting to us for one reason or another, to serious, and possibly repeated trauma. If we recall the way implicit memory is stored from chapter 2, we remember the more upsetting or repetitive the initial life's challenge, due to the biochemical impact or reactions then, the more deeply they are wired in our implicit memory. Sometimes our implicit memory is wired so strongly it has become our primary operating pattern and most of our perceptions are filtered through it. However, it is important to remember that the dynamic of implicit memory patterns are originally there to protect us in some way.

In other words, our implicit memory patterns, or reactivities, stored within our fear response system were encoded there, for some reason, to protect us. And sometimes are wired so strongly that they 'overprotect' us for what is now appropriate in our current life. When this happens our 'spiral of becoming' gets locked in a cycle of unbalanced reactivity, and we remain steeped in our fear response system, either most of the time, or in any similar circumstance to that which has hurt us before. We develop perceptions, behaviors, choices and reactions, which just further cement these ways of being.

Kendra's fear response system began to work overtime to build walls. Her fear response system did not want anyone close again that could hurt or abandon her. Her fear response system adapted behaviors that began to push people away. Of course this behavior from her fear response system only furthered her perception of abandonment, and she began to adopt beliefs like: "Everyone always leaves me", "Nobody will ever really be there for me", "This always happens to me." She truly believed she could not be happy and she truly believed she would always be alone. Her friends and other relatives loved her dearly, but something in her implicit memory, or perception, blocked her receptivity to this love.

When a problematic perception, or 'pattern of being' is deeply ingrained in our implicit make up it needs to be rewired at its source. And it takes direct intervention to help us do that.

How do we know if this is the case? Recall the heartful awareness charting exercise in chapter 4. Above the line on the chart I had you write words that, for you, brought up a 'felt sense' of 'rightness', calm or clarity.

Below the line I asked you to write words that, for you, felt emotionally chaotic. We also examined the concept that staying steeped in the chaotic states below the line perpetuated the cycle of reactivity, and those above the line were conducive to a physiological state of healing. Too, we entertained the idea that for states above the line to be ones of healing, they have to be authentic. Your body knows. Remember it is quite often more honest than your conscious mind.

If you cannot *authentically* engage in a state above the line, there are most likely chaotic emotional states demanding your attention. They need your awareness, compassion, desire and action to re-balance them.

Let us go back to the HEAR scale in chapter 4. Remember the HEAR scale is a simple tool designed to measure your reactivity, and gauge its intensity to judge if you can make an authentic heartful shift. On the left side is 0% heartfully engaged awareness, as opposed to 100% on the right side. While breathing deeply, and attempting to rest in your deepest sense, imagine where you fall on the scale in your ability to rest in your Inner Being. If you are somewhere between 0% and 50%, chances are parts of you need healing attention. If you fall somewhere between 0% to 25%, something in you is most likely yearning for deeper, more immediate healing attention. Somewhere you know.

Although Kendra knew from a cognitive sense that her past experience may have something to do with her perception and behavior, her 'felt sense' was one of abandonment. She tried to find something about the situation to appreciate, she tried to focus on the love that others tried to give her, she tried to shift her awareness. Her perceptions, however, were so clouded from her implicit memory, and she was so consumed by the biochemistry and neural memory of her past, she could not authentically feel anything different. On the HEAR scale she was so steeped in feelings of loneliness and despair, she knew she needed direct healing.

Again, this is where I find the language of parts developed by Richard Schwartz especially beneficial.[45] If we can view those states below the line on the heartful awareness chart as 'parts' of us, but not our deepest Inner Being, we can gain a get a little distance on their reactivity, but still entertain them enough to heal. They are various stored response patterns of experience that have somehow helped us navigate our past. Imagine all the states below the line as either emotional manifestations of implicit memory (e.g. hurt, separation, loneliness etc.), or our learned responses to the discomfort of that emotional memory (e.g. anger, jealousy, depression, etc.), but really not the deepest part of who we are. They are developed from various life experiences, and ingrained implicit memories, and have been formed to serve a function. And may have outlived their usefulness.

Kendra had a part that was profoundly lonely, and sincerely felt that no one would ever be there for her. She had a part that was so protective of her, and wary of her being abandoned again it would not let anyone close; it caused her to build walls. She had a part that 'left' anyone that did get close, before they could leave her. She had a part that just went numb and would not let her feel anything. And she had parts that ate, drank, and slept to excess to suppress the pain.

Again, our typical responses to reactive states are to take off with their reactivity, suppress them, or blame, shame or judge ourselves for having them. All of which keep us below the line on the chart and none of which lead to a physiological state of healing.

There is another possibility. If we truly grasp that the *process* of implicit memory storage is good, and actually protective, we can appreciate the work of these 'parts', and at the same time fully embrace the fact that they may need to be healed and brought back into balance. If my anger at one time was a protective mechanism from previous hurt, but now is wreaking havoc in my life, I can recognize that 'part' of me has worked really hard to protect me in the past. From the understanding of implicit memory, I can see that it is only a part of me, and I can get some distance on its reactivity.

I can also see that it may be way out of balance for any hope of heartfully engaged awareness, and begin to help it heal. I can even hold myself in a state of heartful awareness, or self-compassion in recognizing how it has tried to protect me. This way we engage the message of the difficult emotion enough to heal it, without having it consume us, and the self-compassion, or self-understanding brings us to a physiological state of healing (those states above the line). At the same time we are re-wiring the original implicit memory pattern. Shortly, we will return to the story of Kendra to see how this all plays out.

Dr. Frank Rogers Jr. does some great work on radical compassion in his book *Practicing Compassion*[46]. A huge component of this work is the development of radical self-compassion, which perfectly fits this paradigm. Radical self-compassion brings us to the physiological state of healing, even when entertaining a difficult emotional implicit memory pattern. And this is the path to healing them.

Unlocking the implicit

How do we truly heal? We heal by unlocking old experience and providing new experience. And this is especially important in regard to those old experiences that are deeply wired. Deeply ingrained implicit memory is just that. Deeply ingrained. And the more deeply ingrained, the more it may need direct access to rewiring. In other words, it needs to be directly engaged, and then unlocked, to rewire a new paradigm. In this 'unlocking,' we are un-learning one perceptual framework and then re-learning another. This unlocking happens at all levels of awareness, including the subconscious.

Research is showing us that to truly and effectively reprogram a deeply ingrained implicit memory pattern, or to change and heal our impaired perception and reactivities, we need to directly engage them at some level without letting them consume us. This 'unlocks' it, if you will, and allows us to rewire a new experience.[47] This is memory reconsolidation at its core. The new experience may be a rewired version of the past experience, or merely the experience of not responding in our typical ways!

The way this may play out is we can recognize we have an implicit memory, or 'nudging' surfacing by the 'felt sense' of emotional un-ease. That is, we are being consumed by an emotionally chaotic reaction. If it is strong, and we cannot authentically shift to a state of heartful awareness, we can use this as an indication that an implicit memory is out of balance; something in our reactive system is screaming so loud it is demanding our attention. I refer to these as 'nudgings'.

The nudging could be in the form of a conscious memory, a familiar feeling, or an unmet need underlying the reactivity. We then can gain distance from its reactive hold by appreciating how and why it was stored in the first place, and hold ourselves in a state of self-compassion while addressing what it is trying to tell us. Most of the time, either consciously, or subconsciously in the form of an image, feeling, or intuitive knowing we will be able to identify the underlying need. In essence, we 'hold' our self, and compassionately listen to the 'nudging' as we would do for a best friend.

The 'unlocking' part comes in when we engage the nudging just enough to open the neural networks, and then give them a different experience to recode. Instead of suppressing the nudging, or taking off with its reactivity, we provide for it a different experience. We can hold, and deeply feel, an image of a healing experience. We can allow ourselves to rest in the 'felt state' of meeting the underlying need. We can bathe our self in self-compassion and provide an alternative memory.

Remember, trauma is no longer in the previous event; that is over. Where it is, is stored in our neural networks. And, with new experience, we can re-program them. Again, the brain does not know the difference between what is vividly imagined, or deeply felt, and what is real.

Kendra knew she needed to heal some of her implicit patterns at their source. She began to use intentional practice and imagery to help her heal. Her practice for healing went something like this:

She began the process by settling into her breath and noticing the activity of her thoughts, emotions, and bodily sensations from a witnessing or observing point of view. She was able to disengage enough from their hold to settle further into her breath and establish a natural, deep and comfortable breathing pattern. She refocused and released all the tension in the tiny muscles around her eyes; she refocused and released the tension in her shoulders. She brought her awareness to her solar plexus, as this place felt comfortable for her, and more deeply and fully engaged in her breath. Once she could feel her body calming, and becoming more receptive, she imagined a fictitious place where she could rest in the sensation of security.

Resting in the feeling of being secure and protected, she allowed herself to feel the 'nudging' of the familiar sense of abandonment. However, she was able to keep this feeling at enough of a distance to remain in the physiological state of security and healing. She 'felt' safe. From a grounded space she could engage that 'nudging' for healing without letting it overwhelm her. She could even appreciate and find some self-love and understanding for the implicit pattern and why it was there in the first place. By engaging the 'nudging' she was able to 'unlock' the emotional memories without letting them flood her. This 'unlocking' gave her the answer.

While remaining physiologically secure and grounded, and still steeped in her breath and her inner experience, she felt an intuitive knowing that she needed to provide a different experience than the one that was wired in her embodied memory. In other words, she needed to allow a sense of connection to be wired where there once was abandonment. As deeply as she could, she 'felt' the sense of security, safety, and love, and what it was like to deeply receive those states of healing. She was all at once the giver, and the receiver, and her embodied experience began to change. She soaked herself in a sense of love and security. She gave herself the love and security she should have gotten as a child.

And her neural networks wired to the new experience.

When we provide an alternative, embodied experience to implicit memory by something that is deeply imagined, or deeply felt, we begin to re-wire our neural networks and create different programming. We retain the conscious or explicit memory of the event or state, but are no longer consumed by its charge.

And this can be done at all levels of awareness. It can be an awareness we bring to every moment, and it can be done in deep healing states. Remember the more deeply felt the alternative experience, the more it is coded. There is huge power in both making it a part of our every day awareness, as well as a deep and sustained practice. HEART for Healing is designed to be a deep and sustained practice formulated from this process. It is my attempt to ground some of the great work already out there, especially that of Frank and Dick, into a physiological paradigm.

Practice: HEART for Healing

In all of the Sustained HEART practices the 'notice' and 'refocus' steps are the same. These steps prepare us psychologically and physiologically for the reprogramming of the nurture step.

Notice – your thoughts, your emotions, and your physical sensations. Disengage from their reactivity, witness and observe. Begin to establish an intentional and comfortable breath.

Refocus – your eyes by releasing all the tiny little muscles around the eyes and behind the eyes, refocus by releasing the tension in your shoulders. Bring your awareness down to your torso, somewhere that feels comfortable for you to focus on your breath. Sustain and deepen a comfortable and natural breathing pattern.

Nuture - the nurture step is similar to the process described in Kendra's experience. It includes grounding yourself in a physiological state of healing by cultivating deep states of self-safety or security. It could be an imagined place, or a 'felt sense' of being totally held, safe, and secure. While resting in this 'felt sense', see if any 'nudgings' for implicit healing are making themselves known. In other words, what symptom is presenting itself, nudging for attention to be healed? While engaging the nudging at a safe distance, tune into what it is needing from you, to be re-wired in a more balanced state. This message may come as an intuitive knowing, and image, or a physical sensation. Hold yourself, and the nudging, in as a compassionate state as you would a best friend. As deeply and as vividly as possible provide an alternative experience by the way of a 'felt sense' or image. This begins to rewire the implicit memory at its source. And the deeper the alternative experience is engaged the deeper it is re-programmed as our new operating pattern.

I was in a workshop once with Dr. Rick Hanson, author of *Buddhas Brain: the practical narrow science of happiness, love and wisdom*[18]. He used the phrase "Never dive into the deep end, if you can't swim back to the shallow end." For some deeply traumatic events you may want to work through this process with a professional, perhaps a therapist, or spiritual director, for example.

Exercise and Reflection # 10 - HEART for Healing

Brainstorm ways you might engage the HEART for Healing practice. Again, the reflective writing is meant to be done as a stream of consciousness writing. You might find it helpful to address the following questions, however they are not meant to be answered verbatim.

1) Do you feel any 'nudgings' for healing attention when you get quiet?

2) Revisit the heartful awareness chart. What 'felt states' below the line might be associated with a deeply ingrained implicit patterns for you?

3) What states, for you, may fall on the 0% – 50% range on the HEAR scale?

4) Can you nurture a state of understanding, self-love or compassion for how the memory was stored in the first place?

5) While cultivating a grounded physiological state of healing, address the 'nudging'. What is the 'nudging' telling you? What does it need? How do you best provide what it needs?

6) Deep experience provides deep change. How can you best provide an experiential process, similar to HEART healing, to re-wire unbalanced implicit patterns? What would that 'look' like?

Last Thoughts

My sister called from San Francisco. From her voice I could tell she was very confused, yet curious. She said: "I want to know what is going on! You do not fight with mom anymore and I want to know why!" She, of course, wanted to know what was going on because in the past my relationship with my mother could be quite contentious, and had been a huge issue in my life - until then. I was taken aback, surprised that from 400 miles away she could sense the internal shift I was feeling. I answered: "I do not know... All I can tell you is this meditation stuff is changing my life."

One of the most meaningful comments I get from people is when the people around them notice a change. It often goes something like this: "I really noticed a shift in myself, but when my (husband, wife, parent, boyfriend, girlfriend, boss, friend, sibling etc.,) noticed, I knew for sure something important was shifting."

Research shows us, and more importantly, peoples' personal experience validates, that routine contemplative practice can foundationally change who we are. We have seen scientifically how it happens, we have heard personal accounts, and we have explored a specific approach. And yet, the biggest hindrance to practice still remains getting people to actually do it.

Some things in life require more than 'knowledge about', they require 'practice of.' Contemplative practice is one of those things. I have said before, and will say again, nothing changes if nothing changes. The block may be in authentic willingness to actually be different; it may be in creating the space and time to move from thinking about it to taking action. The next chapter begins to address what it means to truly embody a heartful way of being, including the question of authentic willingness to embrace change.

What can you do to make contemplative practice a part of your life? How can specific practices be modified to truly honor who you are, and what your life is all about? How can you move from intent to action?

6

Heartful Awareness in Action

Heartful awareness changes us. Every moment we spend authentically engaged in heartful awareness for ourselves, others, or our outside world is a transformative moment of experience; our fear response system quiets, and our calm and connection system flourishes. These are the moments that create our days, and our days create our years.

And every moment is an opportunity.

Or it is an opportunity for the opposite.

But the moments matter immensely, as it is the momentary experiences of our lives that determine who we are becoming. Embodying heartful awareness in our everyday existence takes conscious intentionality. 'Knowledge about' life changing ways of being remains untapped potential until it is manifest, or embodied in the momentary choices of our lives. 'Knowledge about' needs to make its way to 'lived experience.' In this chapter we begin to grasp what heartful awareness might look like in the tapestry of our everyday lives, tangible and specific ways to weave heartfulness in the threads of our existence.

When one walks a labyrinth, it is customary to pause in the middle and reflect on the journey. As the path in quite often reflects the journey to our own center, the path out can reveal specific and tangible steps we might take to outwardly manifest the lessons learned. Too, the path outward starts at the innermost point, and broadens and widens before emerges again with the outside world.

Throughout this book we explored how experience forms us and continually changes us. We have seen this from looking at our habitual ways of being, to fostering non-reactivity, and stopping habitual spirals. We have looked at the intentionality of cultivating something different, and the importance of micro moments of our day. We have looked at how new and intentional experience can heal. And we have seen that all the moments of our day add up, and become our lived experience.

The rest of our journey is on specific and tangible ways we might cultivate heartful awareness in the moments of our every day life. Also, as in the outward journey of a labyrinth, we will start at our deeper internal experience and ways of being, and progress to more tangible, day-to-day experience. The specific practices presented are directed at both increasing our own heartful awareness, and building our own personal foundation to clear our blocks and allow a sense of heartfulness to automatically emerge in our day-to-day lives.

To get a better grasp on how we might embody heartful awareness and its foundational benefits in our every day life, it is helpful to look at major concepts and themes, as well as everyday behaviors. The major concepts and themes represent over-arching considerations that deepen the texture of what heartful awareness is, as it is manifest in lived experience. These over-arching concepts are 1) the importance of, and critical choice every moment brings, 2) the all-important transition from intention to action, and 3) the question of true and authentic willingness to embody a different way of being.

As such we will see that it is the awareness of, presence we bring to, and choice in *each moment* that matters most. With 'baby steps' of presence and engagement in the small moments of our life, the choice between love and fear is no longer a daunting task, but a natural extension of our new 'spiral of becoming'. Too, we will see that the critical component is action, for without action everything remains the same. We will see that the path to action is paved one step at a time. Action in the context of heartful awareness is the choice to truly shift, and engage in momentary heartful opportunities as they present themselves. We will also examine our willingness to truly be different. Although a difficult question to address, it is at the heart of embodying heartful awareness, for our selves, and how we are in the world.

A heartful look at our willingness gives us perspective on our appropriate transformative process.

Lastly, we will look at tangible and specific ways to plant the seeds of consciousness for our own heartful awareness to blossom. As we begin to shift to specific and tangible ways heartful awareness plays out for us in our every day lives, we will look at the behaviors our moments are built on, that subsequently determine who we are becoming. Everyday behaviors create the moments of our lives. The thoughts we think, the words we say, to others, and ourselves, and the way we interpret everyday events profoundly influence our capabilities to cultivate, and live from states of heartful awareness. Every moment we are transforming, and the behaviors that comprise those moments matter a lot.

The second half of this chapter focuses on every day behaviors that permeate our existence. They are woven throughout our existence, and profoundly affect our capabilities for heartful awareness and who we are becoming; and we may not even be aware of their enormous impact. We have seen throughout this book the great impact our attention has. Our thoughts and words, to our selves and others, are a primary determinant of our attention. The words we speak, and our language in general, is constantly molding who we are becoming.

With those considerations in mind, we will take an in-depth look at the language we speak. We will look at our language in various its manifestations, including: 1) our inner chatter, and the nature of our inner dialog, including the damaging effects of 'catastrophizing' and the made up 'conversations' in our head, 2) the stories we tell, the scripts we write, and their incredible impact on who we are becoming, 3) our conversations with others, including the huge impact of what we 'say' non-verbally, and 4) what we 'tell' ourselves by our subjective interpretation of events, and how those interpretations mold subsequent events.

Every moment is a heartful opportunity

Throughout our journey to heartful awareness we have defined it as a sense of presence and engagement that we bring to every moment.

Heartfulness invites us into an awareness of every moment, including ours, and other's internal world, and the outside world; however, it then invites us to make an intentional heartful shift. Every moment not only offers the opportunity of *awareness*, it offers the opportunity of *engagement*. Heartful awareness invites active engagement in whatever life-generating emotional state is presenting itself in that moment. It is the momentary choice, from a non-reactive and accepting state, to intentionally seek, and actively engage in, love, compassion, gratitude, or whatever heartful opportunity is available in that moment. When we can truly embrace and appreciate this concept, we can see that we only have endless moments of opportunity to heal, or intentionally create a new paradigm.

And the power is in the moment itself.

It is not about forcing our lives into attunement, pretending we feel something we do not, or grasping at external events or behaviors that might change us. Indeed that just impedes us. It is changing from the inside out.

How do we heartfully engage our existence in this manner? I love the description of how Michelangelo came to sculpt the statue of David. He said that as he chipped away at the marble, he removed all the pieces that were not David, and David began to appear. The presumption of this book has been that if we can cut through enough of the chaos, static and overwhelm of our programming and fear response system, what lies at our internal core is a perfectly loving and compassionate state.

This is our calm and connection system rooted in our deepest self or Inner Being. And this is the system under which we flourish. If we can begin to focus our awareness on, and routinely experience this internal state our brain changes, our biochemistry changes, our heart waves calm, and the way we function in the world changes. And it all begins in each moment. We are no longer dominated by our fear response system, and choices of love, compassion or gratitude become second nature. We develop greater clarity and a larger way of being in the world. Because our calm and connection system is more often dominant than our fear response system, when faced with choices between love and fear, the choice to love is a 'doable' shift.

Love and fear re-visited

I was sitting on a cliff, meditating over the Pacific Ocean. I had been dealing with some tough issues in my life, and was trying to get some clarity. As I came out of an especially powerful meditation, I was surprised to see a man standing next to me. Without pause, Steve promptly and directly asked me if I had experienced any powerful insights during my meditation. I was surprised by his question and I was surprised by his presence. The depth of conversation also surprised me, because I had, in fact, had some powerful insights.

*I shared with him that, from a very experiential level, I felt that every moment had the capability of either being steeped in love or steeped in fear. And if we could really tap into our inner most self, and **feel** the truth, we would know. Further, the choice we made in that moment, and subsequent moments, would begin to determine the texture of our life.*

Steve shared a similar idea. He said he thought that every decision, behavior, or choice was made out of love or out of fear. Those made out of love became the life-affirming choices that increase or vitalize our life force. However, he added, it takes incredible awareness and strength to make those based on love. The choice to love somehow seems scary, and fear is so much more readily available. Although we may know, and deeply believe this fundamental truth, it is not so easy to play out in our every day life. I was reminded of the lyrics to the Bruce Springsteen song "Cautious Man":

"On his right hand Billy'd tattooed the word "love"And on his left hand was the word "fear"And in which hand he held his fate was never clear.[49]

I have thought of that conversation many times since. I still deeply believe in its fundamental truth, however I also believe there are ways to help us 'get there.' And those ways need to be an essential component in the love versus fear discussion. In other words, just the question of love versus fear, with out any tools of implementation, may seem daunting at times, an impossible ideal. Too, it seems to carry the potential of blame, shame or judgment if we do not, or cannot make the choice of love every time.

What I have come to realize is that the 'spiral of becoming' that we have spoken about so often in this book is **always** at work. And that little changes add up. Indeed, it maybe the little changes that have the biggest impact. Too, we can begin to intentionally create circumstances and adopt behaviors that begin to reverse the spiral and then the choice to love becomes a natural extension. It is not really about a few monumental choices as it is our day-to-day behaviors, attitudes and choices that accumulate. And when the monumental ones do appear, we are much more equipped to handle them.

If the choice is just one of love and fear, with no understanding of what that means, or tools to get there, we may become paralyzed, consumed with blame, or shame or self-judgment, and unintentionally take the fear route. It is like expecting to run a marathon with no previous training. Too, if we perceive that it is only the monumental events that change us, we completely miss the opportunity that every moment offers. And the monumental changes are much more likely to appear when we are ready. We may not even see, or perceive them if we are not.

Heartful presence changes us. It is a decidedly different way of being than the 'status quo'. Every moment is an opportunity, or choice to rest in either state. Little shifts become big shifts, and big shifts become foundational changes. The choice between love and fear no longer seems a daunting task, and the small moments and choices of our lives become our lived experience. And our lived experience becomes one of heartful awareness.

It is all in the moment.

~~But it requires action.~~

From intent to action

Training begins with the first step. This is action. But action must be taken. If nothing changes, nothing changes. Or as is often attributed to Einstein, "insanity is doing the same thing over and over again and expecting a different result." In the world of neuroscience, little changes add up. Indeed, they may be the ones that lead to long-term change. Even major transformative moments need follow through, or they will revert to previously programmed experience. The 'spiral of becoming' is happening every moment of every day. It takes intentional action to nurture it in the direction of life.

Behavior change theorists break behavior change into stages. The first stage, pre-contemplation, is the stage where we may not feel good, we know something needs to change, but we're not really aware of how to make it better. In the contemplation stage we may learn about it, read about it, plan it; we may even become experts on 'how to do it', but nothing changes until something changes. Nothing changes until we take action. The action phase is where we actually do something about it. That is where transformation occurs. And when we realize it all begins with momentary baby-steps, we are much more likely to begin. Heartful awareness requires the momentary choice of shift. It requires action in the moment – that fundamental moment in time where we have a choice. But it also requires willingness. Many of us profess to want change, but at a fundamental level we are not really willing to except that change. Discerning your own willingness, from a heartful posture, is the first step in taking appropriate action.

Authentic willingness

As we have seen throughout this book, specifically through an embodied approach to heartfully engaged awareness; a different way of being in this world is possible. However, it is my belief that although most people profess to want this type of existence, they are really not authentically willing to embrace that change. The dynamics of captivating and paralyzing fear, a belief that we are not capable, or a lack of deep internal willingness to be different causes us to unknowingly deny the invitation of growth.

Although we think we want it, and it may even appear that it just does not work out for us however hard we try, I believe there are quite often subconscious blocks in our ability to move forward. Until we entertain these blocks and take an in-depth look at what may be at the root of the unwillingness or fear, from an internal sense, our efforts will be muted.

We have seen throughout this book the terrible damage we are doing to ourselves by ruminating on, or functioning from states of anxiety, threat, fear, shame, self-loathing, judgment, insecurity, etc. We have also seen the tremendous possibilities for our bodies, brains, behaviors and relationships by intentionally cultivating, and living in states of heartfully engaged awareness. We have seen that the state of our emotional attention becomes our internal experience, and our internal experience becomes who we are. And yet most of us remain in status quo.

For most of us, emotional chaos, anxiety, and stress have become such familiar places to be we are subconsciously not really willing to replace them with another way of being. As hard as it may be to accept, we are not really ready to allow ourselves to drop our habitual ways of acting, and reacting, and create a different internal ideal. We may be afraid of the unknown, we may lack the resources, we may not truly know, or believe there is a different way. We may not be able to give up our ingrained definitions of who we are, or we may have some subconscious blocks that need healing first. We may believe we are just not capable.

This book is full of transformative information, specific paths, and resources. An important question remains, however. Are we truly ready and willing to accept the invitation of growth and healing? Are we sincerely open for the transformation that heartfully engaged ways of being will bring to us? What blocks may we need to face to truly embrace this transformation, healing and higher baseline of living? As difficult as the question of willingness may be, it must be spoken to.

We have the knowledge and know-how. We have seen some practical steps, activities and practices for creating a larger or more expansive way of being. And we have seen the possibility of very real, and very measurable changes in our body, mind and spirit as we walk this path. So why don't we? What is the payoff in staying stuck?

When I look up the word 'willing' in various dictionaries the main definition that keeps appearing is the word 'ready'. When I look up the word 'allow' I get the definition 'give permission for something to happen.' So the question is, are we really ready to give permission for heartfully engaged awareness to transform us? Are we truthfully ready for an internal shift? Are we ready to let go of the definitions of ourselves that hold us back, and work through the physiological discomfort of change? Are we ready to address our blocks and engage the invitation of healing? These questions may be the key to cultivating authentic willingness.

At this point I think most, although not all would say, "Yes, I am willing." However, when we dig deeper and get more specific those answers may change. For instance, the next time you are feeling reactive, are you willing to disengage from that reactivity and cultivate a heartfully engaged way of being? Or hold yourself heartfully within your reactivity? Are you ready to incorporate the intentional ways of being that it takes to transform in your everyday life? Are you ready to take the specific steps from intent to action?

What is keeping us stuck? – Examining the pay off

An honest look at willingness requires us to examine the dynamics of what keeps us stuck. Four main concepts stand out for me when I look at this question. First, we need to look at the advantages, in any specific situation, of staying stuck. In all situations there are positives and negatives, and honestly looking at the advantages of remaining in the status quo may be the key to understanding, and curing, our inertia. Second, we need to realize that there is a very real physiological and psychological discomfort in change. Chaotic emotional patterns, in many cases deeply ingrained, may not be healthy or conducive to a thriving existence, but usually are familiar states of being. This familiarity, in some ironic way, carries its own set of comfort. Too, because being able to 'see' ourselves beyond the struggle already carries the biochemical impact of change; we may be unknowingly blocking ourselves from another vision of what is possible. Third, an honest look at the underlying fear associated with change can help dissipate that fear and help us move forward. Lastly, because difficult emotional states are most often judged as 'bad', 'dark' or 'afflictive', they are frequently suppressed or denied, and the underlying invitation for healing or growth is unrealized. Remember, for every difficult emotion there is usually an associated implicit memory yearning to be healed.

Weighing the advantages and disadvantages

An authentic look at willingness requires us to look at the advantages of staying stuck. You may find, after an honest look at all the advantages and disadvantages of change, that for you, right now, it is not advantageous. Or, you may decide that you prefer change, however, it required an honest examination of the payoffs of staying stuck to be able to move forward. In other words, I have had certain circumstances in my life that I had thought I wanted to change, but after examining the situation in its totality, including the payoffs in staying stuck, I decided that I needed to wait until I was truly willing and ready for that change to occur. Other times, when I honestly looked at the payoffs of staying stuck, I realized that they needed to be a trade-off for moving on. I was then more willing to make the necessary changes and sacrifices to do so.

Professing to want change, without a true examination of willingness, only increases our stress and blocks us off from our internal selves. We beat ourselves up for not taking action, when in reality we just are not ready. We need to be kind to ourselves in the process, and know that when the time is ready we will take appropriate action. Only when an examination leads us to an affirmative and receptive 'yes' are we ready to authentically allow the change to happen. Conversely, examining the payoffs of staying stuck, and genuinely deciding they are worth giving up, only serves as motivation to change and a blueprint to do so.

The payoffs of staying stuck can be tangible or psychological. Many times the psychological payoff, unfortunately, is that it feeds into our already ingrained perceptions of our self-identity or self-worth.

Travis is a 40-year-old college student. He lives at home with his mother, does not have a job, and hates himself because he feels he does not have the internal resources to move on. The payoff for him is that he is in a comfortable existence, he does not have to work on the discomfort of growth, and it plays into his perception of himself as being worthless — a perception he is comfortable and identifies with. When Travis examined the pay-offs of staying stuck he realized that moving on did not just mean getting a job and leaving the comforts of the home he knew, he realized it also meant being willing, and working to see himself in a new light. Once he addressed the deeper block, he was more willing to work through the discomfort of change.

Every person has many different opportunities in their lives to question authentic willingness. If you find yourself rationalizing: "This is the way I have always been," "This is because of my childhood," "This is what my former partner (or parent, or sibling, or child) used to do," but you are using it as a reason to stay stuck instead of an invitation to heal, you might question your willingness to change.

Susan has had some issues in her life that have been difficult for her. However, she has neither embraced the healing, nor been willing to let go of how they have defined her. Although she professes to want substantial change, her moment-to-moment choices do not reflect that. She quite often makes statements like, "That is just what my husband used to do," or, "All men only want one thing". She continually sees herself as a victim in relationships, and yet she admits she wants a romantic relationship above all else. When she looked at the payoff of staying stuck – being able to blame all men for her husband's shortcomings – she realized until she healed she would never be truly open to moving on.

Looking deeply enough, with honesty, may reveal some hidden inner subtleties that want to keep us in the status quo. Maybe it feels too vulnerable and risky to really be in the space we think we want. Maybe there is something that we hang on to – even an interpretation of our self – that we need to acknowledge is part of the dynamic before we can fully examine our willingness. Maybe there is a peripheral piece that we will have to give up. Maybe we really do not want what we think we want. These blocks often subconsciously hold us back, and then we blame ourselves for another failed attempt. Bringing them to light illuminates our path to better decide if it is one we want to take, or not.

The physiological discomfort of change

The second reason we choose to remain stuck is the physiological discomfort of change. As we learned earlier, certain emotional states carry biochemical reactions that flood our bodies and brains. It is as if our cells actually become addicted to that biochemical state. If fear or anger keeps me in a specific biochemical state, my cells crave that state because it is familiar and I will want to keep experiencing the associated emotional states because it feels comfortable.

Conversely, it actually feels physiologically uncomfortable to adapt to a new state. The discomfort is more a 'felt sense' of apprehension, newness, or unfamiliarity, rather than actual pain, but understanding and embracing it as part of the change process can be an important component of transformation. We can even learn to embrace it as an indication of growth. Most often, however, we just notice it does not feel good and revert back to emotional states that will deliver the chemistry we're used to. I love the quote, "Feel the fear, and do it anyway".

Willingness in this sense may be the understanding and awareness that there is a new biochemical state to establish, and it takes routine, acknowledgment, choice, and engagement to do that. In other words, when we are noticing, and disengaging, from reactive patterns as they happen, we need to also pay attention to the fact that it may be a little physiologically uncomfortable, and that is actually a good thing. This biochemical shift is necessary to reformulate our blood, and brain, to new ways of being.

Understanding that there might be biochemical discomfort through growth is important in the willingness process. Too, because the 'spiral of becoming' is a circular process, we can actually use an intentional shift in biochemistry to help facilitate change. Further, being able to 'see' our self in the transformed state already carries the biochemical imprint of that state and begins the process. Notice if you are reluctant to really 'see' your self beyond status quo. The moment you can *authentically* do this is the moment change begins.

Learning to ride a bicycle for Michael was quite a traumatic event, complete with tantrums and emotional upheavals. He would scream, yell, pick up the bicycle and throw it down again. It was almost as if the bicycle itself carried the version of himself (as a non-bicycle riding little boy) he so desperately wanted to leave behind. He HATED that bicycle and was quite dramatic about expressing it, but at the same time could not walk away from it. He was obsessed. I knew he was completely capable of it; he was just not ready to perceive himself that way. I tried reasoning, playing the 'cheerleader', instructing bicycle techniques; nothing worked.

And then his grandfather, 'Papa Ray' came along. Papa Ray excitedly expressed to Michael how cool it was that his bicycle was magical! Michael paused a moment, took in the new information about the magical nature of his bicycle, got on, and effortlessly rode away like he had been riding for years. The moment he was willing to perceive himself, and the bicycle, differently, was the moment he succeeded. It was the moment he created the physiological changes necessary for success.

Obviously, in Michael's case, he had assistance seeing himself beyond the struggle, but the concept remains true. The moment we are authentically willing, or able to truly see a vision of our self 'on the other side' is the moment it begins to happen in an adaptive sense. Too, we can also intentionally create the biochemical shifts that have the potential to shift a situation.

My children and I were going through an especially rough period, as with two adolescent boys can be typical, and I found myself much more frustrated and angry then usual. Of course this frustration and anger only made the situation a whole lot worse, but I felt completely justified by those responses, as my boys were making some very poor choices. Just at the point I felt completely overwhelmed, I decided to try an experiment.

Every day for the first 10 minutes when I woke up, and most often during my daily, sustained practice, I would completely focus on, and literally bathe myself in the gratitude I feel for my children. Admittedly, at first this was hard to do because of their current behavior, but I was persistent in my practice. Even though that practice was seemingly unrelated because it was at a different time of the day then when we were having difficulties, our relationship at that point began to transform. I found myself reacting, more often then not, from a caring stance, and my positive reactive behavior began to stimulate a change in their behavior.

They could feel the love, gratitude and care I felt for them, and responded positively. Because a good deal of my attention was on care, I could set down caring and safe guidelines, instead of angry reactive ones, and we all transformed in our relationship. The power in that change was obvious and truly the only initial behavior change was in my sustained focus of gratitude, but I could feel the difference. My reactive patterns were profoundly changed and we more often began to operate from love and care as the foundation of the relationship than from the opposite.

Ask yourself what it would really 'feel' like to already be in the condition or conditions you want to create, or free of the unease you want to be free of. Just being willing to feel those states begins to create the physiological conditions necessary for change. It is as if your brain believes you have already created those external conditions, and begins to act accordingly. However, once again, it needs to be authentic.

Fear and reluctance

Part of willingness involves staying grounded through the discomfort of growth. Even if it is positive growth there may be some aspect of fear of the unknown or fear of growing out of the familiar. Understand that this is part of the process. What is it about change that scares us? Is it the fear of the unknown? Is it that, although we may not like the current circumstance that we are trying to grow out of, we are accustomed to them; they feel familiar and that is what we know?

I love the metaphor of a car driving through the dark. When a car travels in the dark, its headlights light the road. Typically those headlights shine less than 200 feet in front of where the car is traveling, but those 200 feet are enough as long as the car is traveling in a safe manner. If I can ground myself in that metaphor when I feel the fear of growth I am a little more at ease. I know that I will see what I need to see as it is appropriate, and if I can stay centered, in a grounded internal experience, that transformation will come.

The invitation of difficult emotion

What about when, no matter how hard we try, we are consumed by difficult emotion? Are we 'bad', or 'weak' because those emotions we define as maladaptive keep re-appearing and we cannot seem to get to the point where we can see beyond the difficulty? As we learned quite in depth earlier in this book, states like that that cut us off from any hope for heartful engagement, or willingness for growth, are most often a cry for growth in their own right. In other words, somewhere beneath that maladaptive and reactive emotion is the invitation of an unbalanced implicit memory pattern longing to be healed, or a need craving to be met.

What does this have to do with willingness? Many times our own blame, shame or judgment of that which wants to be healed, ironically, prevents the healing. The willingness lies in the ability to recognize, accept and take action on the invitation, and hold it all from a grounded and loving place of exploration, healing and self-appreciation.

Authentic willingness requires a fundamental internal shift. And for this shift to take place we also need to look at the stories we tell ourselves and examine if we are willing to create new ones. We need to examine if we are truly willing to allow different perceptions of ourselves, work through the discomfort of change, cultivate heartfully engaged ways of being, and embrace our own healing.

Exercise and Reflection # 11 - Questions of willingness

After reading the previous section stop and pause. Reflect on, for you, what are genuine considerations of willingness. Which of the components of willingness, discussed above, speak most to you? How might you engage them? How do the questions of willingness play out for you in your own life? In what areas of your life would it be helpful to bring a heartful awareness to your own questions of willingness? Reflect and process in a way that is appropriate for you.

The Language we speak

As we have seen throughout this book, attention molds us. And the language we speak, both internally and externally, largely forms our attention. Heartful awareness both determines the words we speak, and is profoundly affected by them. Words are powerful. Words come from thoughts and feelings and create more thoughts and feelings. Every word we say, or thought we think, to ourselves, and others, create measurable changes in our neural networks and biochemistry, and become encoded as our typical way of thinking and functioning. In other words, the words we say, and the stories we tell, silently, and to others, wire our brain and body to think, perceive, and behave in accordance with those words. Inner and outer words mold us.

We use words in our constant personal chatter, catastrophizing, made up conversations in our head, or creating and replaying our personal stories.

We use words with, or about others, and in the stories we hold about others. We use words in the way that we interpret events. To say it another way, we are constantly perceiving our version of reality and telling ourselves stories, either spoken, or silently, about what we perceive. These words, then, if left unchecked, become powerful determinants of who we are becoming. Again, every thought or feeling we have creates a cascade of biochemical, electrical, and neural reaction patterns that permeate our body. The stories we tell our self, our internal words, and the words we use in communication with others, are powerful conductors of this physiologic cascade.

Your brain does not know the difference between what is real and what is imagined. And will adapt accordingly.

The nature of inner chatter

How do you speak to yourself? What are the stories you tell? What are the 'scripts' you write?

It is estimated that we have somewhere between 50,000 and 80,000 thoughts per day. What makes this statistic even more staggering, is that most of those thoughts are negative, and most are repetitive. They are almost never in the moment, nor really appropriate to our momentary reality. When we ground this information in the fact that we, as humans, are systems of adaptation, and will reflect and embrace any routine experience as our new way of being, we begin to see the phenomenal impact our 'words' have.

Our brain does not know the difference between what is real and what is vividly imagined. Our bodies and brains, then, reflect and adapt to what we are continually 'telling' ourselves. Our amygdala gets activated, and our synapses fire and get stronger with the information they are fed. The laws of associative memory, and state dependent recall kick in, and our 'chatter', unknowingly to us, subconsciously takes us to another place and time. Our conscious mind wants to ground it in the here and now, and we take off with the chatter. And the chatter consumes us.

How and why does this all happen? Remember our amygdalas and fear response systems are giant databases of, mostly subconscious, emotional information. Their job is to constantly scan our environment and release feelings associated with any threat they perceive. And their function, at least in the fear response system's role, is to perceive almost everything as a threat. When it reaches our conscious mind the chatter starts its engine. The huge problem, and main point here, is that when we take off with the chatter we begin to cement those ways of being and perceiving. And we have the potential to do this almost 80,000 times a day!

We all have endless loops of chatter, and we cannot begin to be grounded in a heartfully engaged way of being, through most moments of the day, until we look at the impact of our chatter.

Growing up, my father was my hero. His presence prompted some of the greatest times in my life, although there were also times when he had difficulty showing love, which also impacted me. For a long time this was a deeply held trigger, and I have worked very hard to heal from it. However, sometimes the chatter takes on a life of its own.

Whenever someone does something that I interpret as hitting this 'bruised bone', I can feel my body responding with anxiety, and then here comes the chatter. The chatter tells me all the things that are wrong with the current situation. The chatter tells me it is valid to feel the way I do. The chatter tells me "here we go again – get out quick." Chatter, chatter and more chatter. The chatter creates more biochemical reactions to validate my point, and creates brain synapse patterns that reinforce my current thought processes. In all honesty, I cannot tell if my response is appropriate for the current situation because the cascade of inner chatter clouds my perception, and has taken me on it is own journey of chaos.

With the concept of inner chatter it is important to be able to determine where on the continuum of the 80,000 thoughts the primary trigger lies. In other words, if it is very strong, and forcefully present chatter it may be an indication that there is something underlying that needs to be healed. However, given the fact that our brain is wired to be hyper reactive to threat, and can do so 80,000 times today, most of that chatter is just empty chatter. And takes on a life of its own.

Again, the HEAR scale presented in chapter 4 may help you make that distinction. For me, the easiest way to tell is if it will not 'shut up'. In other words, I have worked very hard to train myself to notice my chatter. When I notice it is off on one of its crazy loops, and I can easily quiet it and become heartfully engaged in the present moment, I do so. But if, no matter how hard I try it will not quiet, I know something is begging for attention. Regardless, the chatter itself only serves to worsen our reactivity. Taking off on its negative spirals is never helpful, and only worsens, and causes resulting adaptations in our mind/body/spirit dynamic.

Notice the chatter, maybe even with a little humor or curiosity, hear its message, and re-engage in the present with heartful awareness. With full engagement and presence in the current moment, find something to appreciate, love, or have compassion for, or lovingly consider what it is in yourself that is screaming for attention. Micro-moments add up, and the more moments you can be 'out of' the chatter loop, the more you can cultivate heartful presence.

Catastrophizing

Catastrophizing, that is, always imagining the worst that could happen in any situation, is it is own specific type of inner chatter. When we anticipate catastrophe, we play scenarios in our heads of all the things that could go wrong, might go wrong, or assuredly will go wrong. The 'loops' of chatter start, and they play over and over in our brain until our brain believes them. The more vividly, and more often we imagine a negative scenario, the more we biochemically and neurally respond as if that scenario has happened. And this makes it more likely. Most of the time we have no idea of this harmful impact, we let it consume us and dominate our thoughts, and unknowingly make our bodies and brains more capable of creating the same catastrophe or scenario we fear.

Conversations in our head

Similar to catastrophizing are the imaginary conversations we play in our head. We may be anticipating a conversation or interaction with another, replaying what we should have, or might have said in a past conversation, or just playing out various scenarios based on our current reactivity. Again, what we do not realize is every time we play out these conversations in our head, our body and brain are reacting as if those conversations are happening. Our bodies are constantly reacting and adapting to our silent, or spoken 'words', and if those words are harsh so will be our physiological responses.

These conversations create an all-over physiological system response and cause changes in our perception and awareness as if they have happened. In other words, our bodies and brains believe they are happening and respond accordingly. They further aggravate the reactivity of our own physiologic system, or state of being, skew our perception of the current circumstance, and further form our judgments. They are decidedly different than heartfully engaged awareness. And, again, most of the time we unknowingly succumb to their detrimental effects. They do not allow for a new narrative.

Exercise and Reflection # 12 - Inner chatter

How do you use your inner words? What is the nature of your inner chatter? How do catastrophizing and inner conversations dominate your thought process? How can you better cultivate present moment, and heartful awareness so you are not consumed by the mostly repetitive, and mostly negative, thoughts that consume our day? Process and reflect in a way that is helpful and appropriate for you.

The 'stories' we tell

Through our constant perception of reality we create stories and narratives that are consistent with our 'programming'. Again, these are through the lenses of our own personal experience, and coupled with the idea that the more we 'tell' the stories, the more they are 'cemented', we leave little room for new interpretation or new growth. In essence, we just perpetuate more of the same. Too, most of our stories come from ingrained 'parts' of us that want us to believe their version of reality. We tell stories about ourselves, we tell stories about others, and we tell stories about our relationships. Sometimes they are verbal, but most often they are held as our own internal narrative.

And this narrative has power. We begin to believe them, fortify them, and perpetuate them.

Further, even when there is some truth to a story, there are usually multiple stories surrounding it. In other words, the story we tell might only be a partial piece, but it is made the only story by the way we tell it. If 'both' are true, but the one we tell becomes our reality, we may need to rethink our narratives. Too, because the nature of inner chatter is based on our fear response system, and is primarily negative, the threat-based story will always be the story that is more prominent. It takes awareness, and attention, to develop a heartfully engaged way of rethinking our stories.

We are constantly constructing our reality with our words and our stories. And we tell our stories from a selective truth. In the world of embodied science, we are quite often literally poisoning ourselves with our own stories. Our nervous, and biochemical systems habituate to any story we tell, and, in the words of Fred Luskin, maybe we need to start telling more honest stories[50]. Too, the stories we tell create expectations of circumstances based on their inherent nature. In other words, if I expect, and act as if a narrative were true, I am much more likely to unintentionally create that condition; my brain and body have already experienced it as the truth.

Robert was a very bright and capable young man. He seemingly had everything going for him, but he was absolutely convinced that every time he walked into any room, everybody in that room was judging him. He was well on his way to professional success, but he could not get over the insecurity of feeling like he was constantly being judged. He told this story to himself over and over again, never realizing that each time he told it he made himself believe it all the more. When he looked at his own reactivies, and the fact that this narrative had become such a big part of who he was, he realized he had no rational reason to believe it was true. It was a huge moment of realization, and transformation for him. Even though the story was originally based on a little insecurity, the story had completely taken on a life of its own. Once he realized this, he felt such a huge shift; he was able to not only tell another, more honest story, he was also able to easily deal with the initial insecurity it was based on.

We have stories about ourselves, and we have stories about others. The more we tell these stories, or live these narratives, the more we confine our reality to living their experience. In addition to telling our narratives, we also have our 'scripts'.

The scripts we write

The scripts we write are based on our expectations from the narratives we tell. In other words, if I am always telling the same story, I behave and act in such a way that that story is true. Our scripts, then, are the way we play out our narratives, and just perpetuate that reality. We write scripts for ourselves, we write scripts for others. If you are using phrases like "This always happens to me", "This relationship is just like my last", " I never can succeed", or "You always do this", "This is just the way you are", there is a good chance your stories, and resulting scripts, are at play. Our scripts may be based on a false, or skewed interpretation of reality, yet we play them out as if they were true.

Too, when we write scripts for others we quite often unknowingly manifest what we expect. In other words, we anticipate, and then act 'as if' what we expect is a given. Just as we have parts, other people do as well. Many times our scripts for others are based on the 'part' or 'parts' of them that we expect to show up. Because there is a phenomenal amount of subconscious processing in the mirror neurons in our brain, our expectations reflect back on that other person, their brain registers our expectations, and we more likely pull that 'part' into the mix. Imagine the possibilities if we expected somebody's Inner Being to show up instead of a preconceived part.

Replaying our Stories

When something unpleasant happens, do you constantly replay the story over and over again in your head? How often do you re-tell the story to willing listeners for attention? Do you somehow become the product of your stories? Retelling a story to deal with it, heal it and release it is a very healthy thing. This is a very different dynamic than retelling, recreating, or replaying a story for the dramatic effect. In all honestly, is there part of you that thrives on the drama, or feels comfortable in the stress it produces?

Replaying our stories re-creates the neural and biochemical patterns as if the experience were happening again. Also, recall what impact any repeated experience has on our bodies, brains and psyches. Constantly replaying any event, or any negative interpretation of an event, only further 'hardwires' it in our perceptions of self, and the likelihood of similar future events. Too, remember our previous conversation about the impact of cortisol, and low-grade cortisol baths. Because cortisol has a 12 hour ½ life, it only takes little doses, or 'baths' all day long to keep the levels sky high. And cortisol baths are primarily due to our thought process.

Years ago, I had a very toxic boss. He was toxic to most everybody in the department, and some people even left their jobs to get out of that environment. He was famous for creating altercations with almost everyone he came in contact with. One altercation could produce a substantial cortisol rush.

There were some challenging issues in our department at the time; issues that I felt passionately about and were very near and dear to my heart. As my boss was prone to saying things without thinking, one run-in with him would leave me feeling like my job and the program I had created were both in jeopardy of being eliminated. Needless to say, because this was such an emotional issue for me, one five minute conversation with him in the morning would flood my body with cortisol and other stress hormones, and send my brain reeling with "what ifs". Catastrophizing and negative chatter would overcome me, complete with all the associated brain synapse patterns.

If I had known about heartful awareness at the time, I could have gauged my reactivity right then, cultivated a compassionate posture towards myself, and the situation, determined my needs, and saved myself from several hours of cortisol flood. What I did instead was catastrophize. What I did instead was replay the altercation over and over in my head all day long, including all the horrible resulting scenarios I could imagine. What I did instead was tell about the exchange to any colleague who would feel sorry for me, activate harmful brain synapse patterns, and send cortisol shots throughout my body all day long like an I.V drip.

In the evening, nearly ten hours later, I would get to re-tell my story in detail. I wanted my family to feel sorry for me. I was not re-telling the story to process it, figure out solutions, and let it go. I was re telling my story to be the drama queen, bask in the fear and negative possibilities, get sympathy from my family, and re-play feeling persecuted. I would take at least 20 minutes to describe a five-minute conversation. Thus, with a vivid re-telling ten hours after the event, I was producing at least enough cortisol to take me back to the original level, which would give me another twelve hours of cortisol! In essence, I had produced enough cortisol from a five minute altercation, by my catastrophizing, reliving and retelling, to last me for twenty four hours - just enough time to have another altercation the next morning. And the truth is my boss was over it within five minutes after the initial event, as I am sure he was off to harassing someone else.

Fred Luskin says reliving our stories like this is like drinking poison and expecting the other person to die[51].

All this catastrophizing, reliving and retelling did nothing to help me deal with the problem constructively, but its wear and tear on my body, brain and psyche was tremendous. I was carrying the stress of that relationship 24/7, and it did not need to be that way. Even in sharing with my family, I could have 'vented' for the purposes of letting go, or processed what constructive action I needed to take.

Had I known then what I know now, it could have been very different. Had I known then what I know now, I could have saved myself many hours of severely damaging neural and cortisol effects. Had I known then what I know now, I could have engaged in heartful awareness towards myself and 'held' myself as I would have a best friend going through the same difficulty.

Exercise and Reflection # 13 - Stories and scripts

What narratives, or stories do you tell about yourself? What about others? What are the scripts that you write for yourself or others? Are you allowing room for growth, or another, more heartful story to be told? Considering all the information you've read this far in this book, how can you bring a deeper sense of heartful awareness into your life's narratives? What could happen if you could let go of your less-heartful stories? Process and reflect in a way that is appropriate for you.

Communication with others

Most of the time our communication with others is based on the narratives we tell, about ourselves, about the circumstance, and about the other person. When you think that every person has somewhere between 50,000 to 80,000 thoughts a day, and when you get two people in communication together they have somewhere between 100,000 and 160,000 thoughts between them, each with their own 'stories' and 'scripts', it is amazing they can hear each other at all. Couple this, with the image of two activated amygdalae, and we can see what a challenge heartfully engaged communication is. Further, if there are more than two people in conversation, the math becomes staggering.

We often unknowingly sabotage relationships by the way we speak to each other. Every word we speak carries the corresponding brain reaction pattern, and when we use hurtful, evaluative, judgmental, or harmful language those patterns are strengthened in both the speaker and the listener. Words themselves can be violent because of the neural influences, emotional reactions, and corresponding adaptations that begin to occur in the bodies, brains and hearts of all those in communication. In short, words matter immensely.

Let us imagine how this might play out. Any perception, interpretation or evaluation we may have of what is going on, or of other people's behaviors, is completely filtered through our own implicit memory, and reactivities. That is, our amygdalae constantly perceive, make meaning, and evaluate through all of our past programming, especially when we are triggered, or in any 'off-balance' state. Remember the power of the congruity of moods, or state dependent recall. Our brain is unknowingly taking us to a place that is colored by the lens of our emotional past. Yet we thoroughly believe its evaluation is the correct one. And we use language that reflects our interpretation or evaluation.

We may make statements like "You are too this" or "You are too that" or "You do this" or "You do that" or any other form of evaluation of the other person or the circumstance. Even questions like "Why can't you do this?" are still evaluative statements; and assume we have the correct interpretation, or answer to the circumstance. When we use blaming, shaming, judgmental, or even slightly evaluative statements, they are coming through our programmed perceptions with the inherent message that we, of course, have the only valid interpretation of 'the truth.'

And, again, every word we speak carries corresponding neural, and biochemical imprints. When we use evaluative or judgmental statements, we further wire our perceptions, and flood our body with harmful biochemicals, which just exacerbate and perpetuate our triggered state. The words, then, invariably further trigger the person or persons we are in communication with, because they, of course, have their own interpretation of events.

If we can take a step back, foster some non-reactivity, remember that the perceptions of all parties are coming from their specific congruity of moods, state dependent recall, and implicit memory, we can better heartfully engage and determine the underlying needs of the people involved. If we can be mindful of the stories we tell, and the scripts we write, without falling victim to them, we can cultivate a more heartfully engaged way of responding.

If we do not, we will most likely revert to violent words that will only perpetuate or aggravate the 'status quo' nature of communication. And our 'spiral of becoming,' in relationship, will begin to spiral down the drain.

Marshall Rosenberg, the creator of non-violent communication, identifies specific types of communication that block compassion. He includes in this "life alienating communication" moralistic judgments, comparisons, and denial of responsibility or placing responsibility on the other person. He also includes demands, and statements that someone 'deserves' a negative outcome or punishment. He calls this the "language of wrongness" and stresses that this type of language encourages people to look outside of themselves for roots and causes rather than be in contact with their own feelings and needs[52].

What would heartful awareness look like in communication with another? First, it would underscore the fundamental truth that 'reality' is always filtered through the perception, or current emotional state of those doing the observing. And hold that truth with heartful engagement. This would allow for different interpretations without evaluation, blame, shame or judgment. Second, it would acknowledge that most triggers or reactivities (those states below the line on the heartful awareness chart) for both, or all parties involved, are usually due to implicit programming, and signify an underlying sensitivity or unmet need. It would hold that in heartful engagement as well. Third, it would invite the parties involved to heartfully engage their own inner processes first, and then those of the other.

Marshall Rosenberg, in his system of nonviolent communication, suggest the following four steps:

1) A non-evaluative statement of the problem
2) Looking inward to identify your own feelings
3) Voicing the unmet need
4) Making a request based on that need

All of the steps are to be done without evaluation, blame, shame, or judgment. Although the steps seem simple, to truly employ them without evaluation, blame, shame or judgment is a challenge. When we truly pay attention to the violent, or accusatory nature of our words, we may be surprised. In his book Nonviolent Communication: A Language of Life, Rosenberg lists words that are evaluative in nature, and very commonly used when we communicate. I urge you to study these lists, and also pay careful attention to the evaluative nature of the words we typically use in communication. Evaluative and judgmental words permeate our interactions with one another.

HEART in Communication might go something like this: Notice your reactive patterns or triggers when you are in communication with another, and disengage from their hold.

Refocus your embodied reaction by releasing your eyes, your shoulders, your chest, and take a few intentional breaths. This will calm your system and distance you from your reactivity.

Nurture a sense of heartful awareness for both yourself, and the other. While being mindful of the stories we tell, the scripts we write, and the influence of our perception and implicit memory, heartfully engage and identify your own sensitivities and underlying needs, and then those of the other. Pause and reflect on what your sincere feelings and needs are in the situation, and without blame, shame, or judgment, make a request.

This is a complete paradigm shift from the way we usually communicate, and it takes sincere willingness to disengage from the reactive semantics to which we are conditioned. Go to your HEART and choose a different response. Sincerely focus on, and express what your underlying feelings and needs are, without evaluation or blame. Your brain, your body, and your spirit will reap the benefits. So will your relationships. Your communication will be rooted in your calm and connection system more often than not, and heartful awareness will be allowed to flourish.

Non – verbal communication

"What you do speaks so loudly that I cannot hear what you say." This quote, attributed to Ralph Waldo Emerson, perfectly describes the power of nonverbal communication. Nonverbal communication is comprised of all of the ways we typically communicate that are beyond the scope of words. It is estimated by research that 93% of communication is actually non-verbal, and the words we speak only comprise 7%[53].

These numbers were discovered through research by Dr. Albert Mehrabian, and presented in his book *Silent Messages: Implicit Communication of Emotions and Attitudes*. He also shows that non-verbal aspects of communication include the tonal and vocal elements we bring to the words we say, which comprises 38% of communication, and facial expressions, gestures, posture etc., that comprise 55% of communication[54]. Although putting specific and quantifiable numbers on human behavior is a daunting task, the fact of the matter remains that most communication is nonverbal. And, in fact, it is the most crucial aspect of communication. Most researchers estimate the percentage of communication that is nonverbal to be somewhere between 60 and 90%.

What does this have to do with heartful awareness? From an embodied perspective: everything. We have learned throughout this book that our bodies are intrinsically connected to our subconscious mind, and, in fact, are often more honest than our conscious mind. Words come from our conscious mind, and nonverbal communication is linked to our emotions, implicit behaviors and subconscious mind. Our bodies know. Our bodies will tell us if we ask them. And our bodies are constantly telling others, whether we know it or not, and whether we like it or not.

How we communicate with others is powerful, and the power lies far beyond the words. To have honest and heartful communication with others we must have honest and heartful communication with ourselves. If our body and tonality are saying one thing, and our words are saying another, we are sending inauthentic and mixed messages. These mixed messages are a symbol of brain dis-integration because the conscious words are saying something other than what is authentically felt. The listener also experiences brain disintegration because a message is received much in the same manner it is sent. In other words, our subconscious or implicit programming are picking up messages sent in that manner, and our conscious brain is hearing, and trying to make sense of the verbal words.

It just feels off.

And we know it.

As in nonviolent communication, when we bring heartful awareness to what we're feeling, and try to articulate it with our words, we engage the part of the brain that integrates both hemispheres. We experience brain integration and a felt sense of calm. Because our body language, then, matches our verbal words, the listener also experiences brain integration, and is able to engage more deeply in the communication.

Too, heartful awareness combined with nonverbal communication invites us into a deeper level of communication overall. As a listener, if we are able to truly engage with all of the communication taking place, not just the words being spoken, we can 'hold' the speaker in a deeper state of heartful awareness. In other words, we may be able to 'hear', and intuitively know, what the speaker is communicating, far beyond the words that are being spoken.

Christina and Ally were partners in a workshop on deep listening. The paired groups were asked to engage in activity where one of the partners spoke and the other listened. The instructions were for the listener to 'hear' all of what was being communicated by paying attention to the verbal words, all of the nonverbal communication, and the energy of the exchange. Christina, deep in a state of heartful awareness, spoke of her worry about her husband's newly diagnosed illness. She spoke of worry and uncertainty. Ally, quietly and without interrupting, listened to all of what was being communicated.

When it was Ally's turn to respond, and relate to Christina what she 'heard', she shared with Christina that she felt like her body language and words did not match. Although her words spoke of worry and uncertainty, what Ally picked up from Christina's body language was a deep trust that everything would be okay. When Ally pointed this out to Christina, Christina cried with relief. She realized that, yes; she truly did feel like everything would be okay. She had not let herself consciously recognize this because she felt that she should be worried. But when she truly tuned into the deepest parts of herself, she knew that all would be okay. It took someone reading her body language, and paying attention to all of her nonverbal communication, to help her tap into what she intuitively knew to be true.

Heartful awareness in the context of nonverbal communication invites us to tap into the deepest sense of ourselves. When we are sending communication outwards, it invites us to tune into our body to 'hear' what it is conveying, identify our feelings and needs from a non-reactive and accepting posture, and connect to a heartful way of relaying that information. When we are receiving communication, heartful awareness invites us into a deeper way of listening. It invites us to 'hold' all of what is being communicated, including all the verbal and non-verbal information being transmitted, and, from a compassionate and non-judgmental posture, receive 'all' of what is being conveyed.

Exercise and Reflection # 14 - Communication with others

Process and reflect on some instances in your own life that could benefit from heartful awareness applied to communication. Do you routinely fall victim to negative communication patterns? What are they? What are the typical situations where this occurs? What might be your underlying feelings and needs in these situations? How can you honestly express these feelings and needs without falling victim to destructive communication patterns? What can you learn from the previous section on nonverbal communication? How do the dynamics of nonverbal behavior play out for you in your communication with others? How can you use the previous information to better apply heartful awareness throughout all of your communication? Process and reflect in a way that is appropriate for you.

Subjective interpretation

I love the quote: "when you change the way you look at things, the things you look at change.[55]" Subjective interpretation, or the story we tell in the moment, has a powerful effect on the moment, the outcome, and any hope we have of being heartfully engaged in both. In most situations we have a choice of how to perceive or interpret that situation. Quite often one way is associated with our fear response drive, and then the other is associated with our calm and connection drive.

Too, when we keep the 'spiral of becoming' in mind, the one that holds our attention is the one that begins to shape our reality. And, because each moment unfolds from the previous, whether our brains are flooded with cortisol or nurtured with oxytocin profoundly affects every moment's subsequent choice. And the choice after that. But it has to be authentic.

My kids and I used to love to take road trips. Music was always a fundamental part of these trips, as we would drive down the road and sing at the top of our lungs. The music kept me awake, alert, and us all engaged in a fun and celebratory atmosphere. I would spend hours before every trip just getting the perfect mix of music prepared.

Once, when my kids were still fairly young, we were heading out on a road trip through the desert. I wanted to make sure we left early enough that we were through the dangerous part of a two-lane highway before dark. I also wanted to make sure we got far enough to find a place to spend the night, because in the desert there were not many choices of where to stay. I had many hours of music ready to keep me awake and alert.

Everything that could go wrong seemed to be going that way. We had delay after delay, and I was beginning to get worried about our timing. It was already dark, we were just heading into the desert, and we still had many hours to go on our journey. We were out in the middle of nowhere, and the music broke. And it started to rain quite heavily. And we had no cell phone reception.

I knew if I got upset and my brain got flooded with cortisol I would not be able to think clearly, and would become overwhelmed with the situation. I also knew that my kids would become upset, and one of them suffered from higher levels of anxiety. I knew it was very important to keep the three of us in a heartful, and calm state of mind, for we had hours to go and very rough conditions to go through. They were little, and scared. And so was their mother.

I began to invite them to look at everything that was going wrong in humorous light. I was also pointing out all the things that we could be grateful for. We made it a game to find the good, or opportunity, in every challenge. Soon we were laughing, and engaging in a whole different way. We were actually laughing at all the setbacks. I knew how important it was for my clarity and emotional stability, especially given the conditions we were facing, to keep nurturing my calm and connection system instead of my threat response system.

Then the windshield-wiper blade broke. I actually figured out a way to fix it with a spoon I found in the trunk – I would have never been able to figure out that one had my brain been flooded with cortisol! When we arrived at our planned destination, we found a town with absolutely no vacancies in any hotel or motel within many miles. I was still desperate to find some music to keep me awake, and found an old Christmas CD in the trunk when I found the spoon to fix the windshield wiper.

Miraculously I found a way to get our only CD working. And we continued to drive down the highway, for many more hours, in the dark, in the desert, in the rain, singing Christmas carols at the top of our lungs on a memorable August night.

Much of the time we have a choice in how to interpret events. And much of the time both interpretations are true. However, the one we focus on is the one that begins to determine our subsequent moments.

While the above story certainly was not a catastrophic event, all the little troublesome events along the way could have caused significant frustration, they slowly, but surely, would have changed the nature of the event itself. The domino effect would have been in full force, and if our perceptions had changed, each event would have increased frustration, and soon it would have been an absolutely miserable time. Too, if I would have become overwhelmed and anxious, it could have been a very dangerous situation.

Sometimes, subjective interpretation greatly influences the way we experience life as a whole. A student of mine, whom I have talked with extensively, struggles greatly with subjective interpretation. She only allows herself to be so happy, and quite often subconsciously sabotages events by the way she interprets them. She may take an event that is 80 to 90% positive, and keep the focus on the one negative aspect to invalidate everything that was good about it. In that way, she creates all the corresponding physiological adaptations of her interpretations, which just perpetuates more of the same.

This dynamic plays itself out over and over again in our everyday lives. Subjective interpretation, or how we choose to see things, can profoundly change what happens in subsequent moments. When we interpret events we create an internal experience of that interpretation. That internal experience, then, creates all the measurable changes in our bodies, brains, and psyches that determine who we are becoming.

Subjective interpretation with regard to heartful awareness is about choosing to interpret events free from our trigger points, reactivities and implicit perceptions. Subjective interpretation, through the lens of heartful awareness, allows a conscious choice of gratitude, joy, compassion and love. Subjective interpretation is not about suppressing that which needs to be healed, it is about embracing heartful opportunities. It is about looking through the lens of heartfulness, when we can, and when it is appropriate, and interpreting our life's events from there. Interpretations matter. And bringing interpretations of compassion, love, joy, or gratitude in to our life changes the experience of being alive.

Exercise and Reflection # 15 - Subjective interpretation

Genuinely and honestly reflect on your tendencies in the area of subjective interpretation. Do you, at a deep level, genuinely allow heartful awareness to play a part in your interpretation of events? Many times, and most events, have a good level of subjectivity if we look deeply and sincerely enough. Looking at subjective interpretation through the lens of heartful awareness for our selves, or external events, allows for the emergence of a different reality. What specific events or situations in your life could change with a heartful lens?

If it feels comfortable to do so, pick a specific event that you could have interpreted differently. Explain it in detail, including the different interpretations you might have been able to make. How might the outcome have been different? What are the ways that you might bring heartful awareness into the way that you interpret every day events? Process and reflect in a way that is appropriate for you.

Conclusion

Opportunities for heartful awareness play themselves out every day in the tapestry of our lives. Every day we are provided with openings; tangible and specific ways to weave heartful awareness into the threads of our existence. By taking 'baby steps' of presence, engagement, interpretations, and intentional ways of being in the small moments of our life, our 'spiral of becoming' becomes one of lived heartful awareness. Again, our path to action is paved one step at a time. It takes willingness, awareness in our words, conversations, and actions, and an acute understanding that every moment is a moment of heartful potential.

Create a plan to bring heartful awareness to the nature of your language. What would happen if you could notice and refocus your catastrophizing or inner conversations before they consume you? How will you remind yourself to pay attention to their activity? How can you begin to tell more heartful stories and write more heartful scripts?

Noticing the heartful opportunity of every moment, acknowledging our level of willingness, and taking action when we can, begins to open up new and heartful spaces, and gives us a defined direction for our heartful journey to progress.

7

Moving Forward

We have seen throughout this book that a different way of being in this world is possible, and that heartful awareness and engagement is the path to get us there. The cultivation of heartfulness completely transforms our inner and outer lives to states of calm, clarity, connection, expansiveness, full inner potential, and a larger way of living. We are not ruled by stress, anxiety, emotional chaos, or our fear response system. We are grounded in our calm and connection system, and we have seen that it takes extreme intentionality to develop this system to its fullest promise.

We have also seen that our bodies are the vehicles for our 'humanness', and, as such, are beautiful systems of adaptation. They are always under the influence of 'the spiral of becoming', constantly adapting to our inner experience, and providing opportunities to more effectively live whatever that inner experience is. We have taken a journey through what it means to truly embody heartful awareness, how it profoundly changes the adaptations in our 'humanness', and the foundational differences it can make in who we are, and how we function in the world.

We have seen the power of intentionally engaging life generating states of being, cultivating micro-moments of opportunity, and the importance of contemplative practice. We have considered the all-important aspect of healing when something may be blocking us. And, in the last chapter, we began to look at important ways, in our everyday lives, to make us more available to heartful awareness. Those included observing the power, opportunity and presence we bring to every moment, genuinely examining our willingness to engage heartful transformation, and the incredible impact of our inner chatter, outer words, stories, scripts, and interpretations.

We have looked at the ever-pervasive challenge of action, and the fact that until action happens everything remains the same. The law of adaptation tells us that if we do not take action to be different, we won't be. However, it is the moments of our life that create our days, and our days that create our years. Small changes add up, and the degree to which we are willing to change our day-to-day ways of being, and the level of heartful engagement we bring to every moment, has a powerful and governing effect on the essence of our existence.

And, again, action in our sense is not about forcing our external lives into attunement, it is about changing from the inside out. It is about allowing a sense of heartful awareness, and heartful engagement, to begin to transform us from the level of our cells, all the way out to our lived existence. Too, there are simple changes and adjustments we can make in our daily lives that allow us to be far more capable of tapping into, and living from a state of heartful awareness. Action, on this part of our journey, concerns simple life adjustments that allow within us a calmer and more generative state for the internal to flourish, and heartful awareness to flow more naturally in our day-to-day existence.

How do we, more often than not, and not just in the midst of practice, live from a heartfully aware state in our everyday lives? How is heartful awareness formed? And transformed? Sometimes, it is the simple things we do that make the most powerful difference. Simple daily changes, and attention to our everyday involvements create new neural networks, new biochemical make-ups and new physiological operating systems. These new operating systems, then, make us much more physiologically and emotionally capable of being, and acting, heartfully aware. In other words, if I feel good, and I feel good about my life and my surroundings, I am much more likely to be able to tap into the deeper and more heartful parts of myself.

This chapter is about cultivating tangible day-to-day experience to better ground us in our calm and connection system. While the last chapter dealt with more overarching concepts, this one focuses on very specific considerations, and practices in our day-to-day life that allow our sense of heartfulness to flourish. It is about making small changes that add up in our day-to-day existence, and make us much more capable of tapping into the deeper parts of ourselves. It is about creating the conditions, or the fertile soil, for our 'seeds of consciousness' to grow in life generating ways. It is about creating the circumstances to better allow our heartful awareness to blossom, for our self and others. It is about quieting the stress and emotional chaos of our external lives so we can better hear what we know to be heartfully true.

In it, we will entertain the idea that our overall level of 'wellness' profoundly affects our ability to engage in heartful awareness, for both ourselves, and others. And, as such, we will look at the dimensions that comprise true 'wellness', look at specifics of each of those dimensions, and examine our strengths, and areas we would like to improve in each of the dimensions. We will look at our 'energy diet', or the things that we expose ourselves to on a daily basis that either detract from, or add to our overall ability to ground ourselves in our calm and connection system and our over all heartful awareness. We will look at self-care and its powerful contribution to our heartful stability. We will focus on gaining some clarity on issues we might be dealing with, and consider our deepest held values. And, finally, we will examine how we might move forward to create heartfully engaged awareness as a foundational part of our existence.

This chapter is experiential in nature. Throughout this book we have looked at transformation through the science of embodiment, and we have seen that the fundamental determining factor is experience. And, in fact, it is experience that is constantly forming us, and reforming us, whether we know it or not, or like it or not. Transformation through heartful awareness is completely dependent on a certain type of experiential presence we bring to the moments of our life. 'Knowledge about' heartful awareness, even if it is interesting and motivating, is not the catalyst that changes us. Throughout our journey we have been slowly transitioning from learning about the profound transformational possibilities of heartful awareness, to examining how they may play out in our own life. This chapter invites you deeper into that process, and deeper into your own experience. The personal processing in this chapter is of utmost importance in assimilating all that our journey has had to offer, and preparing you to move forward and make it your own.

There is a moment right before stepping out of a labyrinth that invites us to pause. The invitation of the pause is to reflect and 'cement' into our awareness all we have learned on the journey in, and prepare to bring it out into our everyday world. As we prepare to exit our metaphorical labyrinth, the invitation of this chapter is to personalize your experience in a way that is true to you. The focus is on your own personal experiences with the material, and the invitation to fully embody them in a way that allows a sense of heartful awareness to grow in your own life, however it is appropriate. The focus is on personalizing your own journey in preparation of stepping out of our labyrinth, and back into your lived experience; but changed from the voyage. This chapter is less of me, and more of you. And it requires your personal, heartful, and experiential engagement.

Dimensions of wellness

What makes a person well? And what does wellness have to do with heartfulness? As we saw in chapter 4, the concept of wellness exists on a continuum. Being well is a state of living that encompasses far more than just 'not being sick,' or existing at 'okay enough.' It is more than just the absence of illness; it is an optimal state of wellbeing. High levels of wellness are individual for each person, but carry with them very specific corresponding psychological and physiological states. In other words, when we are living from a high sense of wellbeing our bodies, brains, and psyches know it, reflect it back, and cultivate capabilities for more of the same. It is a pathway to optimal living, maximizing our potential, and living our life to the fullest. Cultivating a high sense of wellbeing gives us a healthier quality of life, and allows us to flourish and thrive.

Too, wellness is generally used to mean a healthy balance of the mind, body and spirit. It is a view of health that emphasizes the state of the entire being; emotional health, mental health, physical health, social health, and spiritual health are all important components. It is an integration, or balance of various aspects of a whole person. While, in reality, these components cannot be separated, it is important to recognize that each play a part in our foundational level of true wellness.

Emotional wellness is generally seen as the ability to feel, and express, the entire range of human emotions without being controlled by their reactivity. Mental or intellectual health is seen as the ability to gather, process, recall, and communicate information. Physical wellness is described as our best, or optimal physical functioning. It includes all of the bodies physiological systems and general health. Social wellness is seen as the ability to have satisfying personal relationships, interactions with others, and the ability to adapt to various social situations. Spiritual wellness is seen as the maturation of higher consciousness as developed through the integration of our relationships, values, and a meaningful purpose in our life. It may include acknowledgement of the Divine in life[56]. Although these definitions are those established by the wellness industry, the dimensions, and their meaning at the deepest sense, are what they represent for you.

When we are living from high states of wellbeing, we are grounded and our calm and connection system. We see, perceive, and behave in life-generating ways, which foster even greater states of wellbeing. It is from high states of wellbeing that heartfulness naturally emerges. When we are functioning from an integrated state of wellness we are much more able to love, be compassionate, feel hope, gratitude or joy and have those manifest in our lives, the lives of those around us, and our outside world. We are more capable of using our resources to make the world a better place.

High levels of wellness both foster greater capabilities of heartful awareness, as well as create a reciprocal pattern where both are nurtured to greater levels. In other words, wellness helps heartful awareness flourish, and greater states of heartful awareness create still higher states of wellbeing. This feedback loop is evidenced in all of our dimensions of wellness; heartful awareness is both nurtured by an integrated approach to wellness, and further develops our capacity to live as a whole human being.

As such, in our journey to heartful awareness it is helpful to look at the specific dimensions of wellness and our relative health in each. When we are living as whole human beings we are much more capable of heartful awareness, as a life out of balance is a life prone to chaos. In addition to looking at our relative health in each of the dimensions of wellness, we will consider a concept I call 'wellness asset building.'

Wellness asset building is based on the concept of community asset building, which invites the mobilization of community capital (physical, human, social, financial, environmental, political, and cultural) to effect positive change. In other words, it looks at the strengths of the community, as a whole system, and examines how those strengths may be mobilized to nurture the system overall. In wellness asset building we look at our personal strengths in each of the dimensions of wellness, how they currently help the functioning of our system over all, and how they might be mobilized for further thriving, and greater levels of heartful awareness. Then, from a heartfully aware posture, and if it is appropriate, we can examine areas that we would like to improve upon.

The process of focusing on our assets, or strengths first is very important. It is most often our nature to be more comfortable focusing on lack, or what is deficient, rather than what is nurturing or abundant. It is hard for most of us to sincerely and lovingly, without arrogance or self-importance, allow ourselves to focus on our strengths. Additionally, when we come from a loving, or heartfully aware state when dealing with an issue or aspect of our lives we would like to develop, constructive perceptions are more abundant. Too, just the act of turning our heartful awareness inward, and recognizing our strengths in the various dimensions helps further cultivate our capacities. The awareness itself helps further nurture our strengths and our ability to engage in life in a heartful way.

Exercise and Reflection # 16 - Dimensions of wellness

This exercise invites you into heartful awareness for yourself and your strengths in each of the dimensions of wellness. Because this is not typically an easy thing for us to do, it is important to start the process from a calm, and physiologically receptive state. As such, HEART in the moment is the first step to ground us in our own sense of heartfulness.

1) Notice, and disengage from any thoughts, reactivities, or tentative feelings you may be having. Again, do not suppress, just notice, without letting them consume you.

2) Take a few comfortable, deep, and slow breaths. As you continue to breathe comfortably and slowly, consciously release all the tension around your eyes and shoulders. Repeat the word 'release' on the out breath, and physically feel the sensation of release throughout your body. Let your awareness find your breath somewhere in your torso were it feels comfortable, and immerse yourself in the experience of your breath.

3) If it feels appropriate, let yourself focus on a sense of gratitude for yourself and your strengths. If it feels appropriate, let yourself genuinely feel a sense of grateful acceptance for your innermost strengths and let this feeling of acceptance engulf your body for a few minutes while you continue to breathe. If gratitude for your self, and your strengths feels uncomfortable, just notice without judgment.

4) For each identified area, focus on and write about your strengths. Be specific, and allow yourself to elaborate. If you feel uncomfortable allowing yourself to focus on your strengths just notice your response, don't judge it.

5) After you have authentically and heartfully explored your strengths, if it is appropriate, identify areas you would like to improve.

◊ Spiritual
◊ Emotional
◊ Relational / Social
◊ Intellectual
◊ Physical

Review

How did you feel when writing about your strengths? Was it easy to do? What strengths are most important to you? (These may not necessarily be your greatest strengths). How can you incorporate your most deeply felt strengths into more of your life? How can they more readily help you adopt a posture of heartful awareness? Reflect and process in a way that is meaningful for you.

Our heartful energy diet

A nutritional diet is made up of all the food sources we take in on a daily basis, and, and in a large part determines our physical health. It is comprised of all the things we consume, whether they are healthy for us or not. Some may add to our physical health, and some may detract from it. In other words, if I subsist on chips and soda, that is my diet, whether it is healthy for me or not. Most of us also have experience with trying to manipulate our diet for health reasons. We may have tried to lose weight, or gain weight, or just merely eat healthier. And energy diet works in the same way.

An energy diet is comprised of all the things that add to or detract from our emotional health. It is comprised of all the things we expose our self to on a daily basis that add to, or diminish our ability to be grounded in heartful awareness. We all have things, people, relationships, media, etc., that simply either give us life-sustaining energy, or detract from it. When we re-visit the idea that our bodies are systems of adaptation, we can see how powerfully important paying attention to our energy diet is. We are molding to our emotional outlook every moment, of every day. The things we expose ourselves to matter a lot.

The creation of a heartful energy diet invites us to take a deep look at the things in our life that may be enhancing or detracting from our ability to rest in heartful awareness. It invites us into uncovering what, in our life, is life-affirming and what is not. It invites us to take a look at our every day activities, relationships, conversations, media exposure, our environment and all the other peripheral pieces that take up our time, and energy, and examine their impact on our lives.

These situations can be as obvious as manipulative, toxic, or emotionally draining people, or a subtle as exposure to specific forms of media, physical environments, or the act of taking responsibility for other's happiness. Some you may be very aware of, but others may take some work to uncover. Some may be seemingly mundane everyday experiences and influences. However you may discover that, in this context, they are throwing you off center and have a negative impact on your body and brain. Perhaps you will see some aspects of your life in a new light. Whether obvious or subtle, the key to remember is that our personal exposure to everything we encounter is measurable in our bodies. By our choices we are determining the level of our ability to be centered in a heartful presence.

At this point in our process, it should be absolutely apparent that where we keep our attention every moment of every day, through a complex psychophysiological process, literally shapes us. Everything we expose ourselves to – every thought, every situation, every relationship, every conversation – affects our bodies and brains in such a way that determines how we adapt, and who we become. In short, the choices of what we subject ourselves to matters a lot. By paying careful attention to those things in our lives that may infuse, or deplete, our life source or personal energy, we can further generate the growth of our calm and connection system, and reduce the onslaught of our fear response system.

This section is built on the concept that the creation of an 'energy diet' is foundational in allowing our calm and connection system to flourish. The term diet was chosen as a metaphor for all the things that fuel our existence, everything we ingest in our daily lives. As a nutritional diet is composed of all the food substances we take in, whether they are good or bad for us, an energy diet is comprised of all the things that we expose our self to on a daily basis. These are the things that, day after day, add to or detract from our inner experience and ability to live a life of heartful awareness.

Living a life of heartful awareness is both allowed by a dominant calm and connection system, as well as is central in developing one. There is a feedback loop resulting from all of our daily choices that either lead to or detract from our physiological capability to cultivate our calm and connection system, and ability for heartful awareness. All our involvements, large and small, contribute to the constant 'spiral of becoming', even those we are unaware of.

In other words, if every moment I am adapting to my inner experience, yet my experience is consumed with a toxic conversation, harmful media images, a chaotic personal environment, toxic substances, media overload, etc., I am only training my body and brain to feel more chaotic. Heartful awareness gets further and further away. Again, when we look at our quality of life and our potential for heartful awareness through the science of embodiment, we can see how profoundly important each moment is. If our moments are full of life degenerating impact, our bodies and brains, unbeknownst to us, will mold to more of the same.

If I engage in a toxic conversation, or any of the other above behaviors that just make me feel bad, my brain and body are adapting to more of those feelings. My neural networks and biochemical reactions are profoundly determining my level of inner experience, and my inner experience is creating the capacity of more of the same biologically, psychologically, and spiritually in my life. They are also affecting my perceptions, behaviors, and choices.

Remember, our bodies and brains are delicate systems of adaptation and do not know the difference between something that is vividly imagined and something that is real. Too, when we are intentionally, or unintentionally emotionally manipulated by something in our environment our bodies adapt to that manipulation. Whatever we are exposing ourselves to is setting off a cascade of positive or negative reaction patterns that are consuming our bodies. Every time we expose ourselves to something – a thing, situation, thought, or word – that exposure strengthens the neural networks and biochemical reactions associated with the underlying feelings attached to it. And they could be so subtle, or so routine, that their impact is beyond our conscious awareness.

This process happens whether we are aware of it or not. It also happens whether we are using it for our benefit or not. Sometimes these influences are subtle and implicit, meaning they are only felt subconsciously or minimally; sometimes they are explicit an obvious. Regardless, because our bodies are intrinsically connected to our subconscious mind, they can give us incredibly valuable information about what is healthy for us. Somatic knowledge means that our bodies are constantly changing in response to what we expose them to, and tuning into our physical responses serves as sort of a compass for our internal health. By paying careful attention to those things in our lives that add to or detract from our personal energy we can begin to manipulate our surroundings for life-generation and heartful awareness to flourish.

Energy diet specifics

When we look at energy diet specifics, we can look at them in terms of energy drainers or energy infuser's. Energy drainers decrease our capabilities to be grounded in states of heartful awareness, and energy infuser's enhance them. Shortly, we will consider specific aspects of our energy diet, but first it is important to consider the all-important aspect of time.

Our time budget

Ponder this. The hours in a day are finite. If every moment we are adapting and transforming to our inner experience, and there are only so many moments in a day, what we expose ourselves to in those moments, matters. A lot. Our time budget is the over-arching element of our energy diet. Are you making 'wise time budget purchases?' Are you making more life affirming choices than not? As we saw in chapter 4 we do not need to be perfect all the time. We merely need to tip the scales 3:1 as a ratio of life affirming to not.

Although in chapter 4 we looked at intentional moments of heartful awareness, this dynamic can play out in all of our daily activities. What can you do to make yourself more aware of how this dynamic plays out in your everyday life? Are you spending more moments exposing yourself to life generating and sustaining circumstances than those that drain? What can you do to acknowledge and reduce the drains? What can you do to create more of those that sustain?

Part of recognizing what inspires you, or what is life-affirming for you is recognizing what is not. Think of your life is a masterpiece in progress. Are you spending your valuable time contributing to that artwork? Remember the story of how Michelangelo created the statue of David in considering how to fashion the masterpiece of your life. Recognize what contributes to the true care and heartful development of yourself and chip away at what does not. Your time is precious, and your capabilities for heartful awareness and transformation are, to a large extent, the sum total of the way you choose to spend your time.

If your time is filled with those things that are less than optimal, they become the experience of your life. Conversely, if you spend your precious time on activities that are life affirming for you, that becomes the experience of your life. Because repeated experience creates and strengthens neural networks in the brain and biochemical changes throughout the body, budgeting your time helps to create the richest experience you can in the time you are allotted, hour after hour, day after day. And we need only tip the scales.

Tune into your body. Reduce the drainers. Enhance the sustainers.

Tuning into your body is basically going to give you one of three answers. The first is that yes, it is life-affirming. In this case, when you pay careful attention to your physical responses you can feel some generative energy throughout your body and brain. And, again, as in other areas of heartful awareness, it is a deep and grounded 'felt sense,' not whimsical, chaotic for grasping. It feels like a 'centeredness' or 'intuitive yes.'

The second possibility is that, no, it does not feel life-affirming. However, this 'no' could indicate one of two things. The first is that it is truly an energy drainer, and something that is more detrimental to your ability to reside in a grounded and heartful state. These may be the things you want to stay away from, or limit your exposure to in a way that is appropriate for you so they do not dominate your existence. The second would be that it is something that is activating an implicit memory in you, and is actually nudging to be healed. Somewhere you know. And tapping into your Inner Being will probably tell you.

More simply, tuning into your body will either give you an 'intuitive yes', meaning it is healing for you, or an 'intuitive no', meaning it is not. The 'no' could indicate it is either associated with an implicit memory yearning to be healed, or something to be avoided altogether because it is toxic for you. I think a good rule of thumb in making this distinction is the level of 'trigger' it may be associated with. Typically a trigger is a call for healing, simply because the type of physicality indicates it is associated with an implicit memory.

A trigger carries that 'whoosh' feeling of 'fight or flight' toxic energy, and just feels bad. It is a different physiologic phenomenon. Turning into your body will help you differentiate the two. However, unfortunately, some situations carry both.

Energy drainers

Energy drainers can be as numerous and as vast as people experiencing them. However, there are a few very common energy drainers that are worth exploring here. The most important piece is that you determine what, for you, are those big and small things in your life that you experience as energy depleting. The immediately following topics can be both drainers and sustainers. What comprises our personal energy diet can be vast and varied. However, there are a few global considerations that seem to impact us all. These are the people or relationships we expose ourselves to, the media we are exposed to, how overloaded or overwhelmed we allow ourselves to get, and the powerful impact our environment may have on us.

People

What are your moments made of? Are they consumed with people who drain your energy, either with their toxic conversations, aggressive or draining behavior or constant drama? Are you spending your moments 'caretaking' people in a way that is neither healthy for them or you? The circumstances in which people and relationships drain your life force or heartful energy are very different than those that enhance it.

There is a night and day difference between heartfully engaged relationships, conversations, and other interactions with people, and those that are not. Your body, or your somatic response is a good gauge for this. Tune into your body. Does it feel life draining or depleting? Or does it feel life sustaining? When we are able to engage with others from an authentic heartful posture it is actually energy producing. Authentic compassionate engagement is one of the deepest states of heartful awareness, and is actually life sustaining, even within whatever difficulty is presenting itself. This is in direct opposition to the energy drain of a toxic involvement.

Too, remember, a requirement for heartful awareness is that it is authentic. If interactions are done out of 'shoulds,' or blame, or shame for yourself, they are not authentic. If a conversation, interaction or relationship is toxic for you maybe the most heartfully aware thing to do is take care of yourself, and not expose yourself to it. Heartful awareness in this instance is about self-care. Heartful awareness also means there is no room for judgment of that which we feel is toxic to us. We are simply noticing, and disengaging from an environment that drains us from our own heartful energy.

Media

In our current culture we are absolutely inundated with all forms of media. While in so many ways this media influx has become an integral part of our life, it is also important to look at the ways it may be draining our heartful energy. Two of the most obvious are its content, and the time that it is taking away from other aspects of our life.

Remember, everything we expose ourselves to creates and strengthens neural networks and biochemical response patterns, and these ultimately go back and shape our perceptions, and ability to be grounded in deep states of heartfulness. Remember, also, that our brain does not know the difference between something that is vividly imagined, and something that is real, and will react and reprogram accordingly. We also have something called mirror neurons in our brain that, if we are deeply engaged, will fire as if another's experience is ours. In other words, there are parts of our brain that will believe, and react as if what we are watching is our own experience. Thus, the content of media, T.V. shows, movies, etc., especially when it is emotionally involving or manipulative, has a profound effect on our body's adaptation and transformation process, and ultimately our ability to ground ourselves in states of heartful awareness. And most of the time we are unaware.

When we revisit the idea of a 'time budget' it is not hard to see the drain that all forms of media may have on our ability to be grounded in our calm and connection system, or develop a deep sense of heartful awareness. Cell phones, the Internet, all of our technological communication, TV, video games, movies on demand, etc., all consume countless moments of our lives. While many of these things have filled our lives with unimagined possibility, and created the ability for even greater connection in some ways, just the sheer amount of time that we spent on them may be something we want to look at. Again, every moment we are transforming, and all the moments we are engaged in some form of media that is not necessarily life sustaining, are moments that aren't engaged and heartful awareness. And those moments and up.

Admittedly, this is a complex question. While all forms of media have the ability to increase our connectivity, they also have the ability to decrease the connectivity to those around us. I am always amazed when I walk around the University and virtually everybody I see is on a cell phone. And not many are talking to, or interacting with each other. There was a comic (Yes, floating around the Internet) that claimed if the "Breakfast Club", the movie from the 1980's promoting understanding and connection between a diverse group of teens, were to occur today, nothing would happen. In this movie the teens were confined to an all day Saturday detention. They were a very diverse group, who, outside of the detention room, had never taken the time to get to know each other. Because of all of their involvements throughout the happenings of the day, they ended up with deep relationships, and found tolerance and understanding for people they would have never known otherwise. The message of the comic was that if the group met today they would be so immersed in their cell phones, they would have never taken the time to actually get to know each other.

The question is not whether media is good or bad. The reality is, in all forms, it is here to stay. The true question involves being able to discern when, and how much contributes to our ability to cultivate deeper states of heartful

241

awareness, both in regard to its content, and the time we spend engaging in it. Our bodies, and our humanness, are constantly adapting to what we expose them to, and we only have so many moments in a day. In what ways, and to what extent, is all the media in your life either draining or sustaining your heartful transformation?

Overloaded and overwhelmed

When we are constantly functioning from overload and overwhelm we are both unknowingly allowing our fear response system to dominate, and thus become our primary operating system, as well as spending less time nurturing our calm and connection system. Both damage any hope of sustaining or developing our ability for heartful awareness. Too, overload and overwhelm are primary producers of cortisol. Couple that, with the fact that the moods that most often accompany these stressed states color the lens of our perception, and we can see how energy depleting they really are.

While our lives are complex, and may carry a certain inherent degree of overload, it is important to examine the changes we can make. Are there big or small steps you can take to reduce the weight? Knowing the damage you are doing to yourself by remaining in constant overload, what adjustments can you make? What can you do to relieve the feeling of overwhelm?

Pay attention to where your emotional focus is. If you find you are feeling overwhelmed, take big or small steps to cultivate a shift in attention. Practice some of the techniques presented in this book, take a break, experience something that for you cultivates a sense of heartful presence, look at the stars, go for a walk, talk to someone you love. Do everything you can to change the overload, but if you cannot, taking small breaks from the feeling of overwhelm can help substantially. Remember the moments and up, and the more moments in overwhelm mean fewer moments in our calm and connection system.

Environmental influences

Our environment fuels subtle emotional changes in us. These changes, of course, create neural and chemical reactions that may be beyond our awareness, except in a subtle shift of how we feel. But they are very real, and have an impact on our subconscious perceptions, reactions and moods. Pay acute attention to your environment, and notice how it makes you feel. It may include noise, physical space, simplicity, or distractions. In particular, be aware of your personal reactions to your environment, and your ability to be heartfully grounded within it all. What changes can you make? What would be more nurturing to grounding you in your calm and connection system?

We are constantly being exposed to environmental cues that either add to or detract from our ability to be grounded in our calm and connection system. Is important to realize and notice their potential and great impact. What can you do in your own life to be aware of these influences, and change the ones that are draining?

Exercise and Reflection # 17 - Energy drainers

Identify what, for you, are energy drainers. They could be people, conversations, media, environments, habits, demands, etc. Brainstorm, and identify his many situations as you can. Keep in mind that some of these may be very subtle and merely create a slight shift in your emotional groundedness. After identifying as many areas as you can, brainstorm, reflect, and process on ways to reduce their presence in your routine experience.

Energy infusers

Aside from reducing the energy drainers in our life we can routinely and intentionally create nurturing and sustaining circumstances. If we can intentionally create life circumstances that are truly generative, through all the physiological foundations discussed, we cultivate our calm connection system to be the dominant force in our life, and allow heartful awareness our primary operating pattern. Routine experience of these circumstances will change our body, brain, psyche, and spirit accordingly. These energy infusers need to be authentic to our own personal inner experience; however, a few suggestions for consideration follow. Some of these have to do with creating a nurturing environment, and the connections we make, and many have to do with heartful self-care.

Heartful self-care is essential in being able to ground our selves in a heartfully aware existence. Although the reasoning of some of these considerations may not be immediately apparent, they can be foundational in our own inner flourishing. The instructions from a flight attendant on a plane are always that you secure your own oxygen mask first before attempting to assist others. So it is the way with heartful awareness. We are most heartful with others, and our world, when we are first heartful with ourselves. The art of heartful self care allows us to be most grounded in our own calm and connection system, and therefore be more capable of tapping into, and sharing the heartful life force from deep within us.

Exercise

What does exercise have to do with heartful awareness? My friend John from the coffee shop, who is a retired pastor and one of the most beautiful souls I know, says plainly, "I am a nicer person when I exercise." I have another friend that says nothing is more influential on how he will feel psychologically and spiritually on any given day, than the way he feels physically. Most of us are so desensitized to the recommendation of exercise that we either already do it, or just ignore the recommendation when it comes up. I encourage you to look at exercise in a new light.

Although all the external changes associated with exercise will certainly come, along with the touted and important health benefits, the internal benefits contributing to heartfelt awareness are immeasurable. These come from reduced stress, anxiety, and emotional chaos as well as increased self-esteem, self-concept and internal coherence. Quite simply, we feel better. Exercise from the outside makes us more available to heartful awareness from the inside. Regular exercise reduces cortisol. Exercising with others produces oxytocin. Exercise helps us cut through the static of life to hear and get in touch with the deepest parts of our selves, and it makes being heartfully present with what life has to offer within our reach.

Exercise is as simple as moving your body. There should be no blame, shame, or 'shoulds' in what you might do. Find a way that you like to move, and move. And moving will change you. Dance. Walk. Run. Ride a bike. Row a boat. Go for a hike. Vigorously garden. Just move. And moving will help you on your journey to heartful awareness.

Although a complete prescription for exercise is beyond the scope of this book, you can get the full dose in my first book *The Power Within: From Neuroscience to Transformation*[57]. Exercise can be an integral part of your path to heartful awareness. Explore its possibilities.

Nutrition

Few things allow me more of a chance to feel good or feel bad, and thus connected to my potential for heartful awareness, then the nutrition I feed my body. Our ability to cultivate heartful awareness is profoundly affected by the way we feel physically. The way we feel physically is profoundly affected by what we put in our body by the way of nutrition. And yet food issues, crazy fad diets, and undue pressure to have a perfect body can be the exact things that cut us off from any hope of heartful awareness. Creating a heartful approach to nutrition and body image is paramount in grounding ourselves in our calm and connection system and allowing the conditions for heartful awareness to flourish. Pay attention; take good care. Your body is the host of your Inner Being.

I always ask people to imagine what they would do if they were just given a car. It could be the car of their dreams. The only catch is they would have to have the same car, and drive it from now until the day they died. I then ask them how they would take care of it. Most say they would take great care, give it great maintenance, wash it every day, only put the best gas in it, etc. Why do we treat our bodies any differently?

How do you create a healthy, yet sane approach to the nutrients you give our body? Nutrition should be about how the food you eat serves you. It should be about how healthy it makes you feel, and the way it sustains you, not about an impossible ideal. Food is not emotion, and emotion is not food. Many times we confuse the two, and eat for reasons other than nutritional sustenance. Unfortunately, in our culture the two are so intertwined it is hard to have one without the other. A genuine and heartfully aware approach to nutrition removes the emotionalism surrounding it, and creates a loving peace with your body and the way you sustain it.

Again, a comprehensive recommendation for nutrition is beyond the scope of this book, however there is one in my first book mentioned earlier[58]. It invites you into an individual and personalized look at creating a healthy and sane approach to the nutrients you are giving your body.

Simplicity

Quite often we create and live our lives flooded with the countless demands overconsumption, overscheduling, and an overdriven mentality that we have no idea how to get in touch with our heartful core, or even that we have such a thing as an Inner Being. One of the main messages of this book has been that we need to cut through it all enough to be able to ground ourselves in our calm and connection system and let a sense of heartful awareness emerge. If our lives are full of the demands of an over-the-top lifestyle, we do not have the time, attention, or energy to be able to develop any sense of heartful presence. How can you be present to the voice of your heart if there's too much psychological or physical clutter to hear it?

Voluntary simplicity means we make conscious choices to reduce our overconsumption, our cluttered environments, our overly burdensome workloads, and our constant technological overstimulation. We make a concerted effort to balance our inner and outer development. This is a complete paradigm shift from the mentality that more is better. This is a complete paradigm shift from the idea that if we accumulate enough possessions, or enough external validation, we somehow will feel better about ourselves.

What does voluntary simplicity mean in concrete terms? The answer is as individual as we are. I believe we all, at some intuitive level, know what the answers are for us. Are you a 'packrat'? Do you impulsively shop thinking that some thing or acquisition will make you feel better somehow? Are you constantly over stimulated with technology, including computers, cell phones, TV, and video games? Does it take more time and effort to take care of your acquisitions than the enjoyment that you derive from them? Have you overloaded your life with so many commitments that you overlook time for yourself, your family, to be silent or spend in nature? Do you always have to be busy? Do you know how to say 'no' when it is appropriate? What is it that you feel especially overwhelmed by, and how can you take steps to simplify the conditions surrounding that feeling?

Part of voluntary simplicity is not just reducing the over-the-top behavior, but also intentionally cultivating the opposite. When was the last time you chose to be silent and felt comfortable in the silence? When was the last time you walked in the woods, on the beach, or looked at the stars? When was the last time you decided to go a day, or a week with no computer, cell phone, or TV? When was the last time you decided to forgo buying something because you really didn't need it, or probably wouldn't use it anyway? When was the last time you to decided to clear the clutter and throw out everything you haven't used in the past year? When was the last time you decided to simplify your environment?

Voluntary simplicity is as individual as we are, and these are just a few questions to consider. We all know at a deep level what is honest in truly simplifying our lives. Again, it is like the metaphor of Michelangelo sculpting the statue of David. What do you need to chip away to have your 'inner David' appear? What keeps you from the time, effort, and energy to sincerely tap into, and further cultivate, heartful awareness? What clutter do you need to clear before the masterpiece that is you is free to emerge?

Creating connections

The desire to belong, the desire for companionship, is a basic human need. Caring, love, connections with others, and moral support all alleviate stress, dampen our fear response system and allow our calm and connection system to thrive. They even contribute to our health and longevity. Connected and supportive communities actually have the power to change our biochemistry and resulting behaviors, neural adaptations, perceptions, and potential. There is heartful power in creating trusting and loving bonds with others.

Oxytocin is produced in relationships based on emotional closeness and trust. In chapter 4 we learned many of the powerful effects of oxytocin. It reduces cortisol, calms our brain, and allows us a more expansive way of feeling and being. And, again, the more often we are in these physiological states, the more they become our primary operating pattern. Creating close connections, social support and intentional community directly impacts our capacity for heartful awareness. It also gives us the opportunity to practice and further develop that awareness in regard to others. What are areas in your life that you can create, and nurture close connections with others?

Generative time and inspired activities

I love the stars. When I am under a star filled sky my stresses melt away. I am in touch with my innermost self and a sense of heartfelt awareness for my whole world seems to permeate my existence. These moments are more sacred to me than anything a building could hold. I am steeped in feelings of life-generation and I feel reborn.

We all have places that, for whatever reason, allow our life force to feel reborn. Our fear response system seems to fade away and we are once again connected to our heartful core. We feel clarity, calm, and connection to all that is around us. The physiological changes are measurable, and we truly are reborn in a physical and adaptive way. Doing this routinely, and often allows us the moments that change our lives, and these moments add up. But they need to be experienced, and re-experienced to continue to matter.

Building routine time into your days, weeks, and life to reconnect with yourself and your loved ones in generative time, and in generative spaces powerfully resets your base functioning. It may be a stroll on the beach, a walk in the woods, stargazing, or swimming in a mountain lake. It may be time in the museum, gardening, or appreciating art. What are the activities that re-ground you? Are there spaces you can build into your days or weeks to re-generate? Can you build a routine time (daily, weekly, monthly, or yearly) in which to honor this dynamic?

Too, just as we all have spaces that inspire us, we also have activities that nourish our soul. Inspired activities come from being 'in-spirit' and invite you to engage with something that resonates from the deepest parts of who you are. Music, art, dance, communing with nature – these activities can stimulate an area in the limbic system that overlaps with an area of the brain we associate with spirituality. Inspired activities are truly a biological reality. They truly touch our soul. And our whole being adapts accordingly. Intentionally and routinely cultivating inspired activities create change from the inside out. What inspired activities can you incorporate in your life? Be creative and think broadly.

Intentional silence and sacred space

Taking an occasional day to be silent, and getting to know our selves powerfully increases our capacities for heartful awareness. So many of us fill our days, hours, and minutes with so many stimuli we lose touch with who we are at our core. My friend Violet Scolinos grew up in the United States, lived for several years on a Greek island, and then came back to live in the United States. As she was having a hard time adjusting to life back in the United States she compared living in the two places. She said that it feels as if everyone here is addicted to life as if it were a frantic treadmill. They are afraid to get off the treadmill, because if they do, they will actually have to look inside themselves. Intentional silence helps us cut through the chaos of daily life and get in touch with our heartful core.

Take a vacation from the overload of stimuli. Remove yourself from the constant demands of cell phones, email, text messages, Internet, and television. Allow yourself the space, time, and silence to just be. As my friend Violet says, get off the frantic treadmill and take time to look inside yourself. You may be amazed at what you see.

Too, creating sacred space can be a fundamentally important aspect of cultivating a state of heartful awareness. When we have a designated space to retreat, re-energize and intentionally re-ground ourselves, we give ourselves a break from the onslaught of our fear response drive, and position ourselves in our calm and connection drive. We can better get in touch with our heartful core and reestablish a state of heartful awareness. The stress melts away, we are once again centered, and we are better in touch with our Inner Being and what we know to be true. When we can do this routinely, we break our habitual ways of being and reacting in the world. We are changed in the moment, and our capacity to live from a heartfully aware state overall increases immensely.

Time for meditation

A large part of this book is been devoted to the importance of contemplative practice in cultivating a high capacity for heartful awareness. And, in fact, heartful awareness itself is a type of practice that is steeped through our everyday existence. However, I believe it is important to mention again here. The benefits of a routine and sustained practice cannot be understated. This is when we are most directly and effectively training our whole system, including our brain, body, psyche, and spirit to function and live from heartfully aware spaces.

What can you do to develop your own practice? One that feels most comfortable for you based on everything that you have learned? You are much more likely to be successful and routine if you have a specific place and time to practice. Pay attention to creating the circumstances that will help you be consistent. Remember all the foundational and physiological changes that can happen with routine practice, and create an approach that works for you. Create a space. Create a time. Join a local group if you are so inclined. Create an altar. Make it your own.

Honor you your uniqueness

Each of us is unique. To be heartfully aware of our selves is to recognize and celebrate this uniqueness.

Joan was struggling with serious life issues and decisions regarding her work and career. As we began to explore her struggles and her decisions I could tell she spoke with much more energy and enthusiasm connected to the first option, rather than the other. This was evident in her facial expressions, her body language, and her energy level as she talked through each scenario. At the same time she was trying to sensibly talk herself into the other decision. She was trying to convince herself that her passions for the first were frivolous and invalid.

I asked her what a wise man once asked me: "Is it possible to not do the thing that most resonates with you and still be happy at the deepest parts of who you are?" I also asked her which choice she felt most passionately about and which gave her that 'intuitive yes.' I shared with her my view that at the core we are all unique and we're given this uniqueness for a reason. If nobody else, at the deepest level, has the strengths and passions you do at your deepest level, are you not obligated to follow these passions?

Heartful awareness both invites us to honor our uniqueness, and is further nurtured by it. Heartful awareness for our selves may be the very thing that allows our uniqueness to blossom.

Be open to synchronicities in coincidences

The biochemistry, psychological and spiritual adaptations of heartful awareness allow us a sense of expansiveness. That expansiveness allows us to see greater possibility where before we were limited. When we transform through heartful awareness our body, brain, beliefs, behaviors, and external actions begin to automatically respond to that transformation. Know that, at the deepest levels, you are functioning differently. And when we function differently, we draw different things into our lives.

These differences may begin to manifest or appear in subtle, and not-so-subtle ways. Where we once saw limits we now see possibilities. Too, these possibilities may show up in unexpected an unexplained ways. Carl Jung defined synchronicity as a relationship between meaningful occurrences that are connected in their own poetically logical way, and are not necessarily causal in nature. In other words, it may not make sense why something shows up, but it is drawn to us by its sheer connection, because it is meaningful to us in our life. If we do not pay attention we may miss out.

Pay attention. Pay attention to synchronicities, pay attention to coincidences. When we are heartfully engaged we are all at once more grounded in our own center, and more open and aware of greater capacities for life.

Heartful self care

Self-care is a powerful path to heartful awareness. It can take many forms and come in many disguises. While the forms it may take are for too many to consider here, there are a few very foundational ones worth mentioning.

Pay attention to attention	Feed your body and soul	Reduce stress
		Find resources
		Nurture your self
Be as kind to your self as you would a best friend	Learn names	Get organized
	Make friends	Sleep
	Laugh	Get a massage
	Get present	Pamper yourself
Find something to be grateful for	Unplug	Relax
	Quiet inner chatter	

Remember it is all the little things that we do, day after day, that nurture growth in life generating forms. The next exercise is designed to help you identify life-sustaining involvements, and the next practice is designed for extreme self-care. It is a deep relaxation practice, and is designed to nurture you at the level of your soul.

Exercise and Reflection # 18 - Energy infusers and heartful self care

Identify what, in your own life, are energy sustainers or enhancers. After identifying as many areas as you can, brainstorm, reflect, and process why this is so. How can you increase their presence in your life? What would happen if you did?

Process and reflect on several of the previous categories. Which ones most resonated with you? Why are they important to you, or why did they resonate? How can you implement them in your life? Process and reflect in a way that is appropriate for you.

Practice: Body Relaxation and Stress Release

Body relaxation practices directly target the physiological components of the body to induce a relaxed, calm and coherent state. In other words, when our body calms, our mind and spirit calm. We feel calm, we feel at peace, and we are more able to connect to the heartful spaces within and without us. Again, because the body is a system of adaptation, the biochemical, neural and electrical components associated with this calmer and more relaxed state become the body's new operating system. Too, this type of self-care can have a profound effect on inner renewal, and our capacity for heartful awareness. You can do this exercise with calming music in the background if you wish.

1) Bring all your awareness to your breath, and maintain a comfortable relaxed breathing pattern.

2) Relax the tension all around the eyes and the tiny little muscles surrounding the eyes. Relax all of muscular structures of the face. Relax the shoulders, and relax down into the chest. Find a spot on your torso that feels comfortable for you to bring your awareness and imagine the breath coming straight in and out of that spot. Maintain this breathing pattern and relaxed state of being throughout the practice.

3) Progressively, and slowly tighten and release various muscle groups throughout your body for a count of three. After the count of three, the next two breaths should be overtly 'releasing' breaths focused on the same body parts you just tightened. Start from your toes to your knees, then your knees to your hips, then your full torso, from your hips to your shoulders, then the entirety of both arms, including the hands.

4) After you are done with the tightening and releasing aspect of this practice, imagine a wave of relaxation very slowly coming up and over your body. Imagining it starting at your toes, then to your ankles, shins and calves, up and through your knees, thighs, and hips, very slowly up your torso, from your shoulders, down both arms, all the way to your fingertips. Bring your awareness, then, to

253

the base of your neck, and imagine the wave slowly progressing up and around your head, encircling and enveloping your scalp and your skull, as if it were a slowly unfolding cap. Imagine the wave as a curtain, lowering slowly down your forehead, over your eyebrows and deep into your eye-sockets, cheeks, jaw, over the chin, and down the throat and neck.

5) Let your awareness find your breath again at a spot in your torso that is comfortable for you, and rest in the experience of the breath. Imagine your body melting into whatever surface you are on. If you feel any left-over stress or tension you can imagine it floating away on a cloud or a balloon if you like. Focus on what it feels like to truly let go, and release it.

6) Rest in this space for 5 to 10 minutes, or as long as is appropriate. If you would like, you can finish the practice with the HEARTful breathing exercise presented in Chapter 4. In other words, once you are fully relaxed, breathe the sensation, or 'felt sense' of whatever outlook you would like to create for yourself, and 'feel' it soaking every cell in your body. As you transition out of the practice, pause and bring your conscious awareness to how you are feeling. This awareness will help you cement this state of being so you can more easily access it with only a few breaths at a later time.

Living heartful values and fostering greater heartful clarity

Throughout this book we have seen that calming our fear response system and developing our calm and connection system, or cultivating heartful awareness, leads to a sense of expansiveness. That sense of expansiveness, then, allows for greater depth and clarity in the way we live our lives, and, conversely, greater depth and clarity allow for ever more expansive degrees of heartfulness. All at once we are more capable of living a life consistent with our deeper values, fostering the clarity that leads to

Spending heartful time

'Holding' ourselves in a place of heartful awareness while engaging in the above exercise helps us gain clarity on our deepest values and what is truly important for us to embody in this life. However, even when we are aware of our deepest values, we may not be embodying them in our lived experience as well as we might be. So often, we are 'waiting till things calm down', or until we finish this endeavor, or that project, or get done with a specific phase of our life (school, relationship, job, into retirement, etc.) to truly live our values. Unfortunately, I know people well into their very advanced years that are still waiting for their life to begin. Like Bruce Springsteen says in his song, Better Days:

"Yeah just sittin' around waitin' for my life to begin...
while it was all just slippin' away[62]"

A life of heartful awareness invites us in to a life based on our deepest values - right now. Imagine the following:

An angel has just visited you. Her message for you is that your time is finite. She has come to let you know that you only have a year left to live. You will not be sick, and you do not have to spend the year 'getting your affairs in order'. Her message is not meant to be morbid in any way. In fact, it is the greatest gift she can give you (other than longer life). It is meant to be the gift of knowing that your time is short, so, in that knowing, you can spend the year in the most meaningful ways to you that are possible. How would you spend that precious time? What would you do with the days and the moments that you have left?

Exercise and Reflection # 19 - Clarifying life values pt. 2

From a place of heartful awareness imagine you only have a year left to live. You are well, but know your time is finite and short. You want to live that year from your deepest values, and have it reflect all that you want to be and do in that time. What would you do? How would you spend that year? Again, write 'stream of consciousness' writing style in a way that is appropriate for you.

Exercise and Reflection # 19 - Clarifying life values pt. 3

Sometimes we can better clarify what we want our life to reflect, and how it might be more heartfully aware, by looking at the contrast of every day life. From the time you awoke, until the time you went to sleep, what did you do yesterday? You can list, you can write narrative. Write in a way that is appropriate for you.

Heartful clarity through contrast

As we saw from the in-attentional blindness exercise, the very first in this book, what we pay attention to is what shows up for us in life. Our brain really does have a limited capacity for conscious awareness, so where we place that awareness matters a lot. Too, as we have seen over and over again, both our subconscious and conscious awareness creates neural, biochemical and electrical functioning, and that functioning becomes our way of perceiving and being in the world. We have seen how we can heal, and reprogram our subconscious, but there is also power in intentionally controlling our conscious awareness. In other words, conscious awareness, or the things we pay attention to, are constantly contributing to the world we see, and who we are becoming. Our moment-to-moment awareness determines our moment-to-moment transformations. If we bring active heartfulness into that awareness, we bring heartfulness into our transformation.

We have also seen that the biochemicals and neural activity of the calm and connection system lead to feelings of expansiveness. Nurturing this system actually activates parts of our brain that perceive expansiveness, where, when under the influence of our fear response drive, we experience restriction, limited thinking and limited awareness. When we bring the feelings of

Practice: HEART for Clarity

Deep states of heartfulness lead to expansiveness, and expansiveness leads to clarity. HEART for Clarity uses the basic steps of the HEART practices as its foundation, except there is an additional purpose. In this practice we use the shift of affect to gain clarity on a question we may have, an issue we may be facing, or how to better manifest a sense of heartful awareness over-all.

Before you begin the practice write down a question, issue, problem, or any life circumstance you would like some clarity on. During the practice do not overtly focus on this question, just go into the practice with the intention of holding a subconscious awareness of this question. You might even request a sacred presence to work at the subconscious level of your awareness as you go through the practice.

Follow the outline steps of the heart practice:

1) **Notice** any reactivity, thoughts, emotions, and bodily sensations that may be presenting themselves. Disengage from any of these states that may be presenting, by witnessing or observing, gaining distance, but not suppressing.

2) **Refocus** the eyes by releasing any tension or stress in the tiny little muscles all around the eyes. Refocus and relax the shoulders, and refocus your attention down into the chest area or an area in the torso that feels comfortable for you to bring your attention. Create a comfortable, natural and relaxed breathing pattern, with all your attention on the breath.

3) **Nurture** a state of affect that feels healing or generative to you in the moment. If an image helps to bring up this "felt sense", again, hold the image in your minds eye. If you are using an image, focusing on the specifics of that image that bring up the felt sense helps to create the state of deep affect. Remember it is the felt sense, or state of deep affect that creates the foundational physiological adaptations in the body.

261

Try to maintain the breathing in the felt sense of this affect at least 20 minutes.

After the practice notice any answers, intuitive insights, bodily sensations or other ways of knowing that may surface. These 'knowings' may appear in a variety of ways. Be open. Pay attention. Bring your conscious attention to the receptivity of the moment and just notice what appears. Write down the first things that come up, without conscious filtering, either through sensation, other knowings, or cognitive awareness. Let the writing lead you. Also, pay attention in the hours, and days, following the practice. Answers and clarity may emerge at the times you least expect it.

Conclusion – Out of the Labyrinth

As was noted in chapter 1, the challenge of the labyrinth is not in navigating the path, as that is circular and continuous in nature. The real challenge of the labyrinth is the willingness to begin the walk. Now we continue that challenge with taking all that we have learned, and incorporating it into our daily life. This part of our journey asks us to fully assimilate what we have learned, and experienced, and through willingness and active engagement, create an individual and unique approach to living a life steeped in heartful awareness.

We have seen that through heartful awareness a different way of being and flourishing in the world is possible. We have seen that our bodies are evidence of, and vehicles for heartful transformation, and living a life of heartful awareness is truly an embodied phenomenon. We have learned that the very blocks to our heartful awareness may lie in our own internal programming, and we have experienced ways to change those programs. We have seen how trauma blocks us, and how healing clears those blocks. We have seen the power of intentional behavior in allowing the heartful seeds of consciousness bloom.

The science of embodiment has shown us the profound transformations that take place when we truly 'embody' heartful awareness. We have seen that our threat response drive is subdued, and our calm and connection system flourishes. We have seen that through our calm and connection system we have greater connection to our outside world, those around us, our deepest potential and our own Inner Being. We have seen that, through the concept of neuroplasticity, simple daily changes add up, and we have also seen that it takes constant stretching to grow neurologically.

We have seen that beyond mindfulness, heartfulness provides the other half to the whole of our existence. Beyond a non-reactive acceptance, it is a life-generating, and active embrace.

And the present moment is all there is.

And it is everything.

We have seen the opportunity that each moment presents, and engaged in tangible and specific behaviors that change those moments. We have seen that it takes awareness, and willingness, and choice, and active engagement to connect to the heartful opportunities that each moment presents. And we have seen that it all needs to be done with complete authenticity, or it is not heartful awareness at all.

We have seen that we do not have to be perfect all the time, and if we can simply shift and connect to the heartful energy around us, more often than not, we will likely experience profound transformation. We have witnessed the power of our words, stories, and scripts, and the wide variety of influences in our daily lives that either increase, or decrease our capacity to rest in heartful awareness. We have seen that micro-moments add up. We have seen that the invitation of heartful awareness is to, from a non-reactive and accepting posture, actively engage with whatever heartful opportunities are presenting themselves.

And the opportunities are endless.

Heartful awareness encompasses it all. We have seen that heartful awareness creates the capacity to connect to all that is around us, and within us. It provides opportunities for us to connect with others, our outside world, and the deepest parts of ourselves. We have seen, and experienced, that every moment is a moment of heartful potential.

Or not.

It depends on you.

The next question is, then, how do you personalize the journey to make it your own? How do you cultivate an authentic approach to heartful awareness in your own life? How do you complete the mindfulness/heartfulness whole through intentional engagement?

We are all at once ending our journey together, and you are beginning your own. This process needs to be as individual as you are, and tailored to your deepest truths. All growth and change carries with it a certain amount of fear or apprehension, as is often with the unknown. However, the process begins with the starting, and each moment of heartful awareness will open up spaces for more.

Truly embodying heartful awareness creates a whole host of transformational changes without conscious intent. Like the process of preparing the soil for a garden, if you put enough love, attention, and preparation into the soil, and then plant a seed, a beautiful flower emerges. You are not actually responsible for the creation of the flower itself; that happens on its own. That is the miracle of heartfulness. Is often said that a butterfly flapping its wings on one side of the world can create a hurricane on the other side of the world. Heartful awareness generates the flutter. Embodied heartful awareness offers us a miracle in the gift of presence, and engagement, we bring to each moment.

And those moments are everything.

In the Wizard of Oz Dorothy leaves Kansas to find her brain, her heart and her courage, and return to Kansas a profoundly changed person. In reality, her journey was to the deepest parts of herself, emerging transformed. This last exercise asks you to make this journey your own. It asks you to take all that you have learned, and experienced, and, in whatever life circumstances you are currently in, find the courage, brain, and heart in taking the journey from mindfulness to heartfulness.

Exercise and Reflection # 20 - Stepping out

Whatever we place our conscious awareness on integrates our brain and body to better manifest those possibilities. This last exercise will be an ever-evolving process. Reflect and process on what resonated with you throughout this journey, and how you will incorporate it in to your every-day life. How con you seize those moments of heartful awareness that present themselves? What can you do to better embody a life steeped in heartful awareness? This exercise requires less of me, and more of you. What are you taking out of the labyrinth, and how will you make it a reality in your every day life? In each moment as it occurs? How will you recognize the opportunity that each moment offers? How, in that moment of recognition, will you find the courage to be non-reactive, accepting, and embracing of the love that it offers? From a deep and heartful space, let the writing lead you. And return to it often. Where will you go from here?

Journal entry - 1998

I had another dream last night. I found the courage to walk through the door I dreamed of earlier. I had the courage to step inside of that room and soak up all it had to offer. This time it was very different. It was nurturing, and inviting, and felt completely like home. Just being in that space gave me this feeling of 'rightness'. I could feel it in my mind, in my heart, and every cell of my body. I could feel it all the way down to my bones. It was like every cell of my body felt at peace and I could finally relax into the deepest sense of who I was, and it was OK. As I soaked up all this room had to offer, it dawned on me that turning inside and allowing heartful awareness to blossom and flourish, from the inside out, changed me at the deepest level of who I was.

As I was pondering the enormity of what that felt like, I looked around and noticed the walls of the room beginning to melt away. I was sitting secure and 'held' in this room and all it had to offer, yet watching the walls slowly melt and disappear. I was all at once grounded in, and connected to a deep sense of inner peace, and beginning to re-connect with what was beyond the walls. As I looked around to fully see, and capture what was beyond the walls, I intuitively knew it was the same world I had left - and yet everything looked and felt completely different. It was the same world I left, and yet it was not. The things I was looking at were not necessarily different; it was more like I was seeing with new eyes. I felt I was being invited to re-engage in the world that I had left earlier, but in a whole new way. I had a new lens to see through, and interact with the world from, and everything seemed eerily different. It seemed full of new possibility. The world was not really different, but I was.

And that changed everything.

In *Man's Search for Meaning*, Victor Frankl states that the deepest meaning any one person can create in their life is to listen to what resonates within[63]. The deepest parts of our selves are the deepest spaces of heartful awareness, and when we are heartfully aware we are better able to connect with those deep spaces within. The more we incorporate heartful awareness into our life, the more this reciprocal pattern expands to include more and more of our existence, and the existence of those around us. Like a pebble dropped in a still pond, with increasingly wider ripples, our heartful awareness reverberates out and begins to encompass everything around us.

Like the flap of a butterfly's wings, heartfulness actively engages in changing the world, one heart, and one moment at a time.

Sacred Transformations

"Everyone sees the unseen in direct proportion to the clarity of their heart... And that depends on how much they have polished it"

Rumi

The journey through heartful awareness never ends; it just keeps getting deeper and richer in transformative heartful experience. This journey all at once encompasses more of our lived existence, and opens up new, and endless heartful horizons. There is no end to the profound transformations that heartful awareness can offer us. Too, everyone's journey is unique to his or her own path. Some people go through great periods of transformation, interspersed with relative periods of quiet, and some people transform little by little over long periods of time. Some experience a combination of both. Honor what is truthful for you, and be continually heartful with yourself along your path.

My own experience with heartfulness is that the deeper I go the more spaces it opens up. And the more spaces it opens up, the less words can begin to accurately describe the depth and expansiveness of those spaces. So much of this book has been about what we know; what science can, and has shown us about the miracle of the embodied journey to heartfulness – the tip of the iceberg, if you will. This last part – my parting words – is less of what we know scientifically, and more of my own experiential truths regarding my own embodied journey to heartfulness. It is out of reverence for the awe and wonder of what we do not know. If it resonates, or rings true for you, allow it in. If not, find what does ring true for you, and actively cultivate it. Regardless, I encourage you to continuously expand and explore your own truths on your own transformative journey through the limitless possibilities of heartful awareness.

What I have come to know is that the more we practice heartful awareness, the more it creates an ineffable presence in our lives. Again, ineffable means something is experienced so deeply it is impossible to accurately describe in words. Jean ValJean, in *Les Misérables* sings "To love another person is to see the face of God[64]." Heartful awareness offers us the opportunity to see, and experience, the face of God in all the moments of our lives. It may be in loving another, it may be in loving ourselves, and it may be in loving humanity. It is that moment of opportunity where the deepest and most heartful parts of our selves are allowed to emerge and connect to the world around us.

And see the face of God

Heartful awareness is a nonreactive, nonjudgmental, and fully accepting presence we bring to every moment, it also means actively engaging in whatever heartful, or sacred connection that moment offers. The more we make those sacred connections, and rest in the heartful spaces they open up, the more we experience expansiveness and depth in our lived existence. The more these heartful spaces are created in our lives, the less words can begin to accurately describe their power and potential for transformation. These heartful spaces may be exactly where we experience the Divine, a specific Sacred Presence, or find the place deep within us where we intersect with God or whatever deep energy guides our life. By bringing a heartful presence to each moment we are better capable of tapping into the Ineffable Presence that permeates our universe. And any moment we are resting in this Ineffable Presence is a moment we are transforming.

The more we cultivate our capacity for heartful awareness the more we are able to find the sacred in all the moments of our lives. If God, or the sacred is everywhere, there is nowhere it is not. Heartful awareness is finding the potential for sacred connection, with others, our selves, or a Sacred Presence, in all the moments of our lives. Heartful awareness, then, becomes our access point for a sacred connection to life itself.

And, as long as we are human, it is facilitated through the human body and human heart.

And it can be polished.

It is often said that we are not human beings having a spiritual experience, but spiritual beings having a human experience. I wholeheartedly believe in this statement. However, as long as we are having our human experience, it is our human bodies that are facilitating that experience. A human body is the soul enfleshed. It is the spirit incarnate. It is where our hearts reside. We can intentionally cultivate a greater capacity to experience the Divine precisely because we are spiritual beings living an incarnate human experience, and human experience is adaptable. The adaptable, and incarnate experience of heartful awareness is our way back home to the Truth.

Our last practice promotes intentional experience of the Divine. Again, anything that we do routinely and often nurtures the capacity for those states to be our primary operating patterns. Sacred Heart intentionally engages a divine presence. Through it, we calm our system, and then create the capacity for a greater connection to whatever sacred or divine presence feels comfortable for you.

Practice: Sacred HEART

Sacred HEART is similar to sustained HEART, except Sacred HEART holds the intention for directly experiencing communion with a sacred source or being. Again, the idea is to hold the sustained affect – in this case Divine Affect – for a specified period of time. In other words, we allow ourselves to bask in the 'felt sense' of communing with a sacred presence. Follow the steps of Sustained HEART, and in the 'nurture' step intentionally engage or commune with a sacred source, being or energy.

1. **Notice** any reactivity, thoughts, emotions, and bodily sensations that may be presenting themselves. Disengage from any of these states that may be presenting, by witnessing or observing, gaining distance, but not suppressing.

2. **Refocus** the eyes by releasing any tension or stress in the tiny little muscles all around the eyes. Refocus and relax the shoulders, and refocus your attention down into the chest area or an area in the torso that feels comfortable for you to bring your attention. Create a comfortable, natural and relaxed breathing pattern, with all your attention on the breath.

3. **Nurture** a state of Divine Affect, or commune with a sacred source or being. If an image helps to bring up this affect, again, hold the image in your minds eye to bring up the felt sense of the affect. The important aspect of this practice is that you immerse yourself in the 'Felt Sense' of communion or engagement with that which is sacred to you, and hold this state for a sustained period of time.

Be aware of intuitive insights or 'knowings' that may surface. Pay attention to bodily sensations. This practice is most akin to the idea of resting in direct experience with a sacred source or being, possibly resting in the space where your deepest sense of self intersects with the divine. Instead of talking to God, as in some prayer, this is more in line with listening to God. It is more in line with letting our hearts open directly to God, as a felt sense of being completely known, and completely held in divine love.

Coming home to the truth

When we truly experience the Sacred, the Divine, or the mystical, it is an embodied phenomenon. Our human bodies are the conduit between the seen and the unseen. Cultivating deeper connections with the sacred is a beautifully choreographed process between the intentionality we bring to every moment, and the adaptations in our human bodies that create the capacity for more of the same. The gift of incarnation is the gift of being fully alive in our humanness, and yet having the capacity to connect to the sacred. What does all this mean? It means that our bodies, including our brain and our body proper, are not only vehicles for transformation in our world; they are vehicles for transformation in our relationship to the Sacred. And the best way to cultivate a connection with the sacred is to create a physiological state of receptivity through heartful awareness.

We are all at once reclaiming our hearts as an embodied way of being in the world, and using them to consciously connect with the Ineffable Presence everywhere. Our bodies are like radio receivers connecting to the sacred energy of universe. The more we fine-tune the receiver, and polish our hearts as the primary connective instrument, the more we are able to connect with that which is unseen.

We have seen throughout our journey from mindfulness to heartfulness that to create the conditions for heartful awareness to flourish we must first clear and calm the chaos that blocks us from it. That is the gift, and miracle of mindfulness. Mindfulness teaches us a nonreactive, nonjudgmental, and fully- accepting way of being present in every moment. The necessary other half, however, is actively engaging in life generating moments of connection. That is the gift and miracle of heartfulness. Heartful awareness fine-tunes our human systems for receiving, and consciously connecting to the sacred energy that permeates our universe. The embodiment of heartful awareness allows us to be fully human and connect with that which is fully divine.

Heartful awareness promotes love, peace and compassion beyond cognitive understanding. It is an embodied presence we bring to the world, and the world is changed because of it. It is trainable through active and intentional engagement, and through it we can cultivate the capacity for greater experience of the Divine. It is found in the nonreactive, accepting, and heartful engagement we bring to each and every moment.

Every moment carries the potential of heartful awareness.

And we are fundamentally changed as human beings because of it.

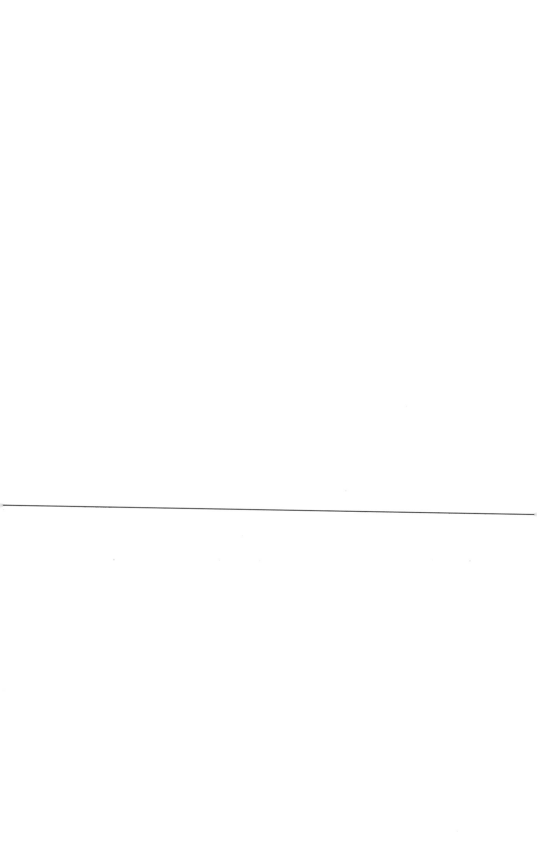

Appendix

Diagram of HEART and other practices:

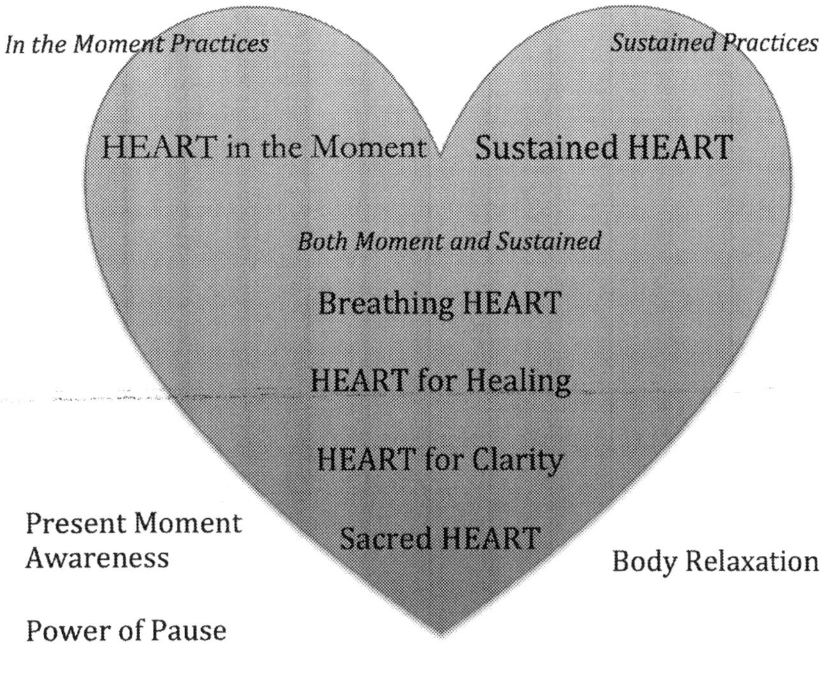

In the Moment Practices   *Sustained Practices*

HEART in the Moment   Sustained HEART

Both Moment and Sustained

Breathing HEART

HEART for Healing

HEART for Clarity

Present Moment
Awareness

Sacred HEART

Body Relaxation

Power of Pause

Figure 8. Diagram of Practices

HEART diagram of practices review

The previous diagram is a representation of how the tools and practices presented in this book might be used. Although it is most important to tailor the practices to how they will best suit you, the diagram makes some distinctions between practices, and this might help you integrate their use in your everyday life. All of the practices, and their components, are described in detail earlier in the text, and, again, shortly. This chart is only meant to help you conceptualize ways in which they might be used.

The practices are divided between practices that you might do in the moment, and practices that you might do for a sustained period of time. Many can be used as both. The practices defined as the HEART practices (inside the heart) are distinctly based on the 'notice, refocus and nurture' steps presented earlier in the text. Those outside of the heart are practices designed for a specific purpose, however not necessarily based on the steps of HEART. They, too, are designed to be done either in the moment, or as a sustained practice.

Although HEARTful breathing, HEART for healing, HEART for clarity and Sacred HEART can be done in the moment, or as a sustained practice, each are primarily grounded in one form or the other. In other words, HEARTful breathing is primarily done in the moment, although it can be done as a sustained practice to further cement your desired emotional outlook. HEART for healing, HEART for clarity, and Sacred Heart typically are more successful if they are done as a sustained practice first, so you more fully understand the dynamics of the practice. Once they are done as a sustained practice it gets easier to recall the steps of the practice, and thus the emotional shift, right in the moment of reactivity.

Once they are all practiced, and a general level of comfort is obtained, you can more easily shift in and out of the practices, and more fully integrate them into the moments of your everyday life.

Resources

For access to audio recordings of the practices
in the text visit www.dralane.com

Practices

Practice : Present Moment Awareness

Present moment awareness, or mindful awareness, means that we are fully present in the moment, mind, body and spirit. We are not hijacked by our thoughts, emotions, or implicit memory patterns. If there is reactivity presenting itself, we notice the reactivity without getting caught up in it. We notice with non-judgmental acceptance, and possibly, even, with a little curiosity. We bring overt attention to being fully present in the moment. And, if appropriate, we become more aware of heartful opportunities as they present themselves.

1. Disengage from the reactivity, if any, and breathe
2. Bring your awareness to the experience of your senses without really engaging in thought about them.
3. Pause and feel what it feels like to be fully present in this absolute now moment.
4. Notice if the moment presents for you a heartful opportunity you might have not been aware of in your reactive state.

Practice: The Power of Pause

A simple pause can break the chain of reactivity or trigger and encourage a more grounded response. It has an overt focus on pausing in the middle of reactivity or trigger, and engaging in an intentionally calming, and focused breath. While in present moment awareness, the focus is outward, or on the presenting moment, the Power of Pause invites an intentional, and inward calming focus. It is typically done in the moment of reactivity.

1. Disengage from the reactivity and bring overt focus to stopping the typical chain of reactive responses.

2. Take a few very intentional and grounding breaths and try to cultivate a sense of clarity through the pause.
3. Try to reassess the situation through the pause rather than through the perception of reactivity.

Practice: HEARTful breathing

While mindfulness practices typically foster non-reactivity through awareness, other practices actively engage the limbic system directly. In other words, actively engaging the limbic system in a specific state trains it to better operate from that state. Compassion, love, gratitude, clarity, and confidence, for example, are all trainable states.

HEARTful Breathing uses the concept of heartful awareness to create the biochemical shifts associated with a desired 'felt state'. Because our brain does not know the difference from something that is deeply felt, and the reality of the moment, the shift to breathing a 'felt sense' of a desired outlook actually shifts our biochemical state to one consistent with that outlook. This shift changes our perception, and, ultimately, creates that outlook.

1. Notice and disengage from the reactivity of the moment and, from an observer or witnessing state, discern its emotional component.
2. Refocus your eyes, and shoulders and bring your awareness to your breath. Establish a relaxed breathing pattern.
3. Nurture what a more desirable, and heartfully engaged outlook would be. Again, this heartfully engaged outlook might be heartful awareness of your own personal needs.
4. Calmly breathe the 'felt sense' of that outlook. If an image helps hold that felt sense, hold the image, but remember it is the felt sense that is most important. In other words, if confidence is the outlook you'd like to create, see if you can breathe what it feels like to be confident. If an image, either of you or someone else, helps you bring up the outlook, then hold the image in your minds eye as you breathe. Breathe the sensation, or 'felt sense' of whatever outlook you would like to create for yourself, and 'feel' it soaking every cell

in your body. As you transition out of the practice, pause and bring your conscious awareness to how you are feeling. This awareness will help you cement this state of being so you can more easily access it with only a few breaths at a later time.

Practice: HEART in the Moment

HEART in the Moment is similar to the Power of Pause, in that it can be done in any moment of the day. It is meant to be done in moments of reactivity, as well as any other moment you would like to cement a heartfully engaged way of being into your physiological makeup. It takes the Power of Pause one step further, in that it intentionally engages in an emotional shift. This emotional shift further intensifies the biochemical shift from chaos to calm, and potentially furthers the state of clarity and expands perception. In other words, we are not just *pausing* from our typical reaction; we are *creating* another one.

The steps follow:

1. **Notice** – Bring your awareness any reactivity you may be having
   - Notice your mental activity
   - Notice your emotional activity
   - Notice your physical response
   - Ground yourself in your breath
2. **Refocus** – While becoming more intentional about a natural, and calming breath
   - Refocus, and release the tension around your eyes
   - Refocus, and release the tension around your shoulders
   - Bring your awareness down to your torso, and rest in your breath
   - Become very intentional about a slower deeper but mostly natural breathing pattern
3. **Nurture** – Nurture a state that, for you, is more life-generative. It may involve holding an image of something that creates feelings of heartfulness, or a 'felt state' that facilitates an emotional shift. Nurture and sustain this feeling as long as it is possible, or appropriate.

Practice: Sustained HEART

The main goal of this practice is to maintain, and genuinely bask in, a state of genuine heartfulness for a period of time. If using an image helps you to create, or maintain this engaged state, it is a good tool to use. However, it is important to remember that the image is just a tool, and a genuine heartful focus is the important aspect of this practice.

1. **Notice-**
   - How you feel mentally, emotionally and physically - scan your body and make a conscious attempt to relax any area that is tight, stressed or anxious.
   - Intentionally disengage from the reactive hold of whatever is present. Hold it from an observing or witnessing point of view.
   - Begin to establish a comfortable breathing pattern

2. **Refocus-**
   - Check your eyes and your shoulders and intentionally relax, 'release' on the out breath if it helps.
   - Bring your awareness to your heart, solar plexus or deep in your belly
   - Breathe- slowly and deeply, but most of all comfortably. Sustain this breathing. If you want, use counting tools to keep your attention keenly focused on the experience of your breath. Vividly feel the sensation of release.

3. **Nurture**
   - When you begin to feel your body release, make an intentional shift to a heartfully engaged state and 'feel' this state. Use an image if it helps to make the shift.
   - Sustain the relaxed breathing and focused emotional state for approximately 15 minutes or more.
   - If you find your mind wandering, gently bring your attention back and continue. Try to not get too caught up in the thought process and instead try and intentionally cultivate a non-conscious feeling state of a heartful engagement.
   - Sustain and breathe.

HEART for Healing

In all of the Sustained HEART practices the 'notice' and 'refocus' steps are the same. These steps prepare us psychologically and physiologically for the reprogramming of the nurture step.

1. *Notice* – your thoughts, your emotions, and your physical sensations. Disengage from their reactivity, witness and observe. Begin to establish an intentional and comfortable breath.

2. *Refocus* – your eyes by releasing all the tiny little muscles around the eyes and behind the eyes, refocus by releasing the tension in your shoulders. Bring your awareness down to your torso, somewhere that feels comfortable for you to focus on your breath. Sustain and deepen a comfortable and natural breathing pattern.

3. *Nurture* - nurture a physiological state of healing by cultivating deeply felt states of self-safety or security. It could be an imagined place, or a 'felt sense' of being totally held, safe, and secure. While resting in this 'felt sense', see if any 'nudgings' for implicit healing are making themselves known. In other words, what symptom is presenting itself, nudging for attention to be healed? While engaging the nudging at a safe distance, tune into what it is needing from you, to be re-wired in a more balanced state. This message may come as an intuitive knowing, and image, or a physical sensation. Hold yourself, and the nudging, in as a compassionate state as you would a best friend. As deeply and as vividly as possible provide an alternative experience by the way of a 'felt sense' or image. This begins to rewire the implicit memory at its source. And the deeper the alternative experience is engaged the deeper it is re-programmed as our new operating pattern.

Practice: Body Relaxation and Stress Release

Body relaxation practices directly target the physiological components of the body to induce a relaxed, calm and coherent state. In other words, when our body calms, our mind and spirit calm. We feel calm, we feel at peace, and we are more able to connect to the heartful spaces within and without us.

Again, because the body is a system of adaptation, the biochemical, neural and electrical components associated with this calmer and more relaxed state become the body's new operating system. Too, this type of self-care can have a profound effect on inner renewal, and our capacity for heartful awareness. You can do this exercise with calming music in the background if you wish.

1. Bring all your awareness to your breath, and maintain a comfortable relaxed breathing pattern.

2. Relax the tension all around the eyes and the tiny little muscles surrounding the eyes. Relax all of muscular structures of the face. Relax the shoulders, and relax down into the chest. Find a spot on your torso that feels comfortable for you to bring your awareness and imagine the breath coming straight in and out of that spot. Maintain this breathing pattern and relaxed state of being throughout the practice.

3. Progressively, and slowly tighten and release various muscle groups throughout your body for a count of three. After the count of three, the next two breaths should be overtly 'releasing' breaths focused on the same body parts you just tightened. Start from your toes to your knees, then your knees to your hips, then your full torso, from your hips to your shoulders, then the entirety of both arms, including the hands.

4. After you are done with the tightening and releasing aspect of this practice, imagine a wave of relaxation very slowly coming up and over your body. Imagining it starting at your toes, then to your ankles, shins and calves, up and through your knees, thighs, and hips, very slowly up your torso, from your shoulders, down both arms, all the way to your fingertips. Bring your awareness, then, to the base of your neck, and imagine the wave slowly progressing up and around your head, encircling and enveloping your scalp and your skull, as if it were a slowly unfolding cap. Imagine the wave as a curtain, lowering slowly down your forehead, over your eyebrows and deep into your eye-sockets, cheeks, jaw, over the chin, and down the throat and neck.

5. Let your awareness find your breath again at a spot in your torso that is comfortable for you, and rest in the experience of the breath. Imagine your body melting into whatever surface you are on. If you feel any left-over stress or tension you can imagine it floating away on a cloud or a balloon if you like. Focus on what it feels like to truly let go, and release it.

6. Rest in this space for 5 to 10 minutes, or as long as is appropriate. If you would like, you can finish the practice with the HEARTful breathing exercise presented in Chapter 4. In other words, once you are fully relaxed, breathe the sensation, or 'felt sense' of whatever outlook you would like to create for yourself, and 'feel' it soaking every cell in your body. As you transition out of the practice, pause and bring your conscious awareness to how you are feeling. This awareness will help you cement this state of being so you can more easily access it with only a few breaths at a later time.

Practice: HEART for Clarity

Deep states of heartfulness lead to expansiveness, and expansiveness leads to clarity. HEART for Clarity uses the basic steps of the HEART practices as its foundation, except there is an additional purpose. In this practice we use the shift of affect to gain clarity on a question we may have, an issue we may be facing, or how to better manifest a sense of heartful awareness over-all.

Before you begin the practice write down a question, issue, problem, or any life circumstance you would like some clarity on. During the practice do not overtly focus on this question, just go into the practice with the intention of holding a subconscious awareness of this question. You might even request a sacred presence to work at the subconscious level of your awareness as you go through the practice.

Follow the outline steps of the heart practice:

1. **Notice** any reactivity, thoughts, emotions, and bodily sensations that may be presenting themselves. Disengage from any of these states

that may be presenting, by witnessing or observing, gaining distance, but not suppressing.

2. **Refocus** the eyes by releasing any tension or stress in the tiny little muscles all around the eyes. Refocus and relax the shoulders, and refocus your attention down into the chest area or an area in the torso that feels comfortable for you to bring your attention. Create a comfortable, natural and relaxed breathing pattern, with all your attention on the breath.

3. **Nurture** a state of affect that feels healing or generative to you in the moment. If an image helps to bring up this affect, again, hold the image in your minds eye to bring up the felt sense of the affect you want to create. If you are using an image, focusing on the specifics of that image that bring up the felt sense, helps to create the state of deep deep affect. Remember it is the state of deep affect that creates the foundational physiological adaptations in the body.

Try to maintain breathing in this 'felt sense' for at least 20 minutes.

After the practice notice any answers, intuitive insights, bodily sensations or other ways of knowing that may surface. These 'knowings' may appear in a variety of ways. Be open. Pay attention. Bring your conscious attention to the receptivity of the moment and just notice what appears. Write down the first things that come up, without conscious filtering, either through sensation, other knowings, or cognitive awareness. Let the writing lead you. Also, pay attention in the hours, and days, following the practice. Answers and clarity may emerge at the times you least expect it.

Practice: Sacred HEART

Sacred HEART is similar to sustained HEART, except Sacred HEART holds the intention for directly experiencing communion with a sacred source or being. Again, the idea is to hold the sustained affect – in this case Divine Affect – for a specified period of time. Follow the steps of Sustained HEART, and in the 'nurture' step intentionally engage or commune with a sacred source, being or energy.

1. **Notice** any reactivity, thoughts, emotions, and bodily sensations that may be presenting themselves. Disengage from any of these states that may be presenting, by witnessing or observing, gaining distance, but not suppressing.

2. **Refocus** the eyes by releasing any tension or stress in the tiny little muscles all around the eyes. Refocus and relax the shoulders, and refocus your attention down into the chest area or an area in the torso that feels comfortable for you to bring your attention. Create a comfortable, natural and relaxed breathing pattern, with all your attention on the breath.

3. **Nurture** a state of Divine Affect, or commune with a sacred source or being. If an image helps to bring up this affect, again, hold the image in your minds eye to bring up the felt sense of the affect. The important aspect of this practice is that you immerse yourself in the 'Felt Sense' of communion or engagement with that which is sacred to you, and hold this state for a sustained period of time.

Be aware of intuitive insights or 'knowings' that may surface. Pay attention to bodily sensations. This practice is most akin to the idea of resting in direct experience with a sacred source or being, possibly resting in the space where your deepest sense of self intersects with the divine. Instead of talking to God, as in some prayer, this is more in line with listening to God. It is more in line with letting our hearts open directly to God as a felt sense of being completely known, and completely held in divine love.

HEART Record Log

Heartfully Engaged Awareness Reprogramming Tools

Date / time	Situation	Tool / technique used	Outcome
1.			
2.			
3.			
4.			
5.			
6.			
7.			
8.			
9.			
10.			
11.			
12.			
13.			
14.			
15.			
16.			
17.			
18.			
19.			
20.			
21.			
22.			
23.			

Acknowledgments

Although in some way my whole life has been a journey to heartfulness, at a very specific point in time, many years ago, it was a conscious choice of complete surrender. Since then has been a very intentional process, and through that process there have been many people that have played a significant role. The gifts I have received from those along my path are far too many to mention here, however there are a few I must thank publicly.

When my inner yearning for more in life broke through to overt behavior, I found myself joining a Zen Vipassana meditation group and a Quaker meeting in very same week, in fact, in the same meeting space. And my life has never been the same. Both became foundational in forming my journey. The Vipassana group offered me an eye-opening journey into the power and process of mindfulness. Quakers, who believe God resides deep in the heart of every single person, find connection to the Divine by sitting in silent communion with each other, and allowing the sacred to emerge. I realize now, that even in the beginning stages of my exploration, mindfulness and heartfulness were present as two halves of a very important whole.

Steve Smith, you were there guiding both, and for that I thank you.

As my path deepened, I realized it needed to encompass my vocational life as well as my personal life, and for that I needed to go back to school – again. Lourdes, you fell into my life like a miracle out of nowhere, and brought with you your infinite wisdom, and all the blessings of the doctoral program at CGU. Thank you. And thank you David for your belief in my potential, and all my friends at HeartMath for the priceless opportunities, and for reaffirming and solidifying my belief in the power of the heart.

I believe the essence of life is communion, and that sometimes we commune in the form of shared knowledge and passion through the spoken and written word. I have been deeply formed by the work of others, many of who are mentioned this text. I have also been formed by many more whose work has become such an ingrained part of me, I'm not sure where the division lies between the two. Thank you for your inspiration, and for sharing with the world what you know.

My work is continually being formed and reformed. One of the greatest blessings throughout this process has been the connection with the thousands of people I've been blessed to share it with. You have become part of me, and have given me far more than I could ever give you. Thank you. Too, eternal gratitude goes to Rick Caughman for your patience, energy and brilliance in designing the cover.

Deep friendships have also been instrumental on my path to discovering the depth and power of heartfulness. Thank you for the conversations and connections over coffee, beer, tears, laughter, kids and cherry stems.

My family of origin has so formed who I have become. Thank you to my mother, siblings, and to my father who has passed on, but who is with me always.

Thank you to my stepson Justin who proofread, and helped keep me focused in the later stages of writing. To my sons, Michael and Sammy, who lived the journey with me. My two little companero's by my side through all the road trips, broken ceramic angels, "wi wot ruin your mdtutacnin" (read: we won't ruin your meditation) apology notes, and our 'coming of age' together. You have seen, and lived my journey with me. Sometimes I don't know where you both end, and I begin. I love you both.

And, to my husband Frank. Finding you along the way was an unexpected wonder. Planned since eternity and yet destined for a specific moment in time. What I know for sure is that had we not been both committed to our own healing and transformative journeys, we would have never recognized each other along the path. And now we walk it together – forever interlaced in peace, love, and compassion… I love you.

Babe, this book's for you.

Endnotes

1   Gendlin, E., 1981. *Focusing.* New York: Bantam Books

2   Campbell, J., 1988. *The Power of Myth.* New York: Doubleday

3   Das, L. S., 1997. *Awakening the Buddha Within: Tibetan Wisdom for the Western World.* New York: Broadway Books

4   LeDoux, J. 2002. *Synaptic Self: How Our Brains Become Who We Are.* New York: Penguin.

5   Lipton, B. 2005. *The Biology of Belief: Unleashing the Power of Consciousness, Matter and Miracles.* Santa Rosa, CA: Elite Books.

6   Springsteen, Bruce. 1992. "You shot through my anger and rage to show me my prison was an open cage..." *Living Proof.* Lucky Town. CD. Columbia

7   Goleman, D. 1994. *Emotional Intelligence: Why it can matter more than I.Q.* New York: Bantam.

8   Schwartz, Richard. 2001. *Internal Family Systems Model.* Oak Park, IL: Trailheads Publications.

9   Siegel, Daniel. 2010. *Mindsight: The New Science of Personal Transformation.* New York: Bantam.

10 Joseph, R., ed. 2003. *Neurotheology: Brain, Science, Spirituality, and Religious Experience.* San Jose, Ca.: University Press.

11 Pert, C. 1997. *Molecules of Emotion: The Science Behind Mind - Body Medicine.* New York: Scribner.

12 Uvnas Moberg, K. 2003. *The Oxytocin Factor: Tapping the Hormone of Love, Calm and Healing.* Cambridge: DeCappo.

13 Lipton, B. 2005. *The Biology of Belief: Unleashing the Power of Consciousness, Matter, and Miracles.* Santa Rosa, CA: Mountain of Love.

[14] Braden, G. 2009. *The Spontaneous Healing of Belief: Shattering the Paradigm of False Limits.* Carlsbad: Hay House.

[15] Siegel, Daniel. 2010. *Mindsight: The New Science of Personal Transformation.* New York: Bantam.

[16] Anissimov, Michael. 2014. *What is the Prefrontal Cortex?.* http://www.wisegeek.org/what-is-the-prefrontal-cortex.htm:wiseGEEK.

[17] Siegel, Daniel. 2010. *Mindsight: The New Science of Personal Transformation.* New York: Bantam.

[18] Carmichael, S. T. and Price, J. L. 1995. "Limbic connections of the orbital and medial prefrontal cortex in macaque monkeys." Journal of Comparative Neurology 363(4): 615–641.

[19] Siegel, Daniel. 2010. *Mindsight: The New Science of Personal Transformation.* New York: Bantam.

[20] Pert, C. 1997. *Molecules of Emotion: The Science Behind Mind–Body Medicine.* New York: Scribner.

[21] McCraty, R., and Atkinson, M. 1995. "The Effect of Emotions on Short-Term Heart Rate Variability Using Power Spectrum Analysis." American Journal of Cardiology 76(14): 1089–1093.

[22] Hasson, U., Ghazanfar, A.A., Galantucci, B., Garrod, S., Keysers, C. 2012. "Brain-to-brain coupling: mechanism for creating and sharing a social world." Trends in Cognitive Science 16(2):114-121.

[23] Fredrickson, B. 2013. *Love 2.0: How Our Supreme Emotion Affects Everything We Feel, Think, Do, and Become.* New York: Hudson Street Press.

[24] Ibid.

[25] McNaughton, N. 1989. *Biology and Emotion.* Cambridge: Cambridge University Press.

[26] Joseph, R., ed. 2003. *Neurotheology: Brain, Science, Spirituality, and Religious Experience.* San Jose: University Press.

[27] Csikszentmihalyi, M. 1993. *The Evolving Self.* New York: Harper Collins.

[28] Frederickson, B. 2009. *Positivity: Top-Notch Research Reveals the 3-to-1 Ratio that will Change Your Life.* New York, Three Rivers Press.

[29] Dispenza, J. 2012. *Breaking the Habit of Being Yourself: How to Lose Your Mind and Create a New One.* Carlsbad: Hay House.

30 Schwartz, Richard. 2001. *Internal Family Systems Model.* Oak Park, IL: Trailheads Publications.

31 Fredrickson, B. 2013. *Love 2.0: How Our Supreme Emotion Affects Everything We Feel, Think, Do, and Become.* New York: Hudson Street Press.

32 Ibid.

33 Ibid.

34 Joseph, R., ed. 2003. *Neurotheology: Brain, Science, Spirituality, and Religious Experience.* San Jose: University Press.

35 Begley, S. 2007. *Train Your Mind Change Your Brain: How a New Science Reveals Our Extraordinary Potential To Transform Ourselves.* New York: Ballantine.

36 Joseph, R., ed. 2003. *Neurotheology: Brain, Science, Spirituality, and Religious Experience.* San Jose: University Press.

37 Fredrickson, B. 2013. *Love 2.0: How Our Supreme Emotion Affects Everything We Feel, Think, Do, and Become.* New York: Hudson Street Press.

38 Frederickson, B. 2009. *Positivity: Top-Notch Research Reveals the 3-to-1 Ratio that will Change Your Life.* New York, Three Rivers Press.

39 Joseph, R., ed. 2003. *Neurotheology: Brain, Science, Spirituality, and Religious Experience.* San Jose: University Press.

40 Johnson, S. 2013. *Love Sense: The Revolutionary New Science of Romantic Relationships.* New York: Little Brown and Co.

41 Kuchinskas, S., 2009. *The Chemistry of Connection: How the Oxytocin Response Can Help You Find Trust, Intimacy, and Love.* Oakland: New Harbinger,

42 Ibid

43 Fredrickson, B. 2013. *Love 2.0: How Our Supreme Emotion Affects Everything We Feel, Think, Do, and Become.* New York: Hudson Street Press.

44 Schwartz, R. 2001. *Internal Family Systems Model.* Oak Park, IL: Trailheads Publications.

45 Ibid.

46 Rogers, F. Jr., In Press. *Practicing Compassion.* Nashville: Upper Room

47 Ecker, B. 2012. *Unlocking the Emotional Brain: Eliminating Symptoms at Their Roots Using Memory Reconsolidation.* New York: Routledge

48 Hanson, R., Mendius, R. 2009: *Buddhas Brain: The Practical Neuroscience of Happiness, Love and Wisdom.* Oakland, Ca: New Harbinger

49   Springsteen, B. 1987. "On his right hand Billy'd tattooed the word "love" and on his left hand was the word "fear" and in which hand he held his fate was never clear." *Cautious Man.* Tunnel of Love. CD. Columbia

50   Luskin, F., 2002. *Forgive for Good: A Proven Prescription for Health and Happiness.* New York: Harper Collins

51   Ibid

52   Rosenberg, M., 2005. *Nonviolent Communication: A Language of Life.* Encinitas: Puddle Dancer

53   Mehrabian, A. 1981. *Silent Messages: Implicit Communication of Emotions and Attitudes.* Belmont, Ca.: Wadsworth

54   Ibid

55   Dyer, W. 2007. *Change Your Thoughts Change Your Life: Living the Wisdom of the Tao.* Carlsbad, Ca.: Hay House

56   Seaward, B. 2011. *Essentials of Managing Stress.* Jones and Bartlett: Sudbury, Mass

57   Daugherty, A.K., 2008. *The Power Within: From Neuroscience to Transformation.* Dubuque: Kendall Hunt

58   Ibid

59   Covey, S. 2013 (anniversary edition). *The Seven Habits of Highly Effective People.* New York: Simon and Schuster

60   Lakein, A. 1989. *How to Get Control of Your Time and Your Life.* New York: Signet

61   Losier, M. 2010. *The law of Attraction: How to Get More of What You Want and Less of What You Don't Want.* New York: Grand Central Life and Style

62   Springsteen, Bruce. 1992. "Yeah just sittin' around waitin' for my life to begin while it was all just slippin' away." *Better Days.* Lucky Town. CD. Columbia

63   Frankl, V. 1992. *Man's Search for Meaning.* Boston: Beacon

64   Schonberg, C., Boubil, A. 2012 "To love another is to see the face of God" *Epilogue.* Les Miserables: Highlights from the motion picture soundtrack. CD. Universal: Polydor

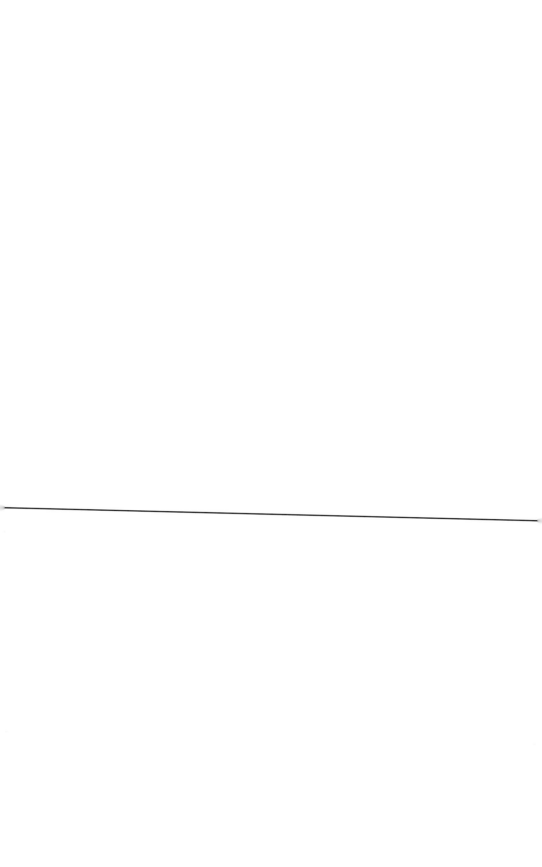